Many Tender Ties

"There is indeed no living with comfort in this country until a person has forgot the great world and has his tastes and character formed on the current standard of the stage . . . habit makes it familiar to us, softened as it is by the <u>many tender ties,</u> which find a way to the heart."

James Douglas
Fort Vancouver, March, 1842

Many Tender Ties

Women in Fur-Trade Society, 1670-1870

By Sylvia Van Kirk

UNIVERSITY OF OKLAHOMA PRESS   Norman and London

Library of Congress Cataloguing-in-Publication Data

Van Kirk, Sylvia.
  Many tender ties.

  Bibliography: p. 255
  Includes index.
1. Fur traders' wives Northwest, Canadian.
2. Northwest, Canadian Social life and customs.
3. Northwest, Canadian Social conditions.
4. Fur trade—Northwest, Canadian—History.
5. Northwest, Canadian—History. I. Title.

F1060.V36 1983   305.4′09712   82-40457

ISBN: 0-8061-1847-4

To the memory of my grandparents,
who sought new horizons in Western Canada.

Part of a map showing Hudson's Bay Company Posts c. 1832. From "Hudson's Bay Miscellany", Volume XXX, Hudson's Bay Record Society, 1975.

Inset

FORT GOOD HOPE

Mackenzie R

GREAT BEAR LAKE

FORT NORMAN

FORT SIMPSON

Liard R

CHURCHILL

Churchill R

Nelson R

T LAKE

RD HOUSE

YORK

SEVERN

MERRY'S HOUSE

GOD'S LAKE

ISLAND LAKE

Severn R

ORWAY HOUSE

WINDY LAKE

GRAND RAPID

BERENS RIVER

BA HOUSE

MARTIN FALL

OSNABURGH

FORT ALEXANDER

LAC SEUL

OWER FORT GARRY

NIPIGON HOUSE

FORT RY

DALLES

STURGEON LAKE

LONG LAKE

ORT FRANCES

PIC

WHITEWOOD LAKE

FORT WILLIAM

LAKE SUPERIOR

BATCHEWANA

MICHIPICOTEN

SAULT STE MARIE

St PAUL

LAKE MICHIGAN

LAKE HURON

MISSISSAGI

LA CLOCHE

WHITEFISH LAKE

NIPISSING LAKE

FRENCH RIVER

BONNE CHERE

GREEN LAKE

NEW BRUNSWICK

FLYING POST

MATAWAGAMINGUE

ABITIBI

Moose R

Abitibi R

MOOSE

ALBANY

JAMES BAY

EASTMAIN

Rupert R

RUPERT HOUSE

WASWANIPI

MIGISKAN

GRAND LAC

TIMISKAMING

FORT COULONGE

CHATS

TEMISKAMAY

MISTASSINI

PIKE LAKE

OBIJUAN

WEYMONTACHINGUE

RAT RIVER

LAC DES SABLES

QUEBEC

MONTREAL (LACHINE)

LAKE OF TWO MOUNTAINS

St Lawrence R

FORT CHIMO

Koksoak R

ACKNOWLEDGMENTS

In its original form, this work was accepted as a Ph.D. thesis by the University of London, England, in 1975. Since that time, it has undergone extensive revision and I would like to express my gratitude to those who have helped in its evolution. It has been a privilege to share ideas and information with Jennifer Brown, a fellow researcher in the field, who has increased my appreciation of the value of interdisciplinary perspectives. Irene Spry has been a constant source of inspiration and encouragement, and I am grateful to her and Alison Prentice for their valuable comments and suggestions. I am also indebted to W. J. Eccles for his critique of an earlier draft of this manuscript. His comments have deepened my understanding of the craft of the historian. Finally, I would like to thank my husband and my parents for their support and interest in a project that has been as time-consuming as it has been fascinating.

The permission of the Hudson's Bay Company to quote from its archives is gratefully acknowledged.

Sylvia Van Kirk
Toronto, Ontario

CONTENTS

ILLUSTRATIONS

John Rowand, Jr, and his bride Margaret Harriott leave Fort Edmonton on their wedding trip, January 1848. The carriole and dog harnesses were decorated for the occasion. From a painting by Paul Kane.

INTRODUCTION

In 1840 on the occasion of his marriage to a Scottish lady, Chief Trader James Hargrave was warmly congratulated by his colleagues throughout the Hudson's Bay Company's vast western territories. His friend James Douglas took the opportunity to muse upon the changing pattern of fur-trade marriages:

> There is a strange revolution in the manners of the country; Indian wives were at one time the vogue, the half-breed supplanted these, and now we have the lovely tender exotic torn from its parent bed to pine and languish in the desert.[1]

This book, which derived its initial inspiration from Douglas's intriguing observation, examines the role played by Indian, mixed-blood and white women in the development of fur-trade society in what is today Western Canada. Such an approach provides valuable insights into the nature of the society which evolved and permits the reconstruction of the complex, human dimension of the fur trade which has been little appreciated.

The fur trade forms the basis of recorded history in Western Canada. For almost two hundred years, beginning with the founding of the Hudson's Bay Company in 1670, the fur trade dominated western development. Although the English laid claim to the huge drainage basin of Hudson Bay known as Rupert's Land, initially they did not venture inland. Instead, they established a line of strategic posts on the shores of the Bay and relied upon the Indians to bring their rich catches of furs down to trade. Soon the English faced relentless competition from French traders with headquarters in Montreal, who pushed west to take their goods to the Indians. By the early eighteenth century, French-Canadian voyageurs had pioneered the vital canoe links through the rock and morass of the Canadian Shield to Lake Winnipeg. At mid-century, French posts were astride the Saskatchewan River, effectively diverting the Indians from trading on the Bay.

The British conquest of Quebec in 1759 shattered the French colonial fur trade, yet the Hudson's Bay Company enjoyed only a brief respite. British-American traders quickly re-organized the Montreal trade and were soon offering such formidable competition that, in 1774, the Hudson's Bay Company was forced to extend its operations inland. For many years, however, the English Company remained completely overshadowed by its powerful Canadian rival, the North West Company, a partnership of traders which emerged under the leadership of Simon McTavish in 1783. It was the intrepid Nor'Westers who first crossed the Rocky Mountains and established posts on the Pacific Slope, creating Canada's first transcontinental economic enterprise. Yet in 1821, the Hudson's Bay Company, largely because of its superior geographical position, finally won the long struggle for the control of the western fur trade. For the next fifty years, this vast region, including the Pacific Slope as far south as the Columbia River, was united under the aegis of the Hudson's Bay Company. Posts were linked by the mighty rivers of the Saskatchewan, the Mackenzie and the Fraser, creating pockets of European habitation throughout the West. It was also with the support of the Company that the earliest colonization ventures in Western Canada were undertaken at Red River and on Vancouver Island.

Detailed accounts of the events sketched above are provided in the works of Harold Innis, A. S. Morton and E. E. Rich, but the rich social history of the fur trade has been ignored until recently.[2] This neglect has marred our understanding of the dynamics of the fur trade because it was not simply an economic activity, but a social and cultural complex that was to survive for nearly two centuries.[3] Like most of the staple industries which characterized the economic development of pre-Confederation Canada, the fur trade generated a distinctive regional way of life; this was reflected in patterns of work, family life, modes of transport, and items of food and clothing. One important difference between the fur trade and other staple industries was that it was the only one which was based on a commodity exchange between two divergent groups of people. The growth of a mutual dependency between Indian and European trader at the economic level could not help but engender a significant cultural exchange as well. As a result, a unique society emerged which derived from both Indian and European customs and technology.

In seeking to discover the norms of fur-trade society, one is immediately confronted with the enormous complexity of the social interaction between Indian and white. The broad categories "Indian" and "white" must be differentiated. While it is convenient to speak in general terms of "the Indian", the traders actually encountered many different tribes with varying languages, customs, and standards of living. In the Shield region, the traders came in contact with bands of Cree and Ojibwa, members of the widespread Algonkian linguistic group. On the prairies were the Plains Cree, the Assiniboine and the populous Blackfoot confederacy. To the north were the Athapaskan tribes, the most important being the Chipewyan, who were drawn into the trading orbit of the Hudson's Bay Company in the early eighteenth century. The Nor'Westers were the first to encounter the numerous tribes which inhabited the Pacific Slope. Significant among these were the turbulent Carrier Indians of the northern interior of British Columbia and the sophisticated, class-conscious Chinook who inhabited the lower reaches of the Columbia River.[4]

As for the traders, it is misleading to think of them as a single group; within the fur trade, the Hudson's Bay Company and the North West Company were two distinct entities with differing social policies and practices. In examining the role played by women in the fur trade, it is important to differentiate their experience within the context of the two companies.

Traditionally the Western Canadian fur trade has been regarded as a totally male sphere. I have often been met with the bemused query, "What women were there in the fur trade?" This study reveals that there were many women in the West who played an essential role in the development of fur-trade society. It is true that for many decades there was a virtual ban on all European women in the West, and this fact in itself is of the utmost importance. Contrary to what might be anticipated, the

Canadian trader did not conform to the image of the "womanless frontiersman". Fundamental to the growth of a fur-trade society was widespread intermarriage between the traders and Indian women. This phenomenon has been remarked upon in previous works, but the nature and extent of these unions have not been subject to detailed scrutiny.[5] A major concern of the present study is to show that the norm for sexual relationships in fur-trade society was not casual, promiscuous encounters but the development of marital unions which gave rise to distinct family units. There were differences in attitude and practice between the men of the two companies; yet fur-trade society developed its own marriage rite, marriage *à la façon du pays,* which combined both Indian and European marriage customs. In this, the fur-trade society of Western Canada appears to have been exceptional. In most other areas of the world, sexual contact between European men and native women has usually been illicit in nature and essentially peripheral to the white man's trading or colonizing ventures.[6] In the Canadian West, however, alliances with Indian women were the central social aspect of the fur traders' progress across the country.

An explanation for this phenomenon can be found in the nature of the fur trade itself. Both the attitudes of the Indians and the needs of the traders dictated an important social and economic role for the native woman that militated against her being simply an object of sexual exploitation. Fur-trade society, as in both Indian and pre-industrial European societies, allowed women an integral socio-economic role because there was little division between the "public" and "private" spheres, between the spheres of work and home.[7] The marriage of a fur trader and an Indian woman was not just a "private" affair; the bond thus created helped to advance trade relations with a new tribe, placing the Indian wife in the role of cultural liaison between the traders and her kin. In Indian societies, the division of labour was such that the women had an essential economic role to play. This role, although somewhat modified, was carried over into the fur trade where the work of native women constituted an important contribution to the functioning of the trade.

An analysis of the evolution in the choice of marriage partners among the traders provides insights into the changing

nature of fur-trade society. Indian wives were "the vogue" during
the initial stages of the fur trade when the traders were dependent
upon the Indians for survival. The important economic role of the
Indian wife reflected the extent to which the traders adopted a
native way of life. Nevertheless, fur-trade society was not Indian;
rather it combined both European and Indian elements to
produce a distinctive, self-perpetuating community. This process
was symbolized by the emergence of a large number of mixed-
blood children.[8] The replacement of the Indian wife by the mixed-
blood wife resulted in a widespread and complex pattern of intermarriage among fur-trade families. It produced a close-knit
society in which family life was highly valued. James Douglas
echoed the sentiments of many of his colleagues when he declared
that without "the many tender ties" of family, the monotonous
life of a fur trader would be unbearable. Fur-trade society was not
static and the shifting influence of its dual cultural roots was
mirrored in the experience of successive generations of mixed-
blood girls. Initially Indian influences were strong, but there was
a noticeable tendency, particularly on the part of Company
officers, to wean their daughters away from their Indian heritage
and to encourage them to emulate the style of European ladies.
After an absence of over a century, the actual appearance of white
women in the Canadian West was to have serious repercussions,
particularly upon the fur-trade elite. Their coming underscored
the increasing class and racial distinctions which characterized
fur-trade society in the nineteenth century. In the Rupert's Land
of the 1830s, a genteel British wife was a conspicuous status
symbol for a Hudson's Bay Company officer, but, ironically, the
white wife also presaged the ultimate decline of the fur trade. Her
presence was most visible in the Red River Settlement, where,
like the missionary, she symbolized the coming of a settled,
agrarian order. This would be a world in which native women
would have little role to play.

This study supports the claims of theorists in women's
history that sex roles should constitute a category of historical
investigation. Traditionally the experience of women has differed
substantially from that of their male counterparts; the lives of
both sexes and how they interact must be examined if we are to
fully understand the dynamics of social change.[9] Much has been

said about the impact of the fur trade upon the Indian, yet little
has been done to differentiate this in terms of the sexes. It appears
that even more than the men, Indian women welcomed the advent
of European technology. Items such as kettles, knives, awls and
woollen cloth considerably alleviated their onerous domestic
duties. The notable instances that can be cited of the Indian
woman acting as ally or peacemaker to advance the cause of the
trader suggests that it was in the woman's interest to do so.
Anthropological studies in other parts of the world have
documented native women playing an active, even leading, role in
promoting the economic change brought about by European
technology.[10] Furthermore, because of her sex, the Indian woman
could be absorbed into fur-trade society in a way not open to the
Indian man. To become the wife of a fur trader offered the Indian
woman the prospect of an alternative way of life that was easier
physically and richer in material ways. An analysis of fur-trade
society from the women's perspective also extends our knowledge
of the role of women in race relations. The existence of numerous
harmonious mixed unions suggests that on an individual level
many traders were able to overcome the racial prejudice of their
parent society. A sharp rise in the expression of racist sentiments
emerges, however, when European women appear upon the
scene, a phenomenon which has parallels in the meeting of races
in other parts of the world.[11]

     In reconstructing the role of women in the fur trade, the pau-
city of sources, in particular those written by native women, presents
a difficult challenge. One is forced to piece together snippets of
information from the extensive collections of traders' journals,
letters and wills which have survived. Although a substantial
body of evidence can be amassed in this way, it is understandably
coloured by the male perspective. As is often the case in the
history of women, an analysis of this material reveals that there is a
significant disparity between the traders' perception of the
women's position and the reality of their actual lives. The
implications of this important paradox are examined throughout
this book as it applies to all three groups of women. With regard
to Indian women, most of the fur traders believed that women
occupied a degraded position within western Indian societies; the
Indian woman in their view had everything to gain by becoming

the wife of the "superior" trader. In reality the Indian woman may have enjoyed an easier existence at the fur-trade post, but she sacrificed considerable personal autonomy, being forced to adjust to the traders' patriarchal views on the ordering of home and family. In the final analysis, it is debatable whether the lot of an Indian woman in marrying a European was improved to the extent that the fur traders claimed.

Similarly, many fur-trade fathers sincerely believed that it was in their daughters' best interests to acculturate them to British standards of womanhood. In many cases, this process simply rendered mixed-blood girls helpless and vulnerable in a society which was becoming increasingly racist and sexist toward native women. Finally, nineteenth-century, fur-trade society presents a fascinating microcosm for the study of the Victorian concept of "the lady". The officers of the Hudson's Bay Company fell into genuine rapture over the charms and accomplishments of the few British ladies who set foot in Rupert's Land. But in this wilderness situation, the impracticality and artificiality of this "ideal" of womanhood was sharply etched. Ironically, the very qualities for which these women were so much extolled made it almost impossible for them to adapt to the rigours of fur-trade life. The "lovely tender exotics" did indeed "pine and languish in the desert".

In examining the experience of women within the male-dominated world of the fur trade, there is a temptation to place the woman ultimately in the role of passive victim. This would accord well with the common stereotype of the Indian being the exploited victim of the greedy, rapacious trader.[12] In both cases, within the fur-trade period, emphasis on the concept of victimization leads to an over-simplification of the dynamics of social and economic interaction. Recently several important revisionist works have appeared which delineate an active role for the Indian in the fur trade, showing that his responses were dictated by his own needs and interests.[13] It is necessary to extend this concept of "active agent" to the women, even though their roles within fur-trade society were restricted. Women's roles were defined in terms of their relationships to men: wife, mother, daughter or worker. Nevertheless, within these spheres, women did act to make the most of the opportunities available to them.

There is considerable evidence that it was not uncommon for Indian women to take the initiative in seeking to become the wives of traders, and for a while at least, they were able to utilize their position as "women in between" two groups of men to improve their status. Mixed-blood wives anxiously sought to preserve their place within the hierarchy, and if white women emerged as agents of racism, this was largely because they felt forced to protect their social status. In a society where marriage defined a woman's position, white women felt threatened by the presence of acculturated native women against whom they might have to compete for husbands. Investigators of women's history are discovering that the view of women as "active agents", instead of the simplistic view of women as "passive victims", promises to provide the key to understanding women's motivations and actions.[14] In this instance, it is believed that the examination of the role played by women as actors upon the fur-trade stage is essential to a full understanding of the complexities of what was an unusual society in early Western Canada.

1

ENTER THE WHITE MAN

History has not recorded the first European to set foot in what is today Western Canada. Before the founding of the Hudson's Bay Company in 1670, unknown coureurs des bois were journeying west of the Great Lakes in company with the Indians. Yet the men who extended the fur trade to the Canadian West were not individual entrepreneurs. The demands of the trade left no room for "the little guy", forcing the traders to group together in ever larger concerns, until by the late eighteenth century there remained only two powerful rivals, the North West Company and the Hudson's Bay Company. Both of these companies had a highly structured social organization. They were organized along hierarchical lines, the basic division being between the officers and the servants or engagés. Fur-trade society within the Canadian context was imbued with concepts of rank and class which cut across the egalitarian, individualistic influences commonly associated with the frontier.[1]

Company ties had an important effect on the traders' experience; so did their interaction with the native peoples. In the fur trade, white and Indian met on the most equitable footing that has ever characterized the meeting of "civilized" and "primitive" people. The fur trader did not seek to conquer the Indian, to take his land or to change his basic way of life or beliefs. The Indian in Western Canada was neither subject nor slave. Even as late as the mid-nineteenth century, the Hudson's Bay Company did not exercise direct authority over the tribes in Rupert's Land. Governor Simpson testified at the Parliamentary Enquiry in 1857 that the fur trade had created a mutual dependence between Indian and white:

They hunt and fish, and live as they please. They look to

us for their supplies, and we study their comfort and
convenience as much as possible, we assist each other.[2]

From the beginning the fur-trade companies had been
concerned to develop an Indian policy, predicated on peaceful
relations, that would ensure commercial success. Literate officers,
such as Hudson's Bay Company men James Isham and Andrew
Graham and Nor'Westers Alexander Henry and Daniel Harmon,
were perceptive observers of native character and custom. Their
writings reflect European cultural and class biases but,
nevertheless, these men had the advantage of long, intimate
experience with the Indians, some of whom were not only their
trading partners but, through intermarriage, their relatives as
well. As men in a foreign environment deprived of the company of
women of their own race, the fur traders took more than a passing
interest in the women of the native tribes. In order to understand
the social interaction that developed between the traders and
Indian women, it is necessary to set the stage by examining the
personnel structures of both companies, the differing Indian
policy developed by each company, particularly with regard to
Indian women, and the general reaction of white men to the
women of the various tribes they encountered.

The Hudson's Bay Company was never a "Canadian"
company to the degree that the North West Company could
claim. Its headquarters was in London where its affairs were run
by the London Committee, a group of well-connected
businessmen who, with one or two exceptions, never set foot in
Rupert's Land. Initially their employees were drawn from the
city of London, notorious for its demoralizing conditions. In
1682, Governor John Nixon at Albany complained that the
drunken, unruly characters sent to him were totally unfit for
service on the Bay. He implored the Committee to:

> . . . send me Some country lads, that are not
> acquainted with strong drink, that will worke hard, and
> faire hard, and are not debauched by the voluptuous-
> ness of the city.[3]

The apprenticeship system advocated by Nixon was adopted
with success by the Company. Orphan boys, often as young as
fourteen, were contracted to the Company for seven years; they
adapted readily to life in Rupert's Land, frequently developing

intimate relationships with the Indians and becoming excellent linguists.

Another of Nixon's recommendations, that Scots be employed as "they are a hardy people both to endure hunger, and could [sic], and are subject to obedience", presaged the Company's policy of hiring Orkneymen, which began in the early eighteenth century. The difficulties of eking out a living on their northern isles attracted the Orkneymen to the Company's service and, on the whole, they proved themselves to be reliable servants. Hardworking, extremely thrifty, and usually sober, the Orkneymen were seldom criticized, except for their closeness and a tendency to conspire to protect their interests.[4] During the eighteenth century, this group came to dominate the servant class of the Hudson's Bay Company and performed the tasks of tradesmen and labourers. The chief factors who governed the posts and their subordinate officers were principally Englishmen. A rigid class and ethnic stratification did not prevail, however, within the ranks of the Hudson's Bay Company. It was possible for William Tomison, an Orkneyman who entered the Company's service as a labourer in 1760, to end his career as chief at York Factory.[5] Occupational mobility was prevalent within the Company largely because it was continually plagued by a lack of experienced men, even though the total number of employees did not number much above two hundred for most of the eighteenth century.

Life on the Bay had little to recommend it. The climate was inhospitable with its merciless cold or insect-ridden heat; the daily routine at the posts was deadly, especially when the London Committee ruled that the men would live under a regime that has been aptly termed "military monasticism".[6] Employees were to be subjected to strict discipline and to live virtuous, celibate lives, performing religious observances and eschewing drinking and gambling.[7] Understandably, the governors had difficulty in enforcing this saintly ideal. Post journals throughout the eighteenth century reveal the persistence of disciplinary troubles — drunkenness, insubordination and illicit trade, particularly during ship time when unruly seamen set a bad example for post servants. The Company's recruitment problems were intensified by Britain's constant demand for manpower to fight her wars on land and sea. The seriousness of the labour shortage in the late

eighteenth century was indicated on one occasion by the reaction
of the native wife of James Spence when she saw the new men
arriving by the annual ship:

> . . . his Indian wife looked steadily at the Men, and
> then at her husband; at length said, James have you not
> always told me, that the people in your country are as
> numerous as the leaves on the trees, how can you speak
> such a falsehood, do not we all see plainly that the very
> last of them is come, if there were any more would these
> dwarfs have come here.[8]

The lack of a large, experienced work force was never a
problem for the North West Company, although it was a much
larger concern, numbering over one thousand men by 1805.[9] The
Canadian company could draw from a skilled pool of French-
Canadians who were thoroughly at home in the wilderness to
man its far-flung enterprises. The engagés were excellent canoemen, renowned for their strength and endurance, but they
were much criticized by their British superiors for their devil-
may-care attitude to life, their ignorant, spendthrift ways and
their love of a good carouse.[10] One of the most significant changes
brought about by the British takeover of the French colonial fur
trade was that the French-Canadians themselves were quickly
relegated to the labouring class in the reorganization which
followed. In the North West Company, ethnicity reinforced class
divisions, making occupational mobility much more difficult
than it was in the Hudson's Bay Company; an expert voyageur
might eventually become an interpreter or a brigade guide, but it
was virtually impossible for him to break into the officer class.

The officer class of the North West Company was dominated
by men of Highland Scots origin. The clan names of Mackenzie,
Macdonald, McTavish, Frazer, Campbell and Cameron
abounded, the Nor'Westers' strong sense of solidarity being
cemented by close kinship ties.[11] Simon McTavish brought
several relatives into the trade, including the son of his clan
chieftain and the three McGillivray brothers, who were his
nephews. The senior Nor'Westers, those in charge of the fur-trade
districts, were known as wintering partners or bourgeois; unlike
their Hudson's Bay Company counterparts, these officers were
not paid salaries but held shares in the Company and shared its

profits. They entered the service as junior officers with the rank of clerk, spurred by the incentive of gaining a partnership when they had proved their mastery of the trade. The North West Company was firmly tied to the London metropolis, but its management was much more in touch with the realities of its trade in the interior than was the Hudson's Bay Company's London Committee. Every summer, agents from the Montreal headquarters were sent to the Company's inland emporium at the western end of Lake Superior to meet with the wintering partners to decide policy and plan the next year's business.

Differences in experience and organization played a role in the formulation of Indian policy in each company. The on-the-spot training of the Nor'Westers confirmed the benefit of continuing the French policy of treating the Indians with lavish familiarity. Assuming La Vérendrye's view that "without the help of the pot you cannot have friendship", they catered to the Indians' love of ceremony, feasting and extensive gift-giving.[12] The Canadians mixed with the Indians on intimate social terms, which was initially an important factor in their success. As Hudson's Bay Company officer Thomas Hutchins lamented:

> The Canadians have great influence over the Natives by adopting all their Customs and making them Companions, the[y] drink, sing, conjure, &c scold with them . . . and the Indians are never kept out of their Houses whether drunk or sober, night or Day.[13]

The formation of liaisons with Indian women was the natural corollary of this policy. The North West Company favoured this development, realizing that an Indian mate could be an effective agent in adding to the trader's knowledge of Indian life.

One must be wary, however, of exaggerating the Nor'Westers' success with the Indians. A. S. Morton's statement that "the relations of the Northwesters, high and low, with the Indians, were of the best" distorts the truth.[14] The Nor'Westers came from the colonial societies of eastern Canada and the United States where, for a long time, the Indian had been regarded in an unfavourable light. They did not scruple to affront native sensibilities if they felt strong enough to avoid retaliation. Like the French before them, the "pedlars from Quebec" had trafficked in Indian captives, taking them down to Montreal for sale.[15] The worst excesses occurred during the trade war when the Nor'Westers felt forced to exert their mastery over both the Indians and their English rivals through coercion and brute force. By the late eighteenth century, relations between the Indians and the engagés seem to have deteriorated into a classic case of familiarity breeding comtempt. Edward Umfreville, who was no admirer of the Hudson's Bay Company, claimed that by this period many of the French-Canadians had become so corrupt and degenerate that the Indians despised them and preferred the sense of propriety shown by the Orkneymen.[16]

The official Indian policy of the Hudson's Bay Company, devised by the remote London Committee, was much more circumspect and formal than that of its rivals. From the beginning English policy had differed significantly from that of the French; they were solely interested in the fur trade, made no effort to Christianize or settle the Indians, and managed to avoid taking sides in tribal warfare, a step which had been costly to the French. Basically, the Hudson's Bay Company attitude toward the Indians may be described as one of benevolent paternalism. As the London Committee instructed Governor Henry Sergeant at Albany in 1683:

It is our Desire that you and all others who are emploied by us in the Bay should treate the Indians with Justice and humanity . . .[17]

The Committee exhorted its officers to treat the Indians "civilly" and "Trade upon an Equal Foundation", but not to fraternize with them. In the Committee's view, such familiarity would be prejudicial to its interests since it might render the Indians impudent and troublesome, lead to illicit trade and undermine discipline. Particularly stringent rules were devised to restrict Indian-white contact during trade time.[18] In the earliest decades of the Company's existence the rule was established that no Indian women were to be harboured in the posts. The Committee was adamant that no intimacies were to be formed with Indian women. Governors who allowed this law to be broken might forfeit their wages, while refractory servants were to be sent home: "for wee cannot . . . Expect good Servises from such, whome neither the Lawes of God or Man can restrain from

Wickedness."[19] Apart from the moral issue, the Committee was even more concerned to avoid any unnecessary expense:

> Indian Weomen resorting to our Factories are very prejudiciall to the Companies affaires, not only by being a meanes of our Servants often debauching themselves, but likewise by embeazling our goods and very much exhausting our Provisions.[20]

The frequency with which the Committee's rulings were broken and the difficulty of enforcing penalties reveal that Company policy was at variance with the social and economic realities of life on the Bay. The contact between the men and the Indians was much more frequent and cordial than the rules would allow, partly because of their developing interdependence. In the earliest years of the Company, the inexperience of its servants, coupled with the fear of French attack, led to the practice of relying upon the Indians to supply the posts with "country provisions". This resulted in the emergence of the "Home Guard", bands of Cree whose lives became oriented to the posts. They frequented an area just outside the fort walls, known as the plantation, and were chiefly employed in hunting for the Company.[21] The proximity of the Home Guard contributed to the development of intimate contact between Company men and native women. In spite of the rules, Indian women were often found within the forts. When Moose Factory, for example, burned to the ground on Christmas Day 1735, twelve Indians were among those celebrating the holiday.[22]

Special attention was always bestowed on leading Indian hunters who were designated "captains", as was Captain Sakie at Moose Factory in the 1740s. Both Captain Sakie and his wife were accorded a ceremonial burial, and the description of "Mrs. Sakie's" funeral reveals the sharing of custom and the closeness of contact which could characterize Indian-white relationships on the Bay:

> In the Afternoon We Buryed ye Queen along side of ye King her Husband after the English fashion we put her into a Gun Chest and Covered it with a flag 4 English Carried her upon there shoulders & 4 Indian women held up ye Pall, old Chicikitie (Sakies own Brother) & his wife walkt next ye Corps & all ye rest of ye Indians in

H B C Archives

"East View of Moose Factory by Wm. Richards, Native of Hudson's Bay, now in the service of the Honble Hudsons Bay Company." Early 19th century.

Order after them being about 30 . . . I walkt before the Corps to ye Burying place when we came there & sett ye Corps down Chicikitie made a short Speach after there way then we put her into ye Grave & Covered the Corps up, Chicikitie Interseeded with me very much to Rail it Round like ye Englishmens Burying Place . . . they all seemed to [be] vastly pleased when I said it should be done.[23]

Such incidents certainly belie the common stereotype of Englishmen as being remote or insensitive in their dealings with the natives.

The Home Guard themselves came to look upon the Company posts as welfare stations which would provide succour, especially for the crippled, sick or starving. J. Jones, a former servant, testified at the Parliamentary Enquiry into the Company's affairs in 1749 that:

> . . . the Indians near the Factories Consider their
> Factories as their Home, The Company relieves their
> distresses, keep their Families for several Months
> together.[24]

This practice, which was motivated by economic as well
as humanitarian considerations, had particularly beneficial consequences for Indian women. In times of scarcity in Indian society,
the women were usually the first to suffer.[25] Before they would
often have perished, but now many sought relief at the Company
posts. At Albany during the hard winter of 1706, Governor
Anthony Beale gave shelter to three starving Cree women whose
husband had sent them away, as he could only provide for his two
children.[26] Many Indian women also received medical attention
from the post surgeons. A notably successful case was that of a
woman who was left at Albany in the fall of 1769 "exceeding Ill";
the following spring her husband returned to find her and her
three children "by Mr. Kitchin's care, and the nourishment
afforded them from Your Honors Fort, hearty and well."[27]

Part of the reason that the traders were prone to take pity on
the suffering of Indian women stemmed from their bourgeois
European notions of how women should be treated. Practically to
a man, fur-trade writers articulate a view of women as being the
fragile, weaker sex dependent upon the chivalrous protection of
men. They were appalled by the drudgery and hardship of an
Indian woman's lot; the fact that a life of toil and premature old
age were the fate of many women in their own country did not
seem to intrude upon their consciousness.[28] Particularly shocking
to the fur traders was the way in which women in northern and
woodland tribes were used as beasts of burden; they were required
to carry or haul the accoutrements of camp from place to place
and fetch home the animals which the hunters had killed. Henry
Kelsey, travelling inland with the Cree in the 1690s, was the first
of several Englishmen to comment on what appeared to him to be
the degraded, slave-like state of Indian women:

> Now as for a women they do not so much mind her for
> they reckon she is like a Slead dog or Bitch when she is
> living & when she dies they think she departs to Eternity
> but a man they think departs to another world & lives
> again.[29]

Even if her carrying role was alleviated by the use of water or animal transport, the division of labour in Indian society subjected the women to an endless round of domestic tasks, rendered all the more onerous by the primitive conditions of the migratory life they led. Writing of the Cree over a century after Kelsey, Alexander Mackenzie declared that a woman's lot was "an uninterrupted succession of toil and pain."

> They are . . . subject to every kind of domestic drudgery: they dress the leather, make the clothes and shoes, weave the nets, collect wood, erect the tents, fetch water [and] perform every culinary service.[30]

Both Mackenzie and Thompson claimed that among the Cree and Chipewyan respectively, women were known to practise female infanticide to spare their daughters the miseries which they themselves had suffered.[31] It is difficult to determine the truth of these allegations. Life was difficult and precarious for both sexes in nomadic Indian tribes, and other commentators felt that the women did not question their role which was essential for survival.[32] However, it did not accord with European notions of femininity for women to be strong. The Hudson's Bay Company men found the unladylike strength of Chipewyan women particularly astonishing. On one occasion David Thompson sent one of his strongest men to help a Chipewyan woman who was hauling a heavy sled; to the man's surprise, it took all his strength to budge the load.[33] The Chipewyan themselves took the superior strength of women for granted. As the famous chief Matonabbee declared, "Women . . . were made for labour; one of them can carry, or haul, as much as two men can do."[34] Samuel Hearne perceived that the Chipewyan evaluated women by different criteria than did the European. Physical prowess and economic skills took precedence over delicate features:

> Ask a Northern Indian, what is beauty? he will answer, a broad flat face, small eyes, high cheek-bones . . . a low forehead, a large broad chin, a clumsy hook-nose, a tawny hide, and breasts hanging down to the belt. Those beauties are greatly heightened, or at least rendered more valuable, when the possessor is capable of dressing all kinds of skins, converting them into the different parts of their clothing, and able to carry eight or ten

stone in Summer, or haul a much greater weight in Winter.[35]

This historical example of Chipewyan women raises the suspicion that the assumed weakness of European women was much more the product of social attitudes and conditioning than innate physical structure.

The traders also observed a sharp difference between European and Indian attitudes in regard to childbirth. Coming from a society which regarded childbirth as the time of women's greatest travail, Europeans were surprised by the scant concern shown for such matters in Indian society.[36] Andrew Graham's observations were typical:

> I can affirm, that women have been taken in travail while on a journey; and they only drop behind the company, bring forth the little stranger, tie it up in a cradle, and carrying it on their backs, proceed as if nothing had happened.[37]

The positions adopted by Indian women in labour, either squatting or kneeling over a low object, seemed to lessen the length and pain of parturition.[38] Concerned at the lack of help and attention which "the sex" received in childbirth, Samuel Hearne endeavoured to explain to Indian women the benefits of the use of midwives as in Britain. He was met with the contemptuous response that such interference was probably the cause of the humpbacks, bandy legs and other deformities which the Indians observed among their English visitors.[39] James Isham, on the other hand, found Indian attitudes commendable. After observing how soon Cree women resumed their heavy work, he was prompted to suggest that Englishwomen were too often unnecessarily pampered: "I think itt's only pride and ambition, that some takes in Keeping their Bed a full month, and putting a poor C—'n to Charge and Expence for aught."[40]

Isham also noticed that Indian women were not very prolific. Children were generally spaced two to three years apart. In attempting to account for this lack of fertility compared with European women, Isham subscribed to a contemporary theory that prolonged nursing prevented conception. Indian mothers suckled their children for several years, never having recourse to wet nurses as was then common practice among the wealthier

"Interior of a Cree Tent, March 25, 1820." This family traded at Cumberland House. Drawing by Lieutenant Robert Hood.

classes in Europe.[41] The traders considered that such a long nursing period had a detrimental effect upon the women because it resulted in premature aging, but the Indians had their own reasons for supporting this practice. If children were weaned before the age of three, the Indian women at Severn House informed William Falconer, they would develop large bellies from having to drink too much water and this would make them poor travellers unable to withstand fatigue.[42] Furthermore, native women had to nurse their children until they were old enough to eat solid, adult fare. As one observer succinctly wrote: "They give babies nothing but milk or else present them with a leg of goose."[43]

The Europeans did comment favourably on the practicality of the Indian cradle which allowed the child, encased in soft skins, to be conveniently carried on its mother's back. A silky, dried, absorbent moss, which was frequently changed, took the place of diapers. Isham thought this was such a "good Saving method", dispensing with the trouble and expense of washing, drying and buying cloth for clouts, that it could be advantageously adopted by "the poor folk's in our own Nation."[44] J. H. Lefroy, a visitor to the Indian Country in the mid-nineteenth century, left a delightful picture of a two-week-old baby which was presented for his inspection:

> It . . . was packed up in that peculiar Indian fashion which I think so excellent. It was so neat and compact, about fourteen inches long, unlike an ordinary baby, which may be put in ones arms, and one does not know which end one had hold of, or which is baby and which is petticoat. It was made to hang up, or set upright. . . . The outside case is made of cloth . . . and embroidery; the inside stuffing is a soft silky moss, very abundant in this country, so that nothing can be so economical.[45]

It was distressing to the traders to see the way in which the onerous duties imposed on Indian women, coupled with the cares of maternity, soon rendered even the most attractive of them old and wrinkled. Unlike the Indian, the European male tended to view a woman as a sexual object, placing much more emphasis on her physical attributes. Thus the traders were constantly evaluating the "looks" of the native women they encountered, their concept of beauty very much reflecting European attitudes. There was widespread agreement that the most comely Indian women were the Cree. According to Alexander Mackenzie:

> Their figure is generally well proportioned, and the regularity of their features would be acknowledged by the more civilized people of Europe. Their complexion has less of that dark tinge which is common to those savages who have less cleanly habits.[46]

The traders commented upon the care which Cree women took in fashioning their hair in elaborate knots and plaits, painting their faces and adorning their garments and persons with beads and bangles. "They omit nothing to make themselves lovely," declared Alexander Henry the elder. Andrew Graham was less impressed, "Like their sisters on the other side the Atlantic, they make too much use of paint."[47]

Opinion varied considerably as to the merits of the women of the other western tribes.[48] The hardened features of Plains

*"Flathead Woman and Child, Caw-wacham." From a painting by
Paul Kane.*

Indian women were not deemed very seductive, but some were attracted by the sweetness of their voices and the way in which their long, soft robes of antelope skin showed their figures to advantage. While the traders could hardly have been paragons of hygiene, they found the Indian women's habit of smearing their bodies with animal grease repulsive. Chinook women who flattened their heads and liberally anointed themselves with salmon oil had little to recommend them, but the Chipewyan women perhaps received the harshest comments. In Samuel Hearne's view, these females were "as destitute of real beauty as any nation I ever saw", some of them being "perfect antidotes to love and gallantry."[49] Yet even among the Chipewyan, Hearne admitted that some of the younger ones were tolerable. Indeed, the traders generally felt a considerable sexual attraction to young Indian women. Cree and Ojibwa girls could be particularly captivating. The Cree were "very frisky when Young & c . . . well shap'd . . . their Eyes Large and Grey yet Lively and Sparkling very Bewitchen . . .; the Ojibwa possessed "pretty black eyes, which they know very well how to humour in a languishing and engaging manner whenever they wish to please."[50]

In the realm of sexual attitudes, the European traders found much to shock, confuse and, in some cases, entice in Indian society. Most of the officers subscribed to a European ideal of womanhood, which emphasized the necessity of female modesty and chastity. In the late eighteenth century, Samuel Hearne, in extolling the virtues of his beloved, praised her for having "a consciousness of innocence, an amiable modesty, and an unrivalled delicacy of sentiment."[51] Thus, the amount of sexual freedom allowed to women in Indian society seemed scandalous to the traders. The more prudish of them, David Thompson and the younger Henry, for example, were disgusted by the fact that some of the women were scantily clad or were so lacking in modesty as to bathe in full view of the men.[52] Even more perturbing was the lack of concern evinced for the virginity of young girls; pre-marital sex was common. As James Isham remarked of the Cree: "Maidens are Very rare to be found at 13 or 14 Years, and I believe m'y Safely say none at 15"; Andrew Graham mused more perceptively that he could not rank fornication as a vice among the Indians as they thought it was perfectly normal.[53]

When it came to marriage, fur-trade observers thought there was a curious lack of romantic involvement between Indian husbands and wives. Individual romantic inclination was not the operative factor in choosing a marital partner. Usually parents and close relations were responsible for arranging a match which was viewed more as a contract between two groups of kin than between two individuals.[54] To the European, it seemed that marriages were contracted with remarkably little ceremony. "When a Young Man had a mind for a Wife" explained Isham, "they do not make Long tedious Ceremony's nor use much formality's."[55] In general, after the consent of the girl's parents had been received, the bargain was sealed by the payment of goods which constituted a bride price. Among the Cree, the custom of bride service was also practised; this required the couple to live with the wife's relations, the husband giving the produce of his hunt to his in-laws until he proved himself capable of supporting his family and the first child was born.[56] Most Indian tribes did not hold the marriage bond to be indissoluble. David Thompson observed, if "they cannot live peaceably together, they separate with as little ceremony as they came together, and both parties are free to attach themselves to whom they will, without any stain on their characters."[57] All the western tribes were polygamous. A plurality of wives was often an economic necessity, a man's prestige being enhanced by the number of wives he could support. The traders, however, were inclined to reflect their own cultural prejudice against polygamy, pointing out that it gave rise to jealous, sometimes murderous, quarrels among the women.[58]

There were times when the Indians' treatment of their women so outraged the chivalrous feelings of the traders that they felt compelled to intervene. Particularly abhorrent was the Chipewyan custom of wrestling for wives; the woman, whatever her own wishes, became the prize of the victor.[59] On one occasion, a young Chipewyan called The Crane lost his wife in a wrestling match at a Hudson's Bay Company post. David Thompson and his men saved the wife by driving the winner out of the fort, but The Crane had won only a temporary reprieve. The other Indian threatened, "You are now under the protection of the White Men, in the summer I shall see you on our lands, and then I shall twist your neck and take your woman from you." When Thompson defended the action of another Chipewyan who had adopted the "white man's way" and actually shot a rival who had wrestled his wife from him, he was contemptuously informed that no woman was worth killing a countryman for:

> Ah, that is the way you White Men . . . always talk and do, a Woman cannot be touched but you get hold of guns and long Knives; What is a woman good for, she cannot hunt, she is only to work and carry our things and on no account whatever ought the ground to be made red with man's blood. Then the strong men take Women when they want them; Certainly the strong men have a right to the Women.[60]

Wrestling for women was probably an exaggerated form of wife exchange which was common in Indian society. An Indian husband deemed it perfectly proper to lend his wife, even to a stranger, for any period of time — from a night to several years — after which she would be welcomed back along with any children born in the interim.[61] The traders had great difficulty in comprehending this custom. To them it seemed indicative of promiscuous sexual behaviour, but to the Indians, wife-lending was important for its social and economic consequences. They considered it "a reciprocal alliance and series of good offices . . . between the friends of both parties; each is ready to assist and protect the other."[62] This practice was not to be equated with adultery. The Indians did not sanction clandestine relationships, and a woman who was discovered with a paramour might be punished with physical mutilation or even death.

While it is true that some of the officers were offended by Indian customs, the liberal sexual attitudes of the Indians served to arouse the white man's desire, especially in a situation where native women were the only females to be encountered. When the Indians offered their women to the newcomers, as was their custom, many of the men were quick to take advantage of this rather extraordinary expression of hospitality.[63] On his journey to the Pacific, Alexander Mackenzie frequently referred to his men sharing the beds of women of various tribes. The generosity of the Mandan of the Upper Missouri in this regard was apparently a potent incentive for trading parties to make the long journey across the plains to their villages.[64] Hudson's Bay Company servant Richard White declared: "The Indians were a sensible People, and agreed their Women should be made use of."[65]

The traders can be accused of ultimately corrupting this Indian practice into outright prostitution. It did not take the Indians long to realize that in their women they possessed a valuable commodity that they could exploit to satisfy what appeared to be the Europeans' voracious sexual appetites. In 1776, Alexander Henry the elder complained that the Indians had little need to trap furs for the "pedlars" because "what with trading Provisions [and] lending their Women to Masters and Men, they obtain more necessaries than they want." He also charged that the Chipewyan were known to take their women hundreds of miles to the Bay for no other purpose than to satisfy the lust of the English.[66] The Plains Indians initially regarded prostitution as dishonourable, but they gradually began to sell the favours of their women if they had nothing much else to trade. By the early 1800s, according to one Nor'Wester, they had become a real nuisance in offering their women to the Company's men, especially since it was "all for the sake of gain, not from any regard for us."[67] Prostitution was also rampant on the Columbia. Here, large numbers of lower-class Chinook women took to camping outside Fort George during the summer, ready to satisfy the needs of the voyageurs who manned the brigades — a situation which was compared with "their frail sisters of Portsmouth" besieging the crews of a newly arrived East Indian fleet.[68]

The corruption of Indian morals was intensified by the Nor'Westers' wholesale importation of liquor into the Indian Country. But even at the Hudson's Bay Company posts where the use of alcohol had been restricted to treating, liquor had begun to have a demoralizing effect, especially among the Home Guards who had come to expect a liberal present of brandy for procuring provisions and trapping small furs. This latter task was often performed by the women who became, it was reported, more rapidly addicted to alcohol than the men; the men at this time considered being drunk "odious" and "not Becoming their Sex". By the mid-eighteenth century, several Hudson's Bay Company officers were lamenting the effect of liquor on the Indians, particularly the women; not only did it make them prone to jealous acts of violence and the neglect of their children, but it debauched their morals. It was tragic, declared James Isham, that the Indian had ever been allowed "to taste of that Bewitching spirit calld. Brandy, or any other Spiritious Liquor's, — which has been the Ruing of a Great many . . . and the Cheif Cause of their Ludness and bad way's they are now given to".[69] One of their "bad ways" was that an Indian would now gladly lend his wife to an Englishman for a bottle of brandy.[70]

Prostitution with its attendant horror, venereal disease,[71] became a problem in the Indian Country, as it already was in Europe. Its extent, however, should not be exaggerated. It is significant that it did not become the usual pattern of sexual interaction between European traders and Indian women, even though it might appear that the fur-trade situation was particularly conducive to unregulated sexual licence. Here, after all, European males, relatively free from the social controls of their own culture, encountered native females who were accustomed to an open expression of their sexuality. What is fascinating about fur-trade society is that there were other important factors which worked toward stabilizing relationships and promoting long-lasting unions. Marriage *à la façon du pays,* not prostitution, became the usual relationship within fur-trade society.

2

THE CUSTOM OF THE COUNTRY

Marriage "after the custom of the country" was an indigenous marriage rite which evolved to meet the needs of fur-trade society. It was practised by both Hudson's Bay Company men and Nor'Westers, although marital patterns within each company framework differed, largely because of the contrast in official company policy toward intermarriage with the Indians. Such was the strength of the social forces promoting the taking of Indian wives that Hudson's Bay Company officers in the field were continually bending the official rules. Finally the London Committee was forced to modify its prohibition of Indian women. The Nor'Westers, on the other hand, did not suffer any split between official policy and actual practice. Deeply influenced by the previous experience of the French traders, the North West Company appreciated the advantages which could accrue from allowing its men to form unions with the Indian women. One of the results of the spread of the fur trade to the Great Lakes region had been extensive intermarriage between the French and the Ojibwa. Although denounced by the Jesuit priests as being immoral, the traders had taken their Indian wives according to traditional native marriage rites and distinct family units had developed.[1] This pattern was to continue after the British take-over of the Quebec fur trade. In the North West Company, all ranks (bourgeois, clerk and engagé) were allowed to marry Indian women.

It is important to emphasize that the Indians initially encouraged the formation of marriage alliances between their women and the European traders. The Indian viewed marriage in an integrated social and economic context; a marital alliance created a reciprocal social bond which served to consolidate his economic relationship with a stranger. Thus, through marriage, the trader was drawn into the Indian's kinship circle. And in return for giving the traders sexual and domestic rights to their women, the Indians expected reciprocal privileges such as free access to the posts and provisions.[2] The marriage of a daughter to a fur trader brought prestige and the promise of security to an Indian family. Among the Cree it became customary to reserve one or more of their daughters specifically to offer as wives "for the white People". This practice was also observed among upper-class Chinook families, where marriage to a trader served to enhance social rank and influence.[3]

Given the Indian view of marriage, a trader's alliance with an Indian woman served the important public function of cementing trade ties, a fact quickly grasped by the Nor'Westers. Successful traders in the Lake Superior region owed much of their fortune to allying themselves through marriage to the prominent Ojibwa bands in the area. In the Athabasca country in 1803, the young clerk William Connolly found his influence among the Cree who frequented Rat River House much increased after he married a daughter of one of the chiefs.[4] It did not take the officers of the Hudson's Bay Company long to realize that marriage to the daughter of a leading hunter or chief could secure not only the bountiful hunt of the father-in-law but that of his relations as well. James Isham, a prominent eighteenth-century governor, declared that marriage alliances created "a firm friendship" with the Indians and were "a great help in Engaging them to trade."[5] Hudson's Bay Company officers took the lead in espousing women who were well connected to leading Indians. Governor Joseph Adams, in the 1730s, had an Indian mate described as being of "ye blood Royal", while Humphrey Marten's wife Pawpitch was a daughter of the "Captain of the Goose Hunters".[6] The men of both companies married most extensively into the Ojibwa, Cree and Chipewyan tribes who inhabited a large area, but as the Nor'Westers moved westward across the Rockies, they contracted unions with women of more remote tribes. In the 1790s James Hughes, a prominent Nor'Wester, married Nan-touche who was probably a Kootenay, as she came from a tribe beyond the Rockies.[7] In 1818 when in charge of Spokane House, the redoubtable Peter Skene Ogden made a valuable alliance with the Nez Percé when he married "Princess Julia" or Julia Rivet, the step-daughter of a French-Canadian trapper.[8]

On the Pacific coast, marriage alliances played a significant role in the traders' relations with the sophisticated Chinook nation. Shortly before transferring his allegiance to the North West Company, Duncan McDougall, the governor of Astoria, had successfully negotiated a match with one of the daughters of Concomely, the powerful Chinook chief.[9] Several more of Concomely's daughters, born of his wives from various neighbouring bands, became consorts of fur traders. The Nor'Wester Alexander McKenzie, while still a clerk, married Concomely's favourite daughter who was dubbed the "Princess of Wales". The importance of this alliance was recognized by the Hudson's Bay Company when it assumed control of the Columbia. Governor Simpson, while visiting Fort George in 1824, declared, "[Mrs. McKenzie] is much attached to us and not only leads her Husband but the whole of the Royal Family."[10] In the early 1820s, another clerk, Archibald McDonald, married the chief's daughter known as "Princess Raven".

The Nor'Westers appreciated that alliances contracted between their engagés and Indian women could sometimes be as effective as those of the officers. Many traders had extolled the virtues of the Flathead women who were reputed to be excellent wives and mothers, but this tribe would sanction the marriage of its women only to those men it esteemed. The skill and bravery of a Métis hunter and interpreter, Pierre Michel, enabled him to win the hand of the sixteen-year-old niece of a hereditary Flathead chief in the spring of 1814; Ross Cox claimed that Michel was the only Nor'Wester he knew to be so honoured by this tribe.[11] The first white man to marry into the Carrier tribe of New Caledonia was Jean-Baptiste Boucher dit Waccan, another Company interpreter, who took to wife a daughter of one of the chiefs in March 1811. Waccan was to remain a personage of considerable influence among the Carrier for nearly half a century.[12]

Marital alliances could also be a factor in trade competition. In 1794 at a post on the Saskatchewan, Duncan

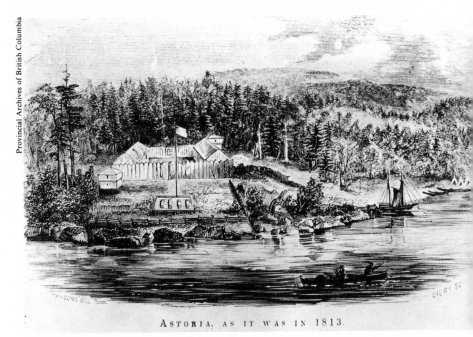

Fort George in 1813 as it was when Nor'Wester Alexander McKenzie married the favourite daughter of Concomely, the powerful Chinook chief.

McGillivray reported that he had secured the furs of a former customer of the English because one of his womenfolk had become the wife of a Nor'Wester.[13] After the union of the two companies, marriages continued to play an important role in promoting good relations between the traders and the tribes in outlying districts. When the Hudson's Bay Company was planning to move into New Caledonia in the interior of British Columbia in the early 1820s, Governor Simpson recommended that the officers should form connections with the principal families immediately upon their arrival as "the best security we can have of the goodwill of the Natives."[14] On a later visit to Fort Stikine in 1841, Simpson gave permission to over a dozen of the men to take Indian wives because these unions would form a useful link with the Tsimshian Indians which would outweigh the increased cost of provisions.[15]

From the many examples that can be cited of European traders marrying Indian women to enhance trade connections, it

Humphrey Marten describes the death of his Cree wife, Pawpitch, in his Albany journal, 24 January 1771. The reference to Pawpitch is bracketed and there is a marginal reference. These annotations were presumably done by the London Secretary for the benefit of the Committee members. Hudson's Bay Company Archives B.3/a/63, fo. 18d.

appears that there was a strong economic motive for the contraction of these unions. Feelings of affection, it might be supposed, did not play a large part in the white man's calculations. This was undoubtedly true in some cases, but what is significant is that many of these marriages *à la façon du pays* developed into lasting and devoted unions. Hudson's Bay Company officer Humphrey Marten revealed intense concern when his Cree wife Pawpitch fell ill of a fever. He must have been watching over her when she died, for he recorded her death in the post journal (an unusual step in itself) as occurring at precisely ten minutes to three on the morning of 24 January 1771. He grieved for the fate of his poor child now left motherless.[16] The experience of parenthood was an important factor in strengthening the bonds between husband and wife. In 1794 at York Factory, Hudson's Bay Company surveyor Peter Fidler took a Cree woman for a wife; Mary, as he called her, proved a valuable helpmate on his wide-ranging excursions. Fourteen children were born to the Fidlers, and the father kept an exact record of their appearance in a little notebook. The eldest, Tom, was born at York Factory at 12:08 a.m. on 20 June 1795; the youngest, Harriett, at Red River at 4:53 on 9 July 1822.[17] As a young clerk in the North West Company, Alexander Ross had been impressed by the virtues of the women of the Okanagan tribe, who possessed "an engaging sweetness, are good house-wives, modest . . . affectionate and chaste." Around 1815, he married the daughter of one of the chiefs; several years later Ross took his Sally to live in the Red River Settlement where they raised a family of thirteen children.[18] Perhaps the most touching tribute to an Indian wife came from William McNeil, captain of the Hudson's Bay Company steamship *Beaver*. He married a Haida woman whose eventual death in childbirth caused him much sorrow:

> . . . the deceased has been a good and faithful partner to me for twenty years and we had twelve children together . . . [she] was a most kind mother to her children, and no Woman could have done her duty better, although an Indian.[19]

An important reason for the strength of the attachment between white traders and Indian women lies in the fact that for

Sally, daughter of an Okanagan chief, who married
Alexander Ross. Undated.

many decades no white women were present in the Indian
Country. In the earliest years of the Hudson's Bay Company, a
singularly unsuccessful attempt had been made to send British
women to the Bay. With the failure of this experiment, strict
rules were imposed prohibiting any women from taking passage
on the Company ships.[20] The Nor'Westers apparently knew
better than to expose white women to the hazards of the
interior. As a result, no white women made their appearance in
the Canadian West until the early nineteenth century, which
placed the traders in an unusual situation. In colonial societies
where white women were present, even if in a minority, relations

Provincial Archives of Manitoba

Henrietta Ross, daughter of Sally and Alexander Ross. In 1854 she married the Reverend John Black. Undated.

between European men and native women were largely restricted to casual or illicit affairs. In seeking to re-establish the domestic life of the mother country, the European woman zealously guarded her status as wife and mother.[21] With the absence of white women, such a pattern could not develop in fur-trade society. Furthermore, it was difficult, if not impossible, for the traders to maintain stable relationships with women in their own country because many of them spent the better part of their adult lives in the Indian Country. Thus, an Indian woman provided the only option for any sort of connubial comfort. For many a trader, an Indian woman filled the place of a white woman as his wife and the mother of his children. The resulting domesticity was a valued aspect of life. Chief Factor James Douglas wrote with feeling that a family was a strong antidote to the loneliness of a trader's existence:

> There is indeed no living with comfort in this country until a person had forgot the great world and has his tastes and character formed on the current standard of the stage . . . To any other being . . . the vapid monotony of an inland trading Post, would be perfectly unsufferable, while habit makes it familiar to us, softened as it is by the many tender ties, which find a way to the heart.[22]

Alexander Ross claimed that the affection which both the bourgeois and the men entertained for their native wives was "one great reason for that attachment which the respective classes of whites cherish for the Indian countries."[23] Indeed, the Nor'Westers realized that to allow their engagés to develop family ties in the West was a good way of ensuring that they renewed their contracts.

Because the Nor'Westers openly sanctioned intermarriage with the Indians, their writings provide considerable information about what constituted the "custom of the country". Significantly, in its early stages, marriage à la façon du pays was mainly derived from Indian practices. A first and essential step for the trader who wished to take an Indian wife was to obtain the consent of her parents. He would then be required to pay a bride price which was determined by the girl's relations, for the Indians were adamant that the traders should follow their custom. According to the younger Henry, the common medium of exchange was a horse for a wife,[24] but bride price could vary considerably among the tribes. At Fort Alexandria in 1801, Payet, one of Daniel Harmon's interpreters, gave the parents of his Cree bride rum and dry goods to the value of two hundred dollars.[25] The marriage of a young clerk to a comely Spokan girl in the winter of 1815 was celebrated by a generous distribution of goods — blankets and kettles to her principal relations; beads, hawk-bells and other trinkets to her lesser kindred.[26] Among the Chinook, marriage involved a mutual exchange of gifts. When Duncan McDougall married Chief Concomely's daughter, he received a rich dowry of sea-otter pelts, but it took the trader almost a year to accumulate the goods to pay for his bride. A total of 15 guns and 15 blankets and a great deal of other property were the cost of "this precious lady".[27]

Marriage *à la façon du pays* apparently did not involve any exchange of vows between the couple, but it was solemnized by other rituals. The smoking of the calumet sealed the alliance that had been formed between the trader and the Indian band, and among some tribes, such as the Flathead, the woman was publicly lectured by her elders on the duties of a wife and mother. Pierre Michel's bride was exhorted "to be chaste, obedient, industrious, and silent, and when absent with her husband among other tribes, always to stay at home, and have no intercourse with strange Indians."[28] The trader usually visited the Indian encampment to claim his wife, and then the couple would be ceremoniously escorted to the fort. It became customary for a new Indian bride to go through a cleansing ritual performed by the other women of the fort, which was designed to render her more pleasing to the white man. She was scoured of grease and paint and her leather garments were exchanged for those of a more European style. At the North West Company posts, wives were clothed in "Canadian fashion" which consisted of a shirt, short gown, petticoat and leggings.[29] Then the trader conducted his bride to his quarters, and from thenceforth they were considered to be man and wife. Since the Hudson's Bay Company officially prohibited its men from taking Indian wives, it is not surprising that no descriptions of marriage *à la façon du pays* have been found in the writings of its officers to date. As early as the 1740s, a few journal entries make reference to certain Indians being the "fathers-in-law" of Englishmen, which indicates that the men on the Bay acknowledged the existence of marital relationships with Indian women.[30] It is safe to assume that these marriages must have been contracted according to rites similar to those practised by the Nor'Westers after the custom of the country.

It appears that Hudson's Bay Company men were even more influenced by Indian attitudes than were the Nor'Westers. The Indians were polygamous and sought to impress upon the traders that "all great men should have a plurality of wives".[31] Hudson's Bay Company officers in their isolation on the Bay were prepared to adopt this custom which enhanced their prestige in Indian eyes. Throughout the eighteenth century, quite a number of notable chief factors at Bayside posts kept more than one Indian wife: men such as James Isham ("the idol of the Indians"), Joseph Isbister and Robert Pilgrim.[32] The most notorious polygamist was reputed to be Moses Norton who, while governor at Churchill, kept a harem of half a dozen of the finest Indian girls.[33] Another prominent officer Matthew Cocking had three Indian wives and in his will of 1797 made provision for the two who were still living, Ke-che-cho-wich and A-pis-taSqua-sish.[34] As late as the founding of the Red River Colony in 1812, Chief Factor William Hemmings Cook at York Factory was indulging in what seems to have become a Bay tradition. Miles Macdonell, the leader of the colonists, who was incensed at Cook's lack of co-operation, acidly observed:

> It may easily be supposed that a chief who occupies himself the Mess room with a squaw occupying an apartment on each side opening into it, would not be very desirous of having his family arrangements deranged by visitors.[35]

In the 1780s the English found themselves besieged with offers of wives at their inland posts, but now some of the officers attempted to follow the example of the Nor'Westers and refused to take more than one Indian wife.[36] This definite stand was taken for economic, if not moral, reasons. Alexander Henry and other Nor'Westers record the persistence of Indian efforts to provide them with wives, but the men limited themselves to one wife at a time. As one former Nor'Wester later testified: "I never heard of any of the men keeping two women at a time, it was not customary. A man could have only one wife."[37]

The North West Company's reluctance to countenance polygamy likely stemmed from its concern for the expense that would accrue from having to support multiple families. It was Company policy to feed, and to at least partially clothe, its employees' wives and families. Hudson's Bay Company officers were, understandably, envious of the liberal way in which their rivals were supported in their domestic arrangements. The bourgeois always had his girl who was carried in and out of his canoe and shared the luxury of his tent and feather bed. When a lowly clerk chose to take a wife, complained Philip Turnor, he was not put to any extra expense, as the Company provided the bride's new "Canadian" apparel.[38] The Nor'Westers were not so generous with their engagés, however; many a voyageur went deeply into debt buying finery for his native wife, owing to the exorbitant prices charged at the Company posts.[39]

By contrast, the Hudson's Bay Company, once it began to realize that it was impossible to prevent its officers from taking Indian wives, was anxious to avoid the resulting expense. In 1739, the London Committee wrote grudgingly to Governor Richard Norton at Churchill:

> As to your Concience in Relation to the Indian Woman and Family, we agree with you that we have no power over that but Certainly the Company ought not to be put to any Charge, or their affairs be Damaged thereby.[40]

Eventually the Committee did accept that the families of active employees might be provisioned at Company expense, but it remained adamant that the Company's economic responsibility ceased with the death or retirement of its employees.[41] The fact that the onus remained on the individual rather than the Company to provide for a family accounts for the large number of Hudson's Bay Company men who left wills granting annuities to their native dependants. The most the Committee would do was to endeavour to have these annuities distributed.

Marriage à la façon du pays evolved from a complex social interaction between the traders and the Indians. Although there were variations in marital patterns, the custom of the country became a commonly understood social practice in the Indian Country.[42] Its acceptance was reinforced by the traders themselves who put considerable pressure on a newcomer to adopt a code of behaviour which had gained its own legitimacy through long usage. One can observe this process of social conditioning working on Nor'Westers Alexander Henry, George Nelson and Daniel Harmon. Arriving fresh from eastern colonial society which recognized only the legitimacy of church marriage, these young men were initially shocked by

fur-trade marriage practices which seemed only a form of
concubinage, "a snare laid no doubt by the Devil himself."[43]
They therefore began by refusing all offers of wives made to
them, but soon all three men were to conform to the custom of
the country. George Nelson's doubts about the propriety of
taking an Indian wife did not last long when he found that his
own bourgeois derided his scruples and the men ridiculed his
prudery.[44] When loneliness finally drove Daniel Harmon to
take a country wife in the fall of 1805 at South Branch House,
he rationalized his decision by declaring that "it is customary
for all the Gentlemen who come in this Country to remain any
length of time to have a <u>fair</u> Partner".[45] It should be emphasized
that the Indians themselves played an important role in ensuring
that the usual patterns for sexual relations between their women
and the white traders took the form of sanctioned marital
unions. Traders who sought to side-step the formalities of
marriage *à la façon du pays* or offended Indian customs ran
the risk of serious reprisal. As one old voyageur explained,
custom had to be observed in the Indian Country; one could not
just grab any woman one pleased:

> Presque toutes les nations sont pareilles, quant aux
> coutumes. On ne se joue pas d'une femme sauvage
> comme on veut. . . . Un homme engagé et un bourgeois
> donnent des présents aux parents de la femme, pour
> l'avoir: . . . Il y aurait du danger d'avoir la tête cassée,
> si l'on prend la fille dans ce pays, sans le consentement
> des parents.[46]

Conflict between the fur traders and the Indians was
relatively rare in the Canadian West. When trouble did occur
it could very often be traced to the traders' failure to understand
or to respect Indian moral standards. During their occupation
of the English posts on the Bay in the early eighteenth century,
the French were taught the perils of trifling with Indian women.
At Fort Philépeaux, an outpost on the Severn River, the French
had forced some Cree women into the fort against their will.
Determined to avenge this outrage, the Indians, according to
James Isham's graphic account, fixed upon an unusual form of
sabotage:

> [the women] therefore unperceivd. informd. their

husbands to be Ready upon a Signal they wou'd make, accordingly the women took an oppertunity to wett all the french fuzes with their 'urin'e, and then gave the Signal, when their husbands Gott in under cover of the Night, and put their Enemies to the rout, when the french run to their arm's and found how they was betrayd, and was Kill'd for their prefidiousness, being 8 in Number.[47]

News of this incident confirmed the London Committee in its suspicion that it was folly to allow Company men to consort with Indian women. In fact, the insistence of the Committee that its unrealistic prohibitions be enforced seriously marred Company operations throughout much of the eighteenth century. Andrew Graham, a prominent eighteenth-century officer, observed "The intercourse that is carried on between the Indian Ladies and the Englishmen is not allowed, but winked at."[48] Ironically, it was the governors or chief factors themselves, on whom the enactment of Committee policy depended, who took the lead in forming marriage alliances with the Indians. According to Graham, who fathered at least two children during his time on the Bay, "the Factors keeps a bed-fellow within the Fort at all times." He maintained, however, that they did try to limit the contact which the lower ranks had with Indian women. "At proper times" a junior officer might be allowed to entertain an Indian lady in his apartment provided she did not stay there overnight, but ordinary servants were allowed no privileges, being restricted to chance encounters or sneaking over the walls at night.[49]

Graham seems to have exaggerated the extent to which the rules were enforced. Earlier in the century some of the governors, most notably James Isham, had allowed their men to form more permanent relationships with Indian women. When in charge of York Factory in the 1750s, Isham not only permitted his servants to have the company of Indian women when posted to the hunters' tents or on short journeys where they were especially useful, but women were allowed as well to reside in the men's quarters in the fort. Like the Nor'Westers, Isham observed that such liaisons had a conciliating effect upon the men; he also recommended the formation of marriage alliances with distant tribes to cement trade ties. The London Committee's response to Isham's initiatives was to sharply censure his actions and demand that his successor Ferdinand Jacobs abolish such licence. Such vacillation in the enforcement of Company policy had a detrimental effect upon business; it alienated both the men and the Home Guard Indians and, ultimately, it resulted in violent conflict.

At places where Company servants had been allowed to form marital relationships with Indian women, the attempts of new governors to bar their families from the posts caused considerable ill-feeling. Jacobs who took over at York Factory in 1761 declared that "the worst Brothel House in London is Not So Common a Stew as the mens House in this Factory". The Indian women, however, regarded the men they were with as "Husbands" and when they were removed from the fort, several servants feigned sickness and refused to work.[50] At Albany in the 1750s when Joseph Isbister was instructed to take similar action against the servants' women, the armourer, who had spent over thirty pounds on his "sweetheart", was so outraged that he threatened to run away.[51] At Moose Factory in 1759, the men were so bold as to declare that if the Committee refused them advances on their wages to meet their families' needs, they would be obliged to leave the post and seek a subsistence elsewhere.[52] The governors particularly incurred the wrath of the men because they exempted themselves from their own rules, deeming it their prerogative to continue to keep Indian women. When Joseph Isbister was temporarily in charge of Churchill in the early 1750s, his rigid rules — especially since he did not follow them himself — provoked much resentment in his junior officers. A sharp altercation took place when Isbister reprimanded James Walker and Robert Bass for trying to take advantage of some Indian women; Walker declared that Isbister had gone too far:

> . . . he began to Vindicate himself . . . telling me that there are no such Strictness at the other factorys as here for here a Man cannot so much as loke at an Indian [woman] he is so watched.[53]

He even claimed that it would be much better to serve under the more lenient Isham at York, although it would mean a cut in wages.

While the governors could resort to threats and corporal

"A North West View of Prince of Wales's Fort in Hudson's Bay, North America, by Sam¹ Hearne, 1777."

punishment if necessary to keep their men in line[54], they were on much more dangerous ground if their policy alienated the Indians. At Moose Factory in the 1740s, one servant Augustin Frost warned the tyrannical James Duffield that the Home Guards were becoming disgruntled under the new regime which denied them access to the post as formerly. Duffield chose to ignore Frost's warnings, claiming that they were only a ruse which he hoped would reunite him with his Indian relations so that the fort would again become "an Indian Factory, with his own wives & Numerous family both in & about it as was ye Custom before."[55] Duffield was fortunate enough to escape the Indians' anger, but when the chief officers at Albany took to ignoring Indian sensibilities, tragedy was the result. The Home Guards around Albany, and especially their captain Woudby, had felt entitled to enter the fort and help themselves to provisions since "ye Englishmen . . . Keeped there Women, they had a Right to there Victuals."[56] Woudby and his followers were thus most insulted when in 1752 Isbister unceremoniously barred them from the post. An opportunity for revenge presented itself several years later when William Lamb was appointed to take charge of Henley House, a small outpost about one hundred miles

Public Archives of Canada

The Home Guard Indians were bands of Cree who lived close to the posts and were employed in hunting for the Company. This Cree hunter and his family were sketched at York Factory by P. Rindisbacher in 1821.

upstream from Albany. In spite of warnings, Lamb insisted that it was his prerogative as master to keep Indian women as Isbister had done at Albany. His two favourites, whom he kept "at Bed and Board" were closely related to Woudby — one was his daughter called Won,a,Wogen and the other his daughter-in-law Nam,a,shis. Their male relatives were not admitted to the house and, outraged by this violation of expected reciprocal privileges and possibly encouraged by the French, Woudby and his sons attacked the English during the winter, killing them and pillaging the house. "Women" lamented Albany's surgeon George Rushworth, "have been the destruction of Your People, Your Goods and Trade." Woudby and his accomplices were eventually tried and executed, but a shocked London Committee recalled Isbister to save him from Indian retaliation and again reprimanded its employees for making "bosom friends" of the Indians.[57]

In reality, the London Committee, with its persistent failure to come to grips with the social situation on the Bay, must share part of the blame for an incident such as the Henley House

Masssacre. Its attitude retarded the stabilizing of relationships between Company servants and Indian women, forcing the men to resort to more clandestine contact which was detrimental to all concerned.[58] In the mid-eighteenth century, it seems that officers on the Bay were enforcing official policy to the extent that the privilege of having an Indian wife became a function of rank, reserved only for officers. Once the Hudson's Bay Company began to move inland new factors contributed to the breakdown of the prohibition against Company servants taking Indian wives. The men could now see at first hand the benefits that their rivals derived from their widespread connection with Indian women. When it attempted to recruit skilled voyageurs into its service, the Hudson's Bay Company was made aware that the right to have an Indian wife was not one which the Canadians would relinquish lightly. At Brandon House in 1798 the recently engaged Jollycoeur insisted upon keeping his Indian consort, informing the master that "every frenchman had a woman & why should we stop him.[59] It is safe to say that well before the end of the eighteenth century, Hudson's Bay Company servants as well as officers had formed extensive marital connections with the Indians.

The growth of definite family ties and a marked concern for the welfare of native dependants is clearly revealed in many of the Hudson's Bay Company wills which have survived from the late eighteenth and early nineteenth centuries. Particularly touching was Matthew Cocking's entreaty to the London Committee to carry out his instructions for his family, not only as "an act of humanity and kindness to my Children and their Mothers" but also as "a testimonial of their esteem and regard for the memory of an old servant."[60] Numerous officers who died on the Bay — among them John Favell, William Bolland and Robert Goodwin — named their Indian wives in their wills and left careful instructions about the management of the annuities which were to provide them with clothing and other necessaries.[61] Many of the Company's servants, although their savings might be quite meagre, also endeavoured to provide for their families. Orkneyman William Flett was not untypical in directing that all his monies be put in trust for "the sole use and benefit" of his "reputed wife Saskatchewan" and their four children.[62]

Lasting relationships (even those that were polygamous) were fostered at Bayside posts where the lives of Hudson's Bay Company men were more stationary than those of the Nor'Westers. With more limited operations, the English did not face the prospect of being posted to a new district hundreds of miles away. The peripatetic experience of the Nor'Westers helps to explain a noticeable difference in the trends in marriage patterns which developed between the two companies. If the Nor'Westers did not believe in polygamy, many of them did practice what can be called serial monogamy. Some of the marriage alliances contracted by the bourgeois were basically for economic reasons, and such unions might not survive the trader's transfer to another region. Quite a number of notable bourgeois, such as J. G. McTavish, John Stuart, Peter Skene Ogden and John Clarke, had different native wives at various stages of their careers, and the Indians were not necessarily averse to this practice. They did not view marriage as a lifetime contract, nor did they consider it to be in their interest to have their women leave the district. On the contrary, observers from both companies reported that an Indian woman who had lived with and borne children to a white man could expect a ready welcome back into her tribe. "When any of the married women has a child by an Englishman" declared Andrew Graham, "the husband is not angry . . . but proud of his present. Indeed the affair rivets her firmly in his favour." Like Graham, the elder Henry stressed that the Indians regarded mixed-blood children as having superior physical attributes which made them better hunters and bolder warriors.[63] It must also be noted that while serial monogamy was an identifiable trend among the Nor'Westers, it was not universal. Other bourgeois, including William Connolly, John Dugald Cameron and Roderick McKenzie, contracted country marriages early in their careers which were to last all of their active service and even a lifetime.[64]

While the bourgeois faced pressures which made the maintenance of lasting unions difficult, they did not encounter the physical obstacles placed in the way of the voyageurs. The bourgeois could transport his woman in comfort on all his journeys, but the voyageur, if only for the sake of space, was usually forced to leave his wife behind during the long summer trip to and from the main depot. It was not unknown for the men's families to follow after the brigades in small canoes often paddled by the women themselves. Most of the voyageurs' wives, however, either remained at the inland posts or returned to the Indians for the summer.[65] Under such circumstances, it is not surprising that the women sometimes changed hands, especially since there was no guarantee that their former partners would return. In the early nineteenth century, uninformed or unsympathetic observers such as Captain John Franklin and certain missionaries made sweeping denunciations about the licentious and demoralized conduct of the French-Canadian voyageurs, but as Marcel Giraud in his massive study on the Métis has emphasized, excess and debauchery were not characteristic of the majority of relationships.[66] Again the development of distinct family units was the dominant trend.

The bourgeois were well aware that many of the voyageurs were deeply concerned about their Indian mates. An engagé had to secure the permission of his bourgeois before taking a wife, and the more unscrupulous officers were prone to taking advantage of this to keep the men in debt. In 1802, one of Alexander Henry's young engagés was prepared to enslave himself to work off his debts if allowed to marry a certain woman. Such an occurrence was not uncommon, declared Henry; he had known others "who would not hesitate to sign an agreement of perpetual bondage on condition of being permitted to have a woman who struck their fancy".[67] Other bourgeois complained that the romantic preoccupations of their men made them quick to neglect their work. According to Chief Factor James Keith:

> A young luscious Rib, surrounded with Gallants, is well calculated to augment a headache, mal de coeur or even obstruction d'estomac to her Protector.[68]

On occasion romance could also spur a man to greater activity. George Simpson recorded in 1820 that Cupid was primarily responsible for making Joseph Greill complete what was normally a four-day journey from Beren's House to Fort Wedderburn in two and a half days. He was returning to claim "a frail fair one" who during his summer absence had put herself under "the protection" of Mr Brown, one of the fort's officers. Both men claimed her, but Simpson settled the affair by allowing the woman herself to choose, and her return to her former husband was celebrated by the customary wedding dram to all hands.[69] No doubt many voyageurs regretted the long separation of the summer months and were motivated to make record time back into the interior in order to be reunited with their families.[70] Quite a number of relationships survived frequent absences. The old voyageur Pierre Marois was not alone when he declared with pride that he had lived with his Indian wife for twenty-three years in a union which he considered as binding as if they had been married in church.[71] Loyalty to their Indian families was a primary cause of many engagés remaining in the West after leaving the service of the North West Company. By the early 1800s, they formed a significant group known as "freemen", who lived a life akin to that of the Indians, supporting their families by hunting and trading with the Company. By 1814, a small community of superannuated voyageurs had also sprung up around the depot at Fort William, some old servants preferring to eke out an existence for themselves and families rather than return to Lower Canada and "give their relatives and former acquaintances certain proofs of their misconduct or their imprudence."[72]

But in becoming freemen, the voyageurs were choosing a primitive lifestyle which most of the Europeans could not stomach. One of the greatest problems facing fur-trade society was that, as comforting and stable as a relationship might be between a trader and a native woman while in the Indian Country, there was no mechanism for ensuring the continuance of the union after the trader had retired. In the Hudson's Bay Company, the rules of the London Committee placed its employees in an agonizing dilemma; they were forbidden to take native dependants to Britain but, at the same time, were prohibited from settling in Rupert's Land until the early nineteenth century with the founding of the Red River Colony. The London Committee's ruling against taking native families to Britain resulted from the unfortunate experience of Chief Factor Robert Pilgrim, the first officer known to have taken his Indian wife to England. In 1750, Pilgrim had retired to Hackney near London, accompanied by his favourite Indian wife Thu-a-Higon[73] and their infant son. Pilgrim was in ill health and several months later he died. By his will, he instructed that the child was to remain in England with his relatives, but Thu-a-Higon was to be sent back to her family at

Fort William as it was in 1845. From "Vie de Mgr Taché" Volume I by
Dom Benoit, published in 1904.

Churchill, all her wants being provided for in the interim.[74] While
the London Committee did arrange for her return to Churchill,
Thu-a-Higon's presence in England was an embarrassment and
may have put them to expense not covered by Pilgrim's estate.
Anxious to avoid the burden which might result from other
families coming to England, the Committee issued a strict order
forbidding all ships' captains to allow "any Indian or Esquemay
Man, Woman or Child to be brought as a passenger to any part of
Great Britain on any Pretense whatever without Our Express
order in Writing for so doing."[75] Thus throughout the eighteenth
century, the accepted course was for an Indian woman and her
offspring to return to her own relations when her Company
husband died or left the Bay.[76]

There were no restrictions against the Nor'Westers taking
their native families with them when they retired to Eastern
Canada or Britain but, for several reasons, only a few of the
bourgeois, such as John Dugald Cameron and James Hughes,
were prepared to take this step. It was argued that the Indian
wife, in particular, would face insuperable problems of adjustment; in the "civilized world" they would only meet with "imper-
tinent insult and unmerited obloquy".[77] The bourgeois were more

reluctant to admit that an Indian wife simply did not fit into their retirement plans. Many were men of education who, having made substantial fortunes, were now determined to enjoy the comforts of genteel living. A number of retired bourgeois felt that their position in civilized society required an appropriate spouse; they therefore severed their connections with their country wives and proceeded to marry white women. William McGillivray, who ultimately succeeded Simon McTavish as head of the North West Company, married Magdelaine McDonald in 1800 when he ceased to be a winterer and took up residence in Montreal; likewise the Honourable Roderick McKenzie of Terrebonne married into the family of a prominent French-Canadian merchant shortly after his retirement in 1803.[78] Such a course was perhaps the ultimate extension of the Nor'Westers' practice of serial monogamy.

Over time it became increasingly difficult for an Indian "widow" to go back to her own people; if her union with a trader had been a long one, she might well end up far away from her own kin.[79] Many abandoned native families, therefore, remained at the posts and looked to the Company for support. The Cree wife of William McGillivray appears to have lived out her days at Fort William, for she was buried in the fort graveyard in 1819.[80] Some Nor'Westers did leave their Indian wives an annuity for the purchase of goods from the Company stores, but they also resorted to a more novel expedient to relieve the burden on the Company. A custom arose known as "turning off" whereby a bourgeois leaving the country arranged to have his spouse (sometimes his entire family)[81] placed under the protection of another officer or, in many cases, an engagé. As Ross Cox explained:

> When a trader wishes to separate from his Indian wife he generally allows her an annuity, or gets her comfortably married to one of the voyageurs, who, for a handsome sum, is happy to become the husband of la Dame d'un Bourgeois.[82]

On the day of his marriage à la façon du pays, Daniel Harmon confided to his journal that he intended to keep his wife

> as long as I remain in this uncivilized part of the world, but when I return to my native land shall endeavour to place her into the hands of some good honest Man, with

whom she can pass the remainder of her Days in this Country much more agreeably, than it would be possible for her to do, were she to be taken down to the civilized world, where she would be a stranger to the People, their manners, customs & Language.[83]

"Turning off" resulted in part from the Indian view that marriage did not constitute a permanent bond, but there were undoubtedly some traders who unfeelingly exploited this attitude to suit their own purposes.

The majority of fur traders, however, were genuinely distressed at the prospect of having to part with their families. "The abandoning of a family, of whatever color they may be, is a severe trial to the feelings" as one expressed it.[84] Hudson's Bay Company officers lamented the want of a refuge in Rupert's Land where a parent might retire with the hope of supporting his family and avoiding "the Miseries of a Separation."[85] One of the reasons that they were prepared to support Lord Selkirk's plan for a settlement was that it would provide a place for them to settle without removing their native families from a familiar environment. The North West Company realized the growing need to make some provision for former employees and their native dependants, but a projected plan for a settlement at Rainy Lake came to naught owing to the bitter trade struggle.[86] Ultimately the Red River became home to the retired men and their families of both companies.

In spite of its many complexities and complications, "the custom of the country" should be regarded as a bona fide marital union. Nor'Wester François N. Annance maintained: "I never knew or heard of a man and woman living together in the North West without being married."[87] The women assumed their husbands' last names, with the engagés respectfully addressing the wives of the bourgeois as "Madame". The way in which William Connolly's Cree wife was regarded in fur-trade society indicates the recognition of the marriage tie:

She passed and was universally acknowledged as his wife at the different posts . . . her children by William Connolly were always acknowledged in public as the lawful issue of their marriage.[88]

A number of Nor'Westers were adamant that their marriages were legitimate even though they had been contracted without benefit of clergy. Around the turn of the century, Charles Oakes Ermatinger had taken *à la façon du pays* a fifteen-year-old Ojibwa girl named Charlotte Kattawabide. In his will, Ermatinger stressed that Charlotte had been "my wife for upwards of thirty years" and "the mother of all my children."[89] Peter Skene Ogden remained devoted to his Indian wife "Princess Julia", who had shared the hardships of his Snake Country expeditions, but he consistently refused to have their union blessed by the church. "If many years of public recognition of the relation and of his children did not constitute sufficient proof," Ogden declared, "no formal words of a priest or magistrate could help the matter."[90] James Hughes was another Nor'Wester who insisted that a marriage contracted according to Indian custom was valid in its own right; even when he took Nan-touche to settle in Eastern Canada, he refused to submit to a church marriage.[91] The Nor'Westers' disdain for the formalities of European marriage may have resulted from the strong Scottish influence in the Company. In Scotland, at this time, it was possible for a legal marriage to be contracted without the sanction of either civil or religious authorities; all that was necessary was for the couple to express their consent in front of a witness.[92]

The development of widespread marital bonds between European traders and Indian women was an important aspect of Indian-white relations in the early Canadian West. The potent interaction of the attitudes and needs of both races caused the fur traders to evolve their own indigenous customs to regulate their social behaviour. Marriage *à la façon du pays* provided the basis for the growth of fur-trade society, which was characterized by the emergence of distinct family units. The desirability of the Indian woman was enhanced by the absence of white women, but the particular demands of the fur trade cast the Indian wife into a much more important role than simply that of sexual partner. Marital alliances cemented the social ties between the Indians and the traders and had a beneficial impact upon the trade itself. In the fur-trade world, the Indian wife, because of her unique work skills, also proved to be a much more valuable mate than a white woman would have been.

3

"YOUR HONORS SERVANTS"

The economic role played by Indian women in fur-trade society reflected the extent to which the European traders were compelled to adapt to the native way of life. The all-encompassing work role of Indian women was transferred, in modified form, to the trading post, where their skills not only facilitated the traders' survival in the wilderness but actual fur-trade operations. At the North West Company posts and at Hudson's Bay Company posts especially, native women came to be relied upon as an integral if unofficial part of the labour force. Their economic assistance was a powerful incentive for the traders to take Indian wives; even within their own tribes, the women exercised a role in the functioning of the trade which has been little appreciated by historians of this period.

The Nor'Westers had a first-hand knowledge of the usefulness of Indian wives which they gained from the French, and this was an important reason for the Company allowing its men to intermarry with the natives. Besides familiarizing the Frenchman with the customs and language of her tribe, the Indian woman had performed a wide range of domestic tasks. When the Jesuit Father Carheil castigated the French traders at Michilimackinac for keeping Indian women, the traders argued that their primary motive was economic necessity. Their wives ground the corn to make the staple food known as sagamité, made moccasins and leather garments, and performed other essential services such as washing and chopping firewood for the cabins. Carheil's remonstrance that the carrying out of these duties provided but "a proximate occasion for sin" was a gross underestimate of the genuine importance of the women's tasks.[1] Given that the Nor'Westers with their large force of skilled engagés still relied upon the services of Indian women, it can be appreciated that the Hudson's Bay Company with its limited and inexperienced personnel had an even greater need for their assistance. Throughout the eighteenth century, officers on the Bay argued with the London Committee that it was essential to keep Indian women in the posts, as they performed important tasks which the British had not yet mastered. The Council at York Factory even protested to the Committee in 1802 that the women should be regarded as "Virtually your Honors Servants."[2]

Perhaps the most important domestic task performed by the women at the fur-trade posts was to provide the men with a steady supply of "Indian shoes" or moccasins. The men of both companies generally did not dress in Indian style (the buckskinned mountain man was not part of the Canadian scene), but they universally adopted the moccasin as the most practical footwear for the wilderness. The first step in making moccasins or other leather apparel such as leggings and mittens was the laborious process of tanning the moose or deer skins:

> The skin they scrape and . . . take the braines of the animal and rub it upon the skin to make it pliable and soft; afterwards they smoke it well and then soak it in warm water for the night in order to render it easy to work with a piece of iron made for that purpose.[3]

Even Joseph Isbister, a stern disciplinarian, stressed the necessity of admitting women into the Bayside forts to provide a constant supply of shoes for the men. Large quantities were needed, for moccasins wore out quickly; at York Factory in 1800, the women made 650 pairs for the men's use in the summer season.[4] On his 1789 expedition, Alexander Mackenzie depended upon the wives of his two French-Canadian voyageurs to keep his party in footwear. The women scarcely ever left the canoes, being "continually employ'd making shoes of moose skin as a pair does not last us above one Day."[5]

Closely related to the manufacture of moccasins was the Indian woman's role in making the snowshoes which made winter travel possible. Although the men usually made the frames, the women prepared the sinews and netted the intricate webbing which provided the support. When Samuel Hearne and his small party went inland in 1774 to establish Cumberland

An Indian woman threading snowshoes in a settlement along the Mackenzie River. c. 1920.

House, the first Hudson's Bay Company post inland, they looked to Indian women for assistance. On October 21, Hearne recorded that all the Indians had gone away "Except 2 or 3 Women who Stays to Make, Mend, Knitt Snowshoes &c for us dureing the Winter."[6] A man could not even venture outside the post to collect firewood or hunt small game in winter without snow-shoes. To be without women to make them was to invite disaster, as Alexander Mackenzie's well-known lament to his cousin Roderic at Fort Chipewyan in 1786 indicates:

> I have not a single one in my fort that can make Rackets [racquettes]. I do not know what to do without these articles see what it is to have no wives. Try and get Rackets — there is no stirring without them.[7]

Without women to provide them with moccasins and snowshoes, Hudson's Bay Company officers stressed, the Company would be seriously restricted in its efforts to compete with its rivals.[8]

In the provision and preservation of food, always a serious concern to the fur traders, Indian women also made an important contribution. For the North West Company, the expense of

importing foodstuffs was prohibitive. The problem of supplying
its canoe brigades was ideally solved by the use of the Indian
food, pemmican — a nutritious, compact mixture of pounded
buffalo meat and fat which kept well and took up relatively little
space. Pemmican became the staple food of the fur trade, and
Indian women performed most of the steps required in its
preparation. At posts on the plains, buffalo hunting and
pemmican making formed an essential part of the yearly routine,
each post being required to furnish an annual quota for the
support of the brigades. In accordance with Indian custom, once
the hunters had killed the buffalo, the women's work began. They
skinned the animals, cut the meat off the carcasses and collected
the marrow and fat for rendering. After the meat was sliced into
thin strips, it was dried on racks in the sun or over a slow fire.
"The women employed all day Slicing and drying the meat" was a
typical diary entry in the early summer months.[9] When the meat
was dry, the women pounded it into a thick flaky mass. About
fifty pounds of this meat would then be mixed with forty pounds
of melted fat and packed in a *taureau* to make up the standard
ninety-pound lot of pemmican. Previously, during the winter, the
women had been kept busy making the *taureaux* which were
flattish sacks of buffalo hide with the hair on the outside.
"Women all busy stretching buffalo hides to make pemmican
bags"; "All the women at work sewing Bags" were common
remarks in many fort journals.[10]

　　Although pemmican was the staple food of the transport
brigades, it was too precious a commodity to form the chief diet
at the posts themselves. Fresh meat could be kept in the
ice-houses at most of the posts on the plains, but to the north,
where game was scarce, the people subsisted mainly on fish and
fowl. The women at the posts of both companies on Lake
Athabasca were adept fisherwomen, since tending the nets was
part of a woman's role in more northerly tribes. After a successful
fall fishery, the women were busily occupied splitting and drying
hundreds of whitefish for the winter.[11] Across the Rockies, the
women preserved vast quantities of salmon, the basic food for the
districts of the Columbia and New Caledonia.[12] At the posts
around Hudson Bay, geese, either dried or salted by the Indian
women, formed an important part of the "country provisions".[13]

Apart from curing the produce of the hunt, Indian women were also responsible for collecting auxiliary food supplies which, besides adding variety to the diet, could sometimes mean the difference between life and death. In the area to the west and south-west of Lake Superior, wild rice was a staple food of the Ojibwa. The women harvested the rice from the marshy shores of the lakes and rivers by shaking the ripe heads into the bottom of their small canoes. The rice was then parched and stored in fawn skins. The traders in the area were frequently grateful for such food,[14] and for maple sugar which constituted an important addition to the diet in the Shield area. The spring trip to the sugar bush provided a welcome release from the monotony of the winter routine, and the voyageurs with their families and Indian relatives all enjoyed the annual event. In April 1805, as a typical instance, all the women from the Nor'Westers' post on Rainy Lake were out making sugar. "Mr. Grant's Girl" seems to have been especially expert at the job and on one occasion traded about thirty pounds of sugar for rum.[15] A kind of sugar could also be made from the Manitoba maple which grew as far west as Fort Carlton. Chief Factor John Stuart noted in April 1825 that the only subject of interest was that all the women were busy making sugar, "some of it very fine."[16]

The entire Indian Country teemed with many varieties of berries which the women looked forward to collecting annually. When the Nor'Westers were tracking up the higher reaches of the Saskatchewan, the younger Henry observed: "the women generally keep on by land, during the use of the line, to gather fruit, which alleviates the labor and revives the spirits of the men."[17] Later at Rocky Mountain House, he reported that the women would all go off on horseback and return with great quantities of poires, raspberries and strawberries. Dried berries, especially saskatoons, were added to the high-grade pemmican made for the officers. But berries were more than a luxury item. David Thompson declared that berries had kept him alive after he became incapacitated by breaking his leg in 1788:

> I became emaciated till the berries became ripe and the kind hearted indian women brought me plenty . . . for my support. This was pure charity for I had nothing to give them and I was much relieved.[18]

"Indian Sugar Camp". From a water-colour by Seth Eastman of an Ojibwa group in Minnesota. Reproduced in Schoolcraft "Indian Tribes of the United States", 1852.

In New Caledonia and the Columbia, berries and "wappitoo root" gathered by the women were necessary to alleviate hunger in the spring when supplies of salmon invariably ran low.[19]

Although the wilds of Western Canada gave the appearance of providing abundant sustenance, all regions suffered from seasonal fluctuations and poorer areas faced frequent starvation. In times of scarcity, an Indian woman's skill and resourcefulness came into their own. At Lake Athabasca, it was common for the women to be sent away to the fishery to support themselves and their children when provisions ran low.[20] After his fisherman deserted to the Nor'Westers at Île à la Crosse in 1810, Peter Fidler's Cree wife Mary virtually saved the English from starvation since she was the only one who knew how to mend and set the nets.[21]

The fact that it was also the woman's role in Indian society to snare small game served the traders well. On one occasion, the Indian wife of the bourgeois John Dugald Cameron reputedly kept the people at her husband's post alive with the catch from her snares.[22] The young Nor'Wester George Nelson was certainly grateful for his Ojibwa wife when he found himself in dire straits at a small outpost north of Lake Superior in 1815.[23] After provisions became almost exhausted in February, Nelson's wife set out, well equipped with snares of wire and twine, to catch small game. At first, she had little success because wild animals were devouring her catch before she could return to the snares. After about a week, however, she came in with sixteen partridges and went off with one of the men next day to bring home the thirty hares which she had cached. Nelson's wife had been accompanied by the wife of one of his Hudson's Bay Company competitors, but although the Nor'Wester knew he might be censured for allowing this, he felt his wife's welfare must come before commercial rivalry:

> I am happy of it because it is company, she will have less trouble to chop wood & if misfortunately she cuts herself or gets otherwise sick, the others will help her.

The "she-hunters" returned with all their equipment after about three weeks, having added much to the kettles of both companies. "My woman brings home 8 hares & 14 Partridges" wrote Nelson with satisfaction on March 3, "making in all 58 hares and 34 Partridges. Good." Occasionally even the well-established post of York Factory could run out of fresh provisions, so essential for the prevention of scurvy. In December 1818, Chief Factor James Swain was forced to send his wife and one of his daughters out to try to catch fish or rabbits. They returned a fortnight later in bitterly cold weather with grim news: there were no fish and they had had to walk many miles to secure a few rabbits.[24]

Although Indian women played an important part in preserving and procuring country provisions, they did not take over the official role of cook at the fur-trade posts as might be expected. Usually an Orkneyman or a French Canadian was specifically designated to serve as cook for the officers' mess. At some posts the servants took their meals in a military-type mess, but as families increased it became common for the women to prepare their families' daily rations in the servants' quarters.[25]

Apart from domestic duties relating to the traditional female roles of making clothes and preparing food, the Indian woman was also involved in specific fur-trade operations. Of particular

Indian women dressing a moose skin at Resolution, N W T. Undated.

importance to the inexperienced Hudson's Bay Company men
was the women's knowledge of dressing furs. As the York
Council emphasized to its London superiors, the Indian women
"clean and put into a state of preservation all Beavr. and Otter
skins brought by the Indians undried and in bad Condition."[26]
Since the North West Company had adopted the birch-bark
canoe as the basis of its transport system, Indian women
continued in their traditional role of helping in its manufacture.
It was the women's job to collect wattappe (wattap), roots from
the spruce tree, which they split fine for sewing the seams of the
canoe. The numerous references in the journals testify to the vast
quantities needed: "Women raising wattap — 33 women, 8
bundles each" — "Mr. Grant's Girl brought us 75 Bundles
Wattap to day." On Lake Athabasca, the women at the Hudson's
Bay Company post were expected to provide an annual quota of
fifty bundles of wattappe each.[27] Having collected the wattappe,
the women helped to sew the seams of the canoes and then caulk
them with spruce gum which they also collected. At Rocky
Mountain House in 1810, Alexander Henry observed the voyageurs' wives busy gathering gum for the Columbia canoes; a
brigade which departed without adequate supplies of bark,
wattappe and gum for repairs could find itself in dire straits.[28] At
York Factory, the women helped to pay for their keep during the
winter by making canoe sails.[29]

Besides assisting in the making of canoes, Indian women,
because of their traditional training, could readily lend a hand to
help man them. Two women assisted in paddling the canoes on
Mackenzie's voyage in 1789,[30] but with a large force of voyageurs,
it was seldom necessary for the North West Company to call
upon this reserve. This was not the case with the Hudson's Bay
Company in the early stages of its moving inland. With few
experienced canoemen, the Hudson's Bay Company turned to
women, who often rendered valuable assistance. John Thomas,
on his return to Moose Factory in 1779, told of meeting another
officer in charge of three small canoes loaded with provisions for
a new inland post; each canoe was manned by an Englishman and
an Indian woman, the woman acting as steersman.[31] In the 1790s
Chief Factor Joseph Colen declared that one of the reasons for
the declining number of canoes coming down to York Factory

A Cree woman gumming the seams of a birch-bark canoe. Undated.

was that the women were no longer allowed to accompany their husbands and help paddle the canoes.[32]

Indeed, the assistance of Indian women on inland journeys had always been of particular importance to the Hudson's Bay Company men. As early as the 1680s, the Committee had urged its servants to travel inland to contact new tribes and bring them down to the Bay to trade, but few Englishmen, lacking as they did knowledge of wilderness survival and native languages, could be persuaded to venture far from the security of the posts in spite of the Committee's offer of reward. As a result, the Hudson's Bay Company's inland exploration during the first century of its existence was restricted to a few isolated sojourns undertaken by individual men who depended entirely upon the Indians they were allowed to accompany. When Anthony Henday made his long trek into the interior in 1754, the women of the Cree party with whom he travelled rendered valuable service; they were constantly pitching camp, drying meat, collecting berries, dressing skins and netting snowshoes.[33] Inland journeys which were not accompanied by Indian women seemed doomed to failure. At Churchill, the Governor had prevented Samuel Hearne from taking Chipewyan women with him on his initial attempts to reach the Coppermine River, ostensibly to reduce the task of feeding a large party. But Matonabbee, the remarkable Chipewyan guide of the third and successful expedition of 1771-72, emphasized that the lack of women carriers had been a prime cause of the failure of Hearne's first two attempts:

> ... for, said he, when all the men are heavy laden, they can neither hunt nor travel to any considerable distance; and in case they meet with success in hunting, who is to carry the produce of their labour? Women ... also pitch our tents, make and mend our clothing, keep us warm at night; and, in fact, there is no such thing as travelling any considerable distance, or for any length of time, in this country, without their assistance. Women . . . though they do everything, are maintained at a trifling expense; . . . the very licking of their fingers in scarce times is sufficient for their subsistence.[34]

Hearne's third expedition, therefore, was well equipped with sturdy Chipewyan women, among them the seven wives of

Matonabbee, all chosen for their strength and skill.[35]

Apart from the assistance rendered by Indian women in general, Hudson's Bay Company travellers found it to their advantage to have their own particular "bedfellow", who could be most valuable in acquainting them with Indian custom. In 1692, when Henry Kelsey returned from the first inland voyage ever undertaken by a Hudson's Bay Company man, he was accompanied by a Cree woman whom he called his wife and insisted that she be allowed to enter the fort.[36] Anthony Henday's "bedfellow" proved invaluable; besides preparing his "winter rigging", she provided him with crucial information about the designs of her countrymen. His woman enabled him to avoid a dangerous confrontation by advising him to stop pressing his party of Cree to hunt for furs because they intended to trade them from the Blackfoot in the spring. Henday protected his ally from the other Indians who might have killed her had they discovered her complicity, and when the scarcity of provisions reduced most of the women to subsisting on berries, he felt obliged to give her a share of his meat.[37]

In the decades prior to the establishment of the Company's first inland post in 1774, the men began to make frequent trips into the interior to counteract the devastating competition of the "Pedlars". The London Committee expressed concern that the men would "go native", but the early Hudson's Bay Company inlanders were unavoidably dependent upon the Indians, and it became customary for them to take a "canoe Mate & Tent Mate".[38] "Women" declared one prominent inlander, "are as useful as men upon . . . Journeys."[39] Certainly, many of the Company's important inland officers in the late eighteenth century — William Tomison, Robert Longmoor, Malchom Ross and William Walker —were greatly assisted in their successful adaptation to life in the interior by their Indian wives.

It was not unusual for an Indian woman to be found in the elevated role of guide owing to her availability and familiarity with the terrain. The elder Henry when going into the Churchill River area in 1776 employed an Indian woman as guide, remarking that she had served Mr Frobisher in the capacity.[40] The importance of the woman as guide is shown in the Nor'Westers' attempt to cripple Hudson's Bay Company operations at Île à la Crosse in 1810 by intimidating the servant's wife who was guiding their brigade. An angry Peter Fidler recorded:

> When our Men passed the Frog portage McTavish frightened our pilot away & it was two Days detention to them before they got her again — without her our men could not have come forward.[41]

Because of her intimate contact with the traders, the Indian woman also played an important role as an interpreter and teacher of language. At least some understanding of the native languages was required to be an effective "Indian trader", a fact readily grasped by the Nor'Westers. The less fluent Hudson's Bay Company men were assisted by Indian women in extending the trade. In 1753, John Potts at Richmond on the east side of Hudson Bay avowed that his sole purpose in sending for a certain woman from Albany had been her perfect understanding of the dialect of the Eastmain Indians which differed very much from what he was used to. She rendered "Great Service to the Company as an interpreter" and taught Potts the language so he could now make the Indians "Sensible" of his intentions.[42] In the Brandon House area as late as 1819, the English still relied upon Indian women to act as interpreters with the Assiniboine, whose language belonged to the Siouan linguistic group and not the more widespread Algonkian.[43] Both companies used women as interpreters to communicate with tribes of the rich Lake Athabasca region. During his first winter at Fort Wedderburn, George Simpson soon discovered one of the reasons for his rivals' strong position: the Nor'Westers' women were "faithful to their cause and good Interpreters whereas we have but one in the Fort that can talk Chipewyan". That one was the redoubtable Madame Lamallice, the wife of the Hudson's Bay Company brigade guide.[44]

Simpson observed that Indian women could often serve as useful diplomatic agents for the traders. In hiring a French-Canadian to help extend the trade into the Great Slave Lake area, he was motivated by the fact that the man's wife was extensively connected among the Yellowknife and Chipewyan tribes there and would be able to overcome any prejudices "that our Opponents may have instilled in their minds against us."[45] In the Columbia District, the Governor was careful to cultivate the favour of one "Lady Calpo", a well-connected Chinook matron, who since the days of the Nor'Westers had been a "fast friend of the Whites". In 1814, she had helped restore peaceful relations after the Nor'Westers had suffered a raid on their canoes, by giving them vital information about Chinook procedures for settling disputes. Simpson found her "the best News Monger in the Parish"; from "Lady Calpo" he learned "more of the Scandal Secrets & politics both of the out & inside the Fort than any other source."[46] The most outstanding female diplomat in fur-trade history, however, appeared very early in the annals of the Hudson's Bay Company. This was Thanadelthur, a young Chipewyan woman, who acted as guide, interpreter, and peace negotiator for Governor Knight's expedition of 1715-16.[47]

Having assumed command of York Factory in the fall of 1714, James Knight was anxious not only to re-establish the English trade, which had lapsed during the French occupation, but to extend it to the north. The existence of the Chipewyan was known, but fear of the Cree, who were the first to obtain firearms, prevented these northern Indians from venturing to the Bayside. Knight's only contact with the Chipewyan was through his chance meeting with female captives held by the Cree. In November he received encouraging information from a Chipewyan woman who had escaped from the Cree and made her way to the post, but his plans for establishing a post at the mouth of the Churchill River appeared to be thwarted by this woman's death. The governor was lamenting his loss, when two days later, Thanadelthur was brought in "Allmost Starv'd."

She had a harrowing tale to tell. In the spring of 1713, she, with another of her countrywomen, had been captured by the Cree in a raid upon the Chipewyan. Over a year later when camped on the north side of the Nelson River, the two women had seized the chance to escape from their Cree master, hoping to travel back to their people before winter set in. They had only the catch from their snares to subsist on and when cold and hunger finally drove them to turn back, they clung to the hope that they might find the traders whose wondrous goods they had seen in the Cree camps. Only Thanadelthur survived. Shortly after her companion had perished, she stumbled across some tracks which led her to the tent of the Company's goose hunters on Ten Shilling Creek.

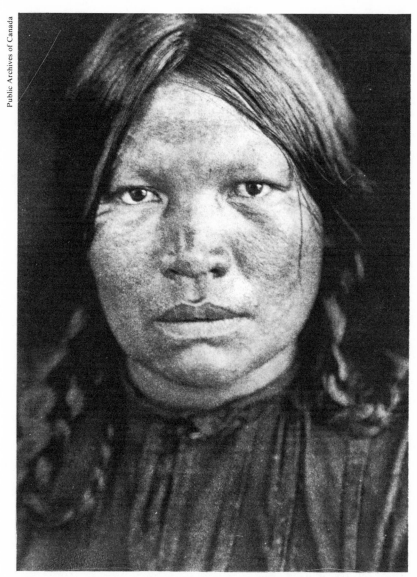

A young Chipewyan woman who would appear to have the Slave Woman's qualities of 'high spirit and firmest resolution'. From a photograph by Edward S. Curtis. c. 1900.

Knight was immediately impressed with his new informant, whom he always referred to as "the Slave Woman". She spoke enthusiastically of her people and their rich fur resources and even though her knowledge of Cree was indifferent, Knight believed that she "will be of great Service to me in my Intention." To ensure the success of his plan, Knight realized that as a first step he must endeavour to establish peace between the Cree and the Chipewyan. Early in June 1715, the Governor gave a feast to his Home Guard Cree and persuaded them to send a peace delegation to their enemies, to be accompanied by one of the Company's servants, William Stuart, and the Slave Woman. Bands of Upland Cree coming in to trade were encouraged to join the peace mission, so that the party which set off on June 27 numbered about one hundred and fifty. Knight entrusted Thanadelthur, who was to act as interpreter, to the protection of Stuart: "take care that none of the Indians abuse or Missuse the Slave Woman." He gave the Chipewyan woman a quantity of presents to distribute among her people, instructing her to tell them that the English would build a fort on the Churchill River in the fall of 1716. Thanadelthur readily appreciated the importance of her position and soon became the dominating spirit of the expedition. Stuart was amazed at the way she kept the Cree in awe of her and "never Spared in telling them of their Cowardly way of Killing her Country Men." But disaster stalked the expedition. Slowed by sickness and threatened with starvation on the long trek across the Barren Grounds, the party had to break up to survive. Most of the bands turned back, leaving only Stuart, the Slave Woman, and the Cree captain with a dozen of his followers determined to find the Chipewyan. Failure seemed certain when Stuart's group came across the bodies of nine Northern Indians, slain by one of the other Cree bands. Fearing the revenge of the Chipewyan, the remaining Cree now wanted to abandon the search.

At this juncture, Thanadelthur took the initiative. She persuaded the Cree that if they would wait ten days she would be able to find her people and bring them to make peace. She left the Cree busily fortifying their camp in case of attack, and within a few days, she came upon a large band of several hundred of her countrymen. It required all Thanadelthur's powers of persuasion to get them to return with her; she made herself hoarse "with perpetuall talking" before the Chipewyan could be convinced of the peaceful intent of their enemies. In true epic fashion, on the tenth day, Thanadelthur and two emissaries came in sight of the Cree camp. When Stuart came out to meet them and conduct them to his tent, she signalled to the rest of the delegation, over a hundred strong, that it was safe to approach. With the help of the Cree captain, Thanadelthur once again assured her people that their party bore no responsibility for the recent raid and that the Cree were most anxious for peace. With those who remained dubious, this forceful woman had no patience: "She made them all Stand in fear of her she Scolded at Some and pushing of others . . . and forced them to ye peace." William Stuart was full of admiration:

> Indeed She has a Devillish Spirit and I believe that if thare were but 50 of her Country Men of the same Carriage and Resolution they would drive all the [Southern] Indians in America out of there Country.

Stuart's party arrived back at York Factory on 7 May 1716, accompanied by ten Chipewyan, one of whom appears to have been Thanadelthur's brother. The Englishman emphasized that the mission owed its success to his remarkable Chipewyan ally who had been "the Chief promoter and Acter" of it.

It had originally been Knight's intention to send the Chipewyan, including Thanadelthur, back to their own country in the autumn of 1716. The season of 1715-16, however, had been a disastrous one at York owing to the non-arrival of the annual ship, and he was forced to postpone his plans for establishing the post at Churchill. Having recently endured the hardship of the long trek to the factory, the Chipewyan themselves were not anxious to return; they were afraid of having to pass through the country of the Upland Cree who had not been party to the peace ceremony. Knight, therefore, allowed them to winter at York: Thanadelthur and three others within the fort, the rest with the Home Guard Cree.

During the course of the winter, Thanadelthur devoted herself to promoting the Company's interests. Knight was fascinated by her stories of rich mineral deposits somewhere to the northwest. Not only would the Chipewyan be able to bring samples of copper to the new post but, she confided to Knight, there were other Indians who possessed a "yellow mettle" which the old man took to be gold. Being highly impressed with the "Extraordinary Vivacity" of Thanadelthur's quick mind, Knight sought her advice in developing his plans, she "Readily takeing anything right as was proposed to her & Presently Giving her Opinion whether it would do or not." Thanadelthur was enthusiastic about Knight's proposal that she should again travel to the Chipewyan to explain that the English had been delayed but would definitely build their fort at Churchill the coming summer. Sometime during this period, Thanadelthur appears to have taken a Chipewyan husband, but she refused to let marriage interfere with this important commission. She informed Knight that she would leave her husband if he would not go with her. She and her companions were to leave in the early spring of 1717, accompanied by the young apprentice Richard Norton.

Unfortunately, the extremely severe winter at York proved fatal for the Chipewyan Indians. On 11 January, Knight recorded in his journal: "ye Northern Slave Woman had been dangerously Ill and I expected her Death every Day, but I hope she is now a Recovering." He worked unceasingly trying to nurse the ailing woman and several other Chipewyan back to health. Not only would the Governor suffer a serious setback in losing his only interpreter, but he was afraid of the "Jealousy & Suspicion" that might result among the Indians should any of their kinfolk die. Although on her deathbed, Thanadelthur struggled bravely. She called the "English Boy", who was to have gone with her to learn the language, to her bedside and told him not to be afraid to go with her people. She assured him that her brother, whom she had asked Knight to designate as an Indian captain, "would love him and not lett him want for anything."

Four days later, on 5 February 1717, Thanadelthur died. "I am almost ready to break my heart" despaired Knight. The old Governor's grief lay deeper than just the fact that this woman's death "will be very Prejudiciall to the Company's Interest." He had come to regard Thanadelthur as one of the most extra-ordinary people he had ever met: "She was one of a Very high Spirit and of the Firmest Resolution that ever I see any Body in my Days and of great Courage & forecast." With bitter irony,

Knight closed his journal entries on the Slave Woman — "the finest Weather wee have had any Day this Season but the most Melancholys't by the Loss of her." So heavily did Knight rely on the interpreting services of Chipewyan women that he managed with great difficulty to secure another slave woman, though she cost him "above 60 skins value in goods". This woman set off with Richard Norton in July 1717 to contact the Chipewyan while an advance party of Company servants sailed to the Churchill River to begin construction on the new post.

The experience of Thanadelthur and subsequent "slave women" indicates the influence which Indian women exercised in trade relations. Nearly a century later, Alexander Mackenzie observed that Chipewyan women, in spite of their burdensome existence, possessed "a very considerable influence in the traffic with Europeans."[48] On his inland journey, Anthony Henday had learned that in order to secure good trade relations it was necessary to cultivate the women; the secret was "to please the Ladys" but not so much as "to Create a Misunderstanding."[49] The astute Nor'Westers readily appreciated the need to cater to the Indian women's love of trinkets and finery. At their posts, they gave away large quantities of lace, ribbons, rings and vermilion:

> . . . such like presents greatly gain the Love of the Women and some of them have great influence over their Husbands particularly the Young people who would carry part of their Furrs to the Canadians if it was for these trinkets only.[50]

The Hudson's Bay Company was reluctant to adopt such "wasteful" measures, although at Moose Factory in 1742, Mrs Sakie, the captain's wife, was given a present of "a brass Coller & a stone ring" in hopes that she might bring them into fashion.[51] It was not until the early 1800s, after Albany chief Robert Goodwin had ordered at his own expense a considerable assortment of ribbons to give to the women when they visited the fort, that the London Committee consented to send out its own consignments, admitting that "the Expence is not great & these little attentions . . . may have good Effect."[52]

Indian women also participated directly in the fur trade itself. Owing to the division of labour in Indian society, it was the women's prerogative to trap small fur-bearing animals; "Among the Natives" observed David Thompson, "the snareing of hares, and trapping of Martens are the business of the Women and become their property for trade."[53] On occasion, an Indian woman even excelled her husband as a trapper. At Fort Alexandria in 1800, the bourgeois A. N. McLeod sent two of his men to The Thunder's tent "to try to prevail with his wife, (the Grey mare being the better horse) to send her fine furs here."[54] Some of the older women were seasoned traders, as Charles Chaboillez discovered when he tried to trade with Old Courtre Oreille. This Cree woman kept threatening to go to the English until Chaboillez had given her "Four Pints M. Rum & ½ fath. Tobc." to induce her to bring in her cache of one hundred thirty beaver skins.[55] Nowhere did the women take a more active part in trading than on the Columbia. With captive slaves to perform the more laborious domestic tasks, Chinook women enjoyed a more elevated status than most Indian women. According to Alexander Ross, it was common to see a Chinook woman, followed by a train of slaves, trading at the fort.[56]

Indian wives of the traders sometimes used their trading acumen to their husbands' advantage. Anastasie, the Ojibwa wife of J. B. Cadotte, played a very active part in conducting her husband's trading operations which were eventually based at Sault Ste Marie. Cadotte, the only French trader of any consequence to remain in the Indian Country after the conquest, formed a partnership with the early Nor'Wester Alexander Henry, who noted that Madame Cadotte was "very generally respected."[57] Indian wives at the Bay posts made an important contribution to the Company's trade by trapping martens and rabbits. Even the unbending James Duffield at Moose Factory in the 1740s was prepared to give preferential treatment to a former officer's Indian wife because she was very industrious in catching martens: "Must use [her] with tenderness on acct of ye Compys Interest," he informed the London Committee.[58] Many decades later, Chief Factor Joseph Beioley reported "The Women belonging to and dependent on this place [Moose Factory] have traded a good many [Made] Beaver, consisting chiefly of Martins and Rabbit Skins."[59] This trade in "small furs" became increasingly important as the supply of beaver decreased, and it helped to offset the cost of the women's maintenance. When the London Committee complained in 1802 that its goods were being wasted on servants' families, they were informed that the women had earned the clothing which they received for themselves and their children. To this the Committee acquiesced: "We do not object to Women being paid for their Service in Trapping Martins."[60]

Altogether, the multi-faceted work role of Indian women in the fur trade merits their description as "Your Honors Servants". But they were servants who never received wages in any real sense and undoubtedly both companies profited by this source of cheap labour. Significantly, in fur-trade society, it was the Indian woman's traditional skills which made her a valuable economic partner, a fact which serves to underscore the initial dependence of the traders upon the Indians. Nevertheless, the Indian woman's life was not left undisturbed by the coming of the Europeans. As has been emphasized, Indian women played an active social and economic role in the functioning of the fur trade; it remains to try to determine how they themselves viewed the intrusion of the white man and his technology.

Hudson's Bay Company Archives

"*A Man & his Wife returning with a load of Partridges from their Tent*". *A water-colour drawing by William Richards. Early nineteenth century.*

4

WOMEN IN BETWEEN

Unfortunately, Indian women have not left a record of their views on the fur trade or their reasons for becoming traders' wives. A reconstruction of their perspective can only be derived from the writings of the fur traders who, perhaps inadvertently, provide some remarkable insights into the behaviour of the women. The general picture which emerges is that of Indian women playing an active role in the promotion of the material and, to some extent, cultural change brought about by the fur trade. Within the tribes, Indian women fostered trade with the Europeans, a phenomenon which suggests that the technology introduced by the traders significantly ameliorated their lives.[1]

As the only females available in the Indian Country, Indian women were taken as marital partners by the traders and actually became an integral part of fur-trade society, an option that was never open to their male counterparts. Indeed some Indian women took the initiative in securing fur-trade husbands and sought to make the most of the opportunities offered by this new role. For a time, they occupied an influential position as "women in between" two groups of men, a situation which could be manipulated to advantage. It is true that in the final analysis the women's role was circumscribed and that when circumstances changed, the Indian women's position in fur-trade society declined; nevertheless, the women must be seen as active participants in the developing complex of Indian-white relations. As Naomi Griffiths has maintained in *Penelope's Web,* a survey of the historical experience of Canadian and European women, it was the lot of most women to take a pragmatic approach to life, trying to

make the best of any possibilities offered to enlarge the limited
sphere of their existence.[2]

Many traders commented upon the assistance and loyalty
which they received from the women within the Indian tribes. It
was a Cree woman called "Mammy" who eventually informed
Governor Isbister of the identity of the perpetrators of the
Henley House massacre.[3] On numerous occasions, Indian
women actually warned the Europeans of impending treachery.
In 1797, Charles Chaboillez, having been warned by an old
woman that the Indians intended to pillage his post, was able to
nip this intrigue in the bud; George Nelson and one of his men
only escaped an attack by some Indians in 1805 by being
clandestinely assisted by the women.[4] "Lady Calpo" was not
alone among the Chinook women in warning the Nor'Westers
of the hostile plans of her countrymen.[5] In seeking to account
for this phenomenon, George Nelson ascribed the women's
actions to the universal maternal instinct. He mused over the
fact that it was "a few old women" who had warned the
"Pedlars" of a plan to drive them out of the country in the early
1780s. As mothers, these women he decided must feel
compassion for the mothers of those whites destined to be
killed, because "women are lovely the world over."[6]

While Nelson's view upholds a popular notion of the
character of women, a more concrete explanation is that women
within the tribes had a vested interest in promoting cordial
relations with the whites. If the traders were driven from the
country, the Indian women would lose the source of European
goods which had revolutionized their lives. It was much easier
to boil water in a metal kettle than to laboriously heat it by
means of dropping hot stones into a bark container. Cotton and
woollen goods saved long hours of tanning hides. "Show them
an awl or a strong needle" declared David Thompson, "and they
will gladly give the finest Beaver or Wolf skin they have to
purchase it."[7] Furthermore, the succour available to the Indians
at a fur-trade post was often of greater relevance to the women
than to the men. Both the Hudson's Bay Company traders and
the Nor'Westers were moved to rescue Indian women from
starvation or maltreatment. The story is told of a young Carrier
woman in New Caledonia who, having been severely beaten by

her husband, managed to struggle to the nearest North West Company post. Being nearly starved, she was slowly nursed back to health and allowed to remain at the post when it became apparent that her relatives had abandoned her.[8]

The presence of the traders allowed certain enterprising Indian women to greatly increase their influence and status; individuals such as Thanadelthur and Lady Calpo were able to work themselves into positions of genuine power. It is paradoxical that in Thanadelthur's case it was her escape from captivity that brought her in contact with the traders. If she had not been a woman, she would never have been carried off as a prize of war by the Cree. Once inside the Hudson's Bay Company fort, she was able to use to advantage her position as the only Chipewyan by acting as guide and consultant to the Governor. The protection and regard she was given by the whites enabled Thanadelthur to dictate to Indian men, both Cree and Chipewyan, in a manner they would not previously have tolerated. Anxious to promote the traders' interests, she assaulted an old Chipewyan on one occasion when he attempted to trade less than prime furs; she "ketcht him by the nose Push'd him backwards & call'd him fool and told him if they brought any but Such as they were directed they would not bee traded."[9] It is possible that the influential role played by Chipewyan women in trade relations stemmed from the precedent set by Thanadelthur. Lady Calpo's connection with the traders gave her a position of influence among the Chinook, second only to that of Chief Concomely. Significantly, she was able to put the seal on her status by successfully pressing Governor Simpson into contracting a temporary marriage alliance with her carefully reared young daughter in 1824. As late as the 1840s, a friend visiting the Columbia wrote to Simpson that Lady Calpo was still thriving.[10]

Other women, after living with the traders, enjoyed considerable prestige when they returned to Indian society. According to Alexander Ross, the women of the Columbia remained "very friendly" to the whites upon rejoining their tribes and "they never fail to influence their connections to the same end."[11] Undoubtedly the most extraordinary example of an Indian woman who used her experience among the traders to later gain wealth and favour was Ko-come-ne-pe-ca or Man-Like Woman.[12] This woman, who may have been a Blackfoot, was for some time the wife of David Thompson's servant Boisverd, but she was reputedly of such loose character that the moralistic Thompson made Boisverd discard her around 1808. Ko-come-ne-pe-ca then took refuge among the Okanagan in the interior of the Columbia District where, being of "a strong and eccentric disposition", she declared that she possessed the power to become a conjurer, a prophet and a man. The secret of her power evidently lay in the "medecine" of certain letters which she had been entrusted to convey for the Nor'Westers. In July 1811, Ko-come-ne-pe-ca, dressed as a man, and a female companion turned up at the mouth of the Columbia and excited considerable interest among the recently arrived Astorians, American traders who hoped to establish posts in the interior. The two women advanced the cause of the Americans by preceding them into the interior, spreading the news among various tribes that white men were coming with free goods and all the luxuries they could desire. By the time Ko-come-ne-pe-ca returned to the Okanagan, she had enriched herself enough to take on the status of a chief, having no less than twenty-six horses loaded with "the fruits of [her] false reports."[13]

Those Indian women who actually became "women in between" were not averse to playing white against Indian in hopes of securing an improvement in their treatment. The Indian woman, declared a rather frustrated Nor'Wester, "has always enough of policy to insinuate how well off she was while living with the white people and in like manner when with the latter she drops some hints of the same purpose."[14] It was observed that when Chipewyan women became the wives of French-Canadian voyageurs they assumed "an importance to themselves and instead of serving as formerly they exact submission from the descendants of the Gauls"; conversely, while the women had to resume their onerous domestic duties when they returned to their tribe, they evinced a greater spirit of independence.[15]

Fur-trade sources indicate that numerous Indian women deliberately sought to become partners of the traders.[16] Generally, the women agreed to being offered to the white men and should they be refused they could become very indignant at this insult.[17] One Nor'Wester noted that Cree women considered it an honour to be selected as wives by the voyageurs, and any husband who refused to lend his wife would be subject to the general condemnation of the women.[18] Alexander Ross observed that Chinook women showed a preference for living with a white man. If deserted by one husband, they would return to their tribe in a state of widowhood to await the opportunity of marrying another fur trader.[19] Nor'Wester Daniel Harmon voiced the widely held opinion that most of the Indian women were "better pleased to remain with the White People than with their own Relations"; his contemporary George Nelson affirmed that "some too would even desert to live with the white."[20]

Alexander Henry the Younger may have exaggerated his difficulties in fending off young Indian women, but his personal experiences underline the fact that the women saw nothing unusual in taking the initiative. On one occasion, when travelling with his brigade in the summer of 1800, Henry was confronted in his tent by a handsome young woman, dressed in her finery, who told him boldly that she had come to live with him, as she did not care for her husband or any other Indian. Henry, however, anxious to avoid this entanglement partly because it was not sanctioned by the husband whom he knew to be violently jealous, forced the woman to return to her Indian partner. A year or so later in the Lower Red River District, the daughter of an Ojibwa chief had more success. Henry returned from the New Year's festivities to find that "Liard's daughter" had taken possession of his room "and the devil could not have got her out." She remained firmly ensconced when he returned the next day from buffalo hunting. By the end of the month Henry thought he had successfully persuaded his "bed-fellow" to return to her father, but after an absence of two days: "The lady returned". In the face of such determination, Henry succumbed. "Liard's daughter", whom Henry referred to as "her ladyship" perhaps because of her demanding nature, became his country wife and bore him at least three children.[21]

In the traders' view, the Indian women were motivated in this regard because they could see that they would be better off with the Europeans. Most traders believed that the condition of women in Indian society was deplorable. Nor'Wester Gabriel Franchère summed it up:

> Some Indian tribes think that women have no souls, but die altogether like the brutes; others assign them a different paradise from that of men, which indeed they might have reason to prefer . . . unless their relative condition were to be ameliorated in the next world.[22]

While the prejudices of the traders resulted in their exaggerating the degradation of Indian women, there can be no doubt that, on a material level, life in a fur-trade post offered an Indian woman an easier existence.

In the first place, she now had a much more sedentary routine. With a stationary home, the Indian woman was no longer required to act as a beast of burden, hauling or carrying the accoutrements of camp from place to place. In fur-trade society, the unenviable role of carrier was assumed by the engagé or servant. The men at the fort were responsible for providing firewood and water, although the women might help. In contrast to Indian practice, the women of the fort were not sent out to fetch home the produce of the hunt.[23] The wife of a bourgeois, benefiting from her husband's rank, enjoyed a privileged status as "la première femme de ce pays."[24] She was carried in and out of the canoe and could expect to have all her baggage portaged by a voyageur. At Fond du Lac in 1804 when the wife of bourgeois John Sayer decided to go on a sugar-making expedition, four men went with her to carry her baggage and provisions and later returned to fetch home her things.[25] Some voyageurs were observed helping their wives in ways which would have been beneath a man's dignity in Indian society. Even the other men at Fort Chipewyan thought that one voyageur, Lambert, had carried chivalry a bit too far when he helped his wife to collect a huge store of moss and then carried it in while "Madame" walked sedately behind carrying nothing but her baby.[26]

While the Indian woman performed a variety of valuable economic tasks around the post, her domestic duties were relatively lighter than they had traditionally been. Now her energies were concentrated on making moccasins and netting

The Indian family of a Hudson's Bay Company steersman watches while trade goods are being prepared for the portage at Grand Rapids. c. 1882.

snowshoes. As one Nor'Wester declared, Indian women could lead "a comparatively easy and free life" with the whites in contrast to the "servile slavish mode" of their own people.[27] It was the prospect of such superior comforts which reputedly motivated some Spokan women to marry voyageurs.[28] The ready supply of both finery and trinkets which bourgeois and voyageurs tended to lavish on their women may also have had an appeal. In 1814 the bourgeois Donald McTavish took to dressing his new Chinook wife in fine black broadcloth for which he paid twenty-three shillings a yard! The voyageurs prided themselves on having well-dressed wives, a fact which contributed to their almost perpetual state of debt.[29] The private orders placed in the 1790s by Hudson's Bay Company officers and servants included a wide range of cloth goods, shawls, gartering, earrings and brooches for their women.[30]

The traders further thought that Indian women benefited by being freed from certain taboos and customs which they had to bear in Indian society. Among the Ojibwa and other tribes, the choicest part of an animal was always reserved for the men: death, it was believed, would come to any women who dared to eat these sacred portions. The Nor'Westers paid little heed to such observances. Duncan Cameron sarcastically commented: "I have often seen several women living with the white men eat of those forbidden morsels without the least inconvenience."[31] The Nor'Westers were also convinced that Indian women welcomed a monogamous rather than a polygamous state. Indeed, one observer went so far as to declare that an Indian woman was better off sharing the semi-nomadic life of a French-Canadian freeman than that of an Indian:

> . . . these men make excellent Husbands and tender fathers & content themselves with only <u>one wife,</u> who never receives any brutal or unkind treatment from them, nor have any of those shameful and distressing drudgeries to perform which the Indians invariably impose on their debased maltreated and wretched partners.[32]

This statement reveals a serious lack of appreciation for the fact that life was precarious and hard for all Indians regardless of sex. Under such circumstances, the women were not averse to polygamy because it provided a means for sharing their heavy domestic burdens. There is evidence, however, that Indian women took quickly to the European view that a man should have only one wife. At the Hudson's Bay Company inland posts in the late eighteenth century, the Indian wives of the officers were themselves a factor in lessening the polygamous tendencies of Hudson's Bay Company men. More than one inland master was diplomatically able to avoid the expense of supporting several wives by making it plain that he already had a woman, and if he were to take another, his own would be very offended.[33] The coming of the fur traders, thus, offered the Indian women the prospect of an alternative way of life; it promised sufficient relief from the burdens of their traditional existence to induce numerous Indian women to choose it.

After they became wives of the traders, Indian women still endeavoured to preserve the domestic autonomy to which they were accustomed. This was an aspect of the women's lives which caused the fur traders considerable confusion; they did not know how to explain the fact that in spite of the onerous burdens inflicted upon the women, they were not without influence in certain areas. Indeed at times some of the bolder ones succeeded in making themselves quite independent and "wore the breeches."[34] In reality, in Indian society, it was the division of labour resulting from the conditions of a nomadic existence which imposed such a heavy burden upon the woman. Within her own sphere, the Indian woman enjoyed an autonomy which was relatively greater than that of her European counterpart at the time. The household was in effect her property; the products of her labour were hers to dispose of as she wished.[35] The value of the services which the Indian woman performed in fur-trade society, when coupled with this tradition of being "mistress in her own house", appears to have enabled individual women to gain dominant positions. This did not accord with the traders' notion of proper wifely behaviour, and a perturbed discussion emerges in their writings over the excessive influence which Indian women could exert over their fur-trader husbands.

The young clerk George Nelson spent considerable time contemplating the insoluble perplexities of womankind. Nelson claimed that initially Cree women were incredibly attentive and submissive when married to whites, but this did not last long. Once they had gained a footing, they knew well "how to take advantage & what use they ought to make of it."[36] On one of his first trips into the interior, Nelson was considerably annoyed by the shenanigans of the Indian wife of Brunet, one of his voyageurs. This jealous, headstrong woman completely dominated her husband by a mixture of "caresses, promises & menaces." Not only did she render her husband an unreliable servant, but she helped herself to the Company's rum. Brunet's wife, Nelson fumed, was as great "a vixen & hussy" as the tinsmith's wife at the market place in Montreal: "I now began to think that women were women not only in civilized countries but elsewhere also."[37]

One of the most remarkable examples of a Chipewyan wife rising to prominence was the case of Madame Lamallice, the wife of the brigade guide at Fort Wedderburn, the Hudson's Bay Company post on Lake Athabasca. During the difficult winter of 1820-21, Madame Lamallice was accorded a favoured position because she was the post's only interpreter and possessed considerable influence with the Indians. George Simpson, then experiencing his first winter in the Indian Country, felt obliged to give in to her demands for extra rations and preferential treatment in order to prevent her defection, and he was amazed by this woman's resourcefulness. In the spring when provisions ran low, Lamallice and the other voyageurs with their families were ordered to go to support themselves at the fishery. Madame Lamallice did not wish to leave the fort and informed Simpson that if she and her family were allowed to remain at the post they would not ask for any provisions for the next twenty days:

> . . . it appears that in anticipation of a scarcity of provisions this thrifty amazon has out of the Rations served to her family (even when the officers' mess was on short allowance) laid up a stock of about 200 fish; I have therefore permitted her to remain.[38]

Simpson was not amused, however, to learn that Madame Lamallice was carrying on her own private trade in pounded meat, beaver tails and moose skins, with a hoarded stock of trade goods, including cloth and ribbons. The Company officers realized that they were almost powerless to stop this traffic; when they attempted to control Madame Lamallice, she threatened to turn all the Indians against the English.[39]

Madame Lamallice's prestige apparently collapsed after the union of the two companies in 1821, but Governor Simpson continued to express general concern about the influence of such "petticoat politicians" whose demands were "more injurious to the Comp[ys] interests than I am well able to describe."[40] He would have rated highly the services of the boat builder at Brandon House, James Inkster, except that this servant was under the control of his Cree wife and her relatives, and was given to drink.[41] Nor were officers exempt; the Governor was critical of James Bird's management of Red River in the early 1820s partly because "I find that every matter however trifling or important is discussed wh. his Copper Cold. Mate before decided on and from her it finds its way all over the colony."[42] Chinook women, when married to whites, were reputed to gain such an ascendancy "that they give law to their Lords."[43]

It is evident that the fur traders did not doubt that they offered Indian women a superior way of life. It is much more difficult to evaluate the accuracy of their claims from the point of view of the women. Quite a number of Indian women probably were under the illusion that life at a fur-trade post had much to offer, judging from their active role in securing white husbands, but there is evidence to suggest that, in the long run, this new life could have detrimental consequences for the women, both physically and pyschologically. It is noteworthy that other Europeans, principally explorers and missionaries who visited Rupert's Land in the early nineteenth century, did not think that an Indian woman had much to gain by becoming the wife of a trader. Some of the officers of the Franklin Expedition in the 1820s felt that the fur traders had been corrupted by Indian attitudes toward women: Indian wives were not treated with "the tenderness and attention due to every female" because the Indians would despise the traders for such unmanly behaviour.[44] John West, the first Protestant missionary in the West, denounced fur-trade marital relations: "They do not admit them as their companions, nor do they allow them to eat at their tables, but degrade them merely as slaves to their arbitrary inclinations."[45] Such statements invite skepticism because of the writers' limited experience with fur-trade society and, in the case of the missionaries, their avowedly hostile view of fur-trade customs. Furthermore, the above comments project a European ideal about the way women should be treated which, apart from being widely disregarded in their own society, would have had little relevance for Indian women. It is doubtful that the women themselves would have viewed the fact that they did not come to the table, a custom partly dictated by the quasi-military organization of the posts, as proof of their debased position.[46] The segregation of the sexes at meals was common in Indian society, but now, at least, the women did not have to make do with the leftovers. The daily individual ration for the women of the forts could be as high as four pounds of meat or fish.[47]

The remarks made by some of these outside observers nevertheless provide insight into the problems suffered by the Indian wives of traders. Paradoxically, the "easy life" at the fur-trade post was seen to have a deleterious physical effect on Indian women. It was as if, mused the Reverend John West, "the habits of civilized life" exerted an injurious influence over their general constitutions.[48] Apart from being more exposed to the dangers of European diseases and alcohol, the wives of fur traders suffered more in childbirth than they had in the primitive state. Dr John Richardson, who accompanied the Franklin Expedition, noted that Indian women now bore children more frequently and over a longer period of time. They were also more susceptible to the disorders and diseases connected with pregnancy and childbirth. It was not uncommon for the wives of fur traders to give birth to from eight to twelve children, whereas the average in Cree society was four.[49]

Several reasons can be advanced for this dramatic rise in the birth rate. The less fatiguing routine and more regular diet of the trader's wife could have resulted in greater fecundity. When Governor Simpson jokingly remarked that the whitefish diet at Fort Chipewyan seemed conducive to procreation, he may have spoken a medical truth.[50] In Indian society sexual activity had been circumscribed by a variety of taboos, and evidence suggests that Indian men regarded their European counterparts as licentious. Indian women had sex more often with their European partners whose attitudes may have interfered with traditional modes of restricting family size. The practice of infanticide was condemned and the traditional practice of nursing each child for two to four years was also discouraged. In the traders' view, this habit resulted in the premature aging of the mothers. However, the theory that lactation depressed fertility is supported by the fact that Indian children were born at intervals of approximately three years.[51]

Differing cultural attitudes about the upbringing of children must have caused Indian mothers considerable anguish. In native society, the women had been used to having complete charge of this sphere, for the children were regarded as virtually the "property" of the mother. In fur-trade society, while it was acknowledged that Indian women were remarkably devoted and affectionate mothers,[52] European fathers exercised patriarchal authority. It was common for the officers in both companies to send very young children, particularly sons, to Britain or Canada so that they might receive a "civilized" education. This must have been hard on the mothers, for it would have been almost impossible to make them understand the reason for such a decision. According to family tradition, Nahovway, the wife of Chief Factor William Sinclair, was so upset at the prospect of having her youngest child Colin taken away from her that her husband pretended to agree not to send him to England as he had all his other sons. When the boy was about nine years old, however, he was quietly spirited away on one of the Company ships.[53] The mothers' grief at being separated from their children was compounded by the fact that the children, who were especially vulnerable to respiratory diseases, often died.[54]

An extreme example of the tragedy which could result from cultural differences related to the Chinook practice of head-flattening. In Chinook society, a flat forehead achieved by strapping a board against the head of the baby when in its cradle, was a mark of class; only slaves were not so distinguished. Thus it was only natural that a Chinook woman, though married to a fur trader, would desire to bind her baby's head. White fathers found this custom abhorrent, and some insisted that their infants' heads not be flattened. As a result the mothers murdered their babies rather than have them suffer the ignominy of growing up to look like slaves. Gradually European preference prevailed. When Governor Simpson visited the Columbia in the early 1820s, he reported that Chinook wives were abiding by their husbands' wishes; no cases of infanticide had been reported for some years.[55]

Despite her important contributions and influence in certain areas, the Indian woman in fur-trade society was at the mercy of a social structure devised primarily to meet the needs of European males. It is true that the flexibility of custom could be taken advantage of by both men and women, but instances of women actually doing so were rare. One of the few recorded cases was that of the Indian wife of Joseph Colen, chief at York Factory in the 1790s. Although Colen had made arrangements for his wife to receive "every attention" during his absence in England, she could not be dissuaded from taking an Indian husband and leaving the factory.[56] The traders, however, were certainly not entirely innocent of the charge levelled at them by the missionaries, that they were guilty of exploiting Indian women.[57] At its worst "turning off" can be seen as a perversion of native custom calculated to suit the traders' transient needs, and the women, understandably, resented it. At a post in the Peace River District in 1798, the Indian wife of an engagé who was growing tired of wintering *en derouine*, did manage to foil her husband's attempt to pass her on to his successor,[58] but resistance was more often futile. An extreme case of an Indian woman who had suffered the vagaries of "turning off" was a "Mademoiselle Censols". By 1825 when she became the country wife of Hudson's Bay Company officer John Hutchinson, she reputedly already had had eight previous husbands, most of them voyageurs.[59] In the summer of 1840, Betsey, an industrious Indian washerwoman at York Factory, was very angry to find herself abandoned by her fourth, or perhaps even her fifth, husband who was going home to England. She declared she would never marry again because she was suspicious that any new suitor would just be after her carefully saved earnings. Within a short time, Betsey, however, had succumbed to the entreaties of the recently widowed cooper David Munro and soon departed with her new family for the Columbia.[60]

Women seem to have been particularly victimized during the violent days of the trade war. By the turn of the century, some of the bourgeois had stooped to the nefarious but profitable scheme of selling women to their engagés. At Fort Chipewyan in 1800, when the estranged wife of the voyageur Morin tried to run away, she was brought back by her Indian relations, only to face the prospect of being sold by the bourgeois to another engagé. James Mackenzie, who seems to have been especially ruthless, confided to his journal:

> Two advantages may be reaped from this affair; the first is that it will assist to discharge the Debts of a Man [Morin] unable to do it by any other Means for he is neither good Middleman, Foreman, Steersman, Interpreter or Carpenter — the next is, that it may be the means of tickling some lecherous Miser to part with some of his Hoard. I therefore kept the woman to be disposed of in the Season when the Peace River Bucks begin to rut most, I mean the Month of May.[61]

Mackenzie's plan to find her a temporary protector in the meantime failed when the woman herself stoutly refused three different possibilities and "to convince them how heartily she hated them all three, she set up her pipes at the bare mention of their names." She only escaped being sold by declaring that if she must be bound to a voyageur she might as well return to her old one. In the fur-trade wars Indian wives were used as pawns by rivals sometimes so desperate as to debauch and intimidate each other's women. A notorious instance involved the Indian wife of Hudson's Bay Company servant Andrew Kirkness at Île à la Crosse in 1810-11.[62] In the late summer, this woman in a fit of pique had deserted her husband and sought refuge at the Nor'Westers' post. She soon regretted her action, for she was kept a virtual prisoner by the Canadians, and all efforts by the Hudson's Bay Company men to get her back failed. Finally Kirkness deserted to the rival post, leaving the English in dire

"Fort Chepewyan — an establishment of the N.W. Co.ʸ on the Athabasca Lake (north America)." From a water-colour by George Back. c. 1825.

straits since he was their only fisherman. Kirkness remained with the Nor'Westers until the spring, intimidated by the threat that should he leave "every Canadian in the House would ravish his woman before his very eyes." Eventually Kirkness was released, but only after his wife had been coerced into saying that she did not want to accompany him. As the Hudson's Bay Company party was evacuating its post, the woman tried to escape but was forcibly dragged back by the Nor'Westers and ultimately became the "property" of an engagé.

Understandably, the Indians did not take kindly to such abuse of their women. In some well-established areas of the trade, women now became a source of friction between Indian and white, instead of the positive link they had been formerly. Relations between the Nor'Westers and the Chipewyan became particularly bad in the 1790s when the traders, desperate to maintain their virtual monopoly on the rich Athabasca area, began coercing the Indians even to the extent of seizing their women in lieu of trade debts. Since they were not powerful enough to mount an attack, the Chipewyan connived at the escape of their women during the summer months when most of the traders were away. Resentful of their treatment, many of the women watched for the chance to slip back to their own people, and the summer master at Fort Chipewyan was almost solely preoccupied with keeping watch over the engagés' women. By 1800 at least one voyageur had been killed by irate Chipewyan, and the bourgeois contemplated offering a reward for the hunting down of "any d-nd rascal" who caused a Frenchman's woman to desert.[63]

By the early nineteenth century many Indians had become openly contemptuous of the white men and their so-called morality. A northern tribe called the Beaver Indians took a particularly strong stand. At first they had welcomed the Nor'Westers, but, having lost respect for them, they now forbade any intercourse between their women and the traders.[64] Elsewhere individual hunters boycotted the traders because of the maltreatment of their women,[65] or sought more violent revenge. At Rupert's House in 1806, Hudson's Bay Company servant John Robertson, in defecting to the Nor'Westers, cast off his Indian wife and took one from among the Indians loyal to the Canadians. His father-in-law was so outraged by this callous abandonment of his daughter that he pursued Robertson and shot him.[66] George Nelson felt forced to admit that some of the traders deserved the hatred of the Indians. In his reminiscences of his days in the West is preserved a most damning speech by an Indian who hoped to pass off his second wife to a white man because he considered her a disgrace to her race:

> . . . she is naturally lazy and dirty; she is so headstrong she will do only as she pleases and she is very fond of men — she is never pleased but when she had them before her. She will not do for me nor for any Indian. — [The] best way is to give her to the whites. With them she will have only snow-Shoes and maggacins to make, & with them she will have as much of men as she desires. . . . they take women, not for wives — but use them as Sluts — to satisfy the animal lust, & when they are satiated, they cast them off, and another one takes

her for the same purpose, & by & by casts her off
again, and so she will go on until she becomes an old
[woman], soiled by every one who chuses to use her.
She is foolish — she has no understanding, no sense,
no shame.[67]

At the height of the trade rivalry in the first two decades of the
nineteenth century, it does appear that the Indian woman's view
of the white man was considerably tarnished; some Indian
women, Nelson observed, showed "an extraordinary predilec-
tion" for their own people and could not be prevailed upon to
live with the traders."[68]

During this time, there was also a noticeable change in the
North West Company's opinion as to the value of taking Indian
wives. In 1806, at the annual meeting in July, the wintering
partners resolved that

... no Man whatever, either Partner, Clerk, or Engagé,
... shall henceforth take or suffer to be taken, under
any pretence whatsoever, any woman or maid from
any of the tribes of Indians now known or who may
hereafter become known in this Country to live with
him after the fashion of the North West.[69]

In part, this resolution was motivated by the fact that in
well-established areas marriage alliances were no longer a
significant factor in trade relations. Too often the traders,
concerned only with besting their rivals, now ran roughshod
over the Indians, who were becoming increasingly demoralized
by the vast quantities of liquor being brought into the country.
Nevertheless, it is noteworthy that the stipulation that alliances
not be formed with Indian women "from tribes as yet
unknown" became a dead issue. The important marriage
alliances in the Columbia District between the Nor'Westers and
the daughters of Chief Concomely took place in 1813 and after,
and Alexander Ross does not appear to have been censured for
taking his Okanagan wife.[70] After the union of the two
companies in 1821, the Hudson's Bay Company men followed
the Nor'Westers' lead in taking wives from among the tribes in
the outlying districts of the Columbia and New Caledonia. In
the latter region the impolitic dealings of an inexperienced
Hudson's Bay Company officer with a Carrier woman led to the

murder of two men at Fort George in 1823 and serious problems
with the Indians.[71] This incident served to underscore once again
that if the traders did not secure the full approbation of the
Indians before contracting liaisons with their women, trouble
would result. Indeed as Governor Simpson declared:

> It is a lamentable fact that almost every difficulty
> we have had with Indians throughout the Country may
> be traced to our interference with their Women or their
> Intrigues with the Women of the Forts in short 9
> Murders out of 10 Committed on Whites by Indians
> have arisen through Women.[72]

If increasing native hostility contributed to a decline in the
practice of taking an Indian wife, the North West Company
was also influenced by the pressing economic need to "reduce
. . . the number of women maintained by the Company." By the
early 1800s, it was estimated that between twelve and fifteen
hundred women and children were being fed and in many cases
clothed at Company expense; the wintering population at Fort
Vermilion in 1810 — 36 men, 27 women and 67 children — gives
a representative distribution of a post's population.[73] Given the
enormous quantities of food consumed by the traders and their
families,[74] the Company could not afford to add to this heavy
burden when faced with the expense of having to fight its
competitors. Another Montreal-based concern, the XY
Company, which had been a strong rival in the trade war since
1798, had set the Nor'Westers an example by prohibiting its
junior clerks and servants from taking Indian wives for
economic reasons.[75]

The Hudson's Bay Company had never officially sanctioned unions between its employees and Indian women, but by
the turn of the century, the London Committee was distressed
to discover that the support of officers' women and children had
grown to a considerable expense.[76] Chief factors were ordered
to keep a detailed account of all goods expended, but irregulari-
ties persisted until a new financial system was introduced in
1810 giving officers a direct share in the profits of the trade.
Only then were certain officers moved to control their Indian
wives who had previously operated as if "the chief purpose of
their existence was to dispense the property of the Company

on the most undeserving of objects for the most selfish purposes."[77] With the prospect of the founding of the Red River settlement which would bring civilization to Rupert's Land, several Hudson's Bay Company officers expressed the view that it was no longer desirable for white traders to intermarry with Indian women. No ruling specifically prohibiting Hudson's Bay Company men from taking Indian wives has been found, however, prior to a resolution passed to that effect, but only for the Southern Department, in 1824.[78]

By the early decades of the nineteenth century changing concerns on the part of both Indian and white actively discouraged the fur traders from forming marital unions with full-blooded Indian women, except in outlying districts. Another significant factor in the decline of Indian wives resulted from their no longer being the "women in between". Decades of intermarriage had in itself produced a new group of marriageable women — the mixed-bloods. The Nor'Westers' resolution in 1806 specifically allowed the traders to continue to marry the daughters of white men after the custom of the country.[79] Mixed-blood women were soon to replace their Indian progenitors in playing an important role in the indigenous fur-trade society that was evolving in the Canadian West.

5

"DAUGHTERS OF THE COUNTRY"

Before the passing of the North West Company's resolution of 1806, the taking of a mixed-blood wife instead of an Indian one had become widespread in fur-trade society. By the mid-eighteenth century, a large mixed-blood population had grown up and James Isham reported that the offspring of Hudson's Bay Company men and Indian women were "Pretty Numerious".[1] It is almost impossible to identify many of these children because so many of them were absorbed into the Home Guard bands. In the annals of the Hudson's Bay Company during this period virtually no distinction was made between Indian and mixed-blood. In the North West Company, the policy of supporting servants' families, coupled with the emergence of a body of "freemen", resulted in the progeny of Nor'Westers being recognized at an early stage as a group distinct from the Indians. They were known as Métis or "bois brulés" and by far the largest number of them were descendants of the French-Canadian engagés and their Indian wives.

Initially, the upbringing of mixed-blood girls was strongly influenced by their Indian mothers who passed on to their daughters the native skills which had proved so valuable to the functioning of the fur trade. But by the end of the eighteenth century the officers, particularly of the Hudson's Bay Company, were concerned to impress upon their daughters "the Ideas and Habits of Civilized Life" and to wean them away from their Indian heritage.[2] In their desire to ensure that their daughters remained within fur-trade society, many fathers came to play an instrumental role in promoting their marriages to incoming traders or to the mixed-blood sons of their colleagues. With her dual heritage, the mixed-blood woman possessed the ideal qualifications for a fur trader's wife: acclimatized to life in the West and familiar with Indian ways, she could also make a successful adaptation to white culture. As fur-trade families began to intermarry extensively, the custom of the country evolved toward European concepts of marriage. Fur-trade society pulled increasingly away from its Indian roots as the mixed-blood wife became "the vogue".

Because it was common for mixed-blood children to be raised among their mothers' people, the number who were fathered by Hudson's Bay Company men has been seriously underestimated. Many such children were adopted by Indian step-fathers who were reputed to be remarkably fond parents.[3] It seems likely, however, that this fate more commonly befell girls than it did boys. The London Committee could sometimes be persuaded to allow fathers to send their sons to England to be educated, but it was reluctant to extend this privilege to daughters. Young female children, the Committee argued, required special care which the ships' captains could not possibly provide.[4] Furthermore, while a civilized education was seen as necessary for a boy's advancement in the fur trade, for a girl such an upbringing would serve only to estrange her from the fur-trade way of life. The experience of the children of Chief Factor Ferdinand Jacobs in the 1770s is illustrative. His son, called Samuel, was sent home to England to be educated; his daughter, Thucautch, was brought up among the Home Guard. Thucautch's education was to learn the skills expected of a native woman, and eventually she became the wife of "one of York['s] best Indian home Guards."[5] In many ways, mixed-blood girls brought up among their mothers' people became virtually indistinguishable from the Indians — as their names Neskisho, Ke-che-cow-e-com-coot and Wash-e-soo E'squaw' testify.[6] A detailed description of the mixed-blood wife of John Lee Lewes, a prominent nineteenth-century officer, reveals that she was much more influenced by her Plains Cree mother than her Orkney father John Ballenden, who had been a Hudson's Bay Company servant:

> She is the daughter of an Indian woman, and much
> more the squaw than the civilized woman herself,
> delights in nothing so much as roaming around with

her children making the most cunning snares for Partridges, rabbits and so on . . . she is moreover very good-natured and has given me two pairs of worked moccasins . . . she also gives me lessons in Cree.[7]

Although mixed-blood children might be absorbed into the Indian way of life, they remained conscious of their paternity. The father's name was remembered, even if the father was long gone. According to popular legend it was a young Cree woman who rescued the Nor'Wester John Rowand after a serious fall from his horse and who soon after became his wife. In reality Louise Humphraville [sic] was only part Indian. Her father was Edward Umfreville, a well-known trader who had served both companies before leaving Rupert's Land in 1788 when his daughter was no more than five years old.[8] Among the descendants of Hudson's Bay Company men brought up among the Home Guard, the tradition was maintained that their paternal origin rendered them superior to true Indians.[9] The advantage of having a Company father also manifested itself in more concrete ways. When Ferdinand Jacobs left the Bay in 1774 he made arrangements for Thucautch to continue to receive an annual supply of goods from the Company's warehouse. In his will, he left his daughter an annuity of ten pounds which she was still collecting in goods as late as 1800.[10] Matthew Cocking was evidently fond of indulging his daughters with treats of "Ginger Bread, Nuts &c", and after his death, the York Council arranged that part of the annuity he had left his daughters be used to continue to supply them with these "little Luxuries".[11]

While there were practical reasons for the acculturation of daughters to the Indian way of life, many fathers had qualms about abandoning their children to such a fate. It exposed them to physical hardship and returned them to a primitive, heathen state, a course which offended the religious sensibilities of some officers in both companies. A number of bourgeois in the North West Company showed considerable concern to provide their children with a Christian education and, for this reason, sent sons and to a lesser extent daughters to school in Upper and Lower Canada. David Thompson paid over sixty pounds a year

John Rowand, Jr, son of Chief Factor John Rowand and his mixed-blood wife, Louise Umfreville.

to board one of his daughters at a school in Lower Canada, but he was reconciled to the heavy expense:

> It is my wish to give all my children an equal and good education; my conscience obliges me to it, and it is for this I am now working in this country.[12]

Among the Hudson's Bay Company officers, several were moved to beg the London Committee to permit them to send their daughters to civilization. Andrew Graham appealed to the Committee in 1772:

> You are many, if not all of you, Fathers, let then what would be feelings of Your own Paternal hearts on such an occasion, plead in my behalf; & let not humanity & Christianity be forgot.[13]

Graham's request was acceded to only when he himself was coming over to England and could bring his daughter with him, but the pleas of the few servants who were anxious to follow this course were flatly refused.[14] The London Committee, realizing that daughters sent to England would soon be alienated from their former life, refused to allow "any Female Children" to return to their native land "after receiving their Education in Great Britian."[15]

This harsh attitude undoubtedly dampened the desire of Hudson's Bay Company fathers to send their children to England, but as the eighteenth century progressed, it is clear that more and more officers were determined to prevent their daughters from living as Indians and began to play an active role in their upbringing. Moses Norton at Prince of Wales's Fort evidently doted on his only daughter Mary; she lived a sheltered life within the fort and was indulged with every comfort.[16] A fascinating glimpse of the efforts of some fathers to "civilize" their daughters is provided by the Book of Servants' Private Commissions which lists imports from England on private account for the years 1790-1810. The officers at Albany seem to have been particularly anxious to have the females in their families adopt English fashions. Large quantities of cloth (mainly calico and chintz), ribbons and lace were ordered, along with the items essential to dressmaking. Among Robert Goodwin's requests were issues of "Ladys Magazines", specifically with pictures of fashionable dresses, and "a Lady's

This pencil sketch by Peter Rindisbacher illustrates the clothing worn by mixed-blood women in the Red River Settlement: high-waisted gowns with low bodices and skirts almost to the ankles. The sketch (c. 1825) forms the basis for his water-colour entitled "A Halfcast and his Two Wives".

Glenbow-Alberta Institute

red Morocco Book for Silk thread with Scissors &c a pretty large one".[17] Jewellery such as ornamental earrings and silver brooches were popular items, while a really stylish lady might complete her costume with an imported shawl and a beaver hat with band and feather which sold for one pound six shillings. The more fastidious officers also decided to do something about the native women's ignorance of undergarments; in 1804, John McKay ordered eight ladies' shifts and six pairs of women's white stockings.[18] Soap was a regularly imported item at all the posts; but at Churchill, Governor Auld endeavoured to set new standards of hygiene and elegance by importing nail and tooth brushes, combs and fine pumice stone.[19] The only item of European apparel that never proved popular were shoes, even those of "flat solid" design. The moccasin remained the most practical footwear, although the effect might seem rather incongruous. By the nineteenth century, the mixed-blood wives and daughters of the officer class attempted to keep up with English fashion. When Harriett Gladman, who was from an old Hudson's Bay Company family and the wife of a chief trader, donned her best to pay a social call at York Factory in 1840:

> [She was] dressed to death in a Waterloo blue Merino [gown], moccasins, a straw bonnet lined with lilac satin with a profusion of lilac blue & white ribbon & a cap border of very broad blonde, the same depth all around no gloves & a silk shawl, the old fashion white around & green pattern.[20]

While the women of fur-trade officers dressed increasingly in the English style, in general, mixed-blood women evolved a more practical costume. The "Canadian" fashion, as the Nor'Westers called it, combined both white and Indian features. The sketches by the Swiss colonist Peter Rindisbacher from the early 1820s show the women wearing high-waisted gowns with gathered but shapeless skirts which reached almost to the ankle. The long-sleeved, jacket-like bodice was very low-cut and filled in with a criss-crossed scarf arrangement, apparently to facilitate the nursing of children. The outfit was not complete without Indian "leggins", moccasins and usually a blanket. Captain Charles Wilkes described the women of Fort Vancouver:

> The ladies of the country are dressed after our own by gone fashions, with the exception of leggins, made of red and blue cloth, richly ornamented. Their feet, which are small and pretty, are covered with worked moccasins.[21]

The Métis women of Red River were acknowledged to be tidy about their person and dress, but Alexander Ross felt that they were overly fond of showy prints and finery. He also believed that their retention of the primitive blanket was a most injurious fashion:

> The blanket as an overall, is considered indispensable; it is used on all occasions, not only here, but throughout the continent, both at home and abroad; if a stick is wanted for the fire, or a pleasure party is to be joined away from home, the blanket is called for. This invariable habit gives them a stooping gait while walking, and the constant use of the same blanket day and night, wet and dry, is supposed to give rise to consumptive complaints, which they are all more or less very subject to.[22]

The blanket was important as a head covering, for mixed-blood women did not wear hats as a rule. They fashioned their hair simply in a single long braid at the back which might be decorated with ribbons and beads, and they were very fond of jewellery such as necklaces, earrings and rings.[23] It also appears that the daughters of the country were loath to give up the unladylike Indian habit of smoking tobacco. Rindisbacher often portrays them holding rather elegant, long-stemmed clay pipes. A story is told of Hudson's Bay Company officer P. C. Pambrun who attempted to bribe his wife to stop smoking; even the promise of a pair of diamond earrings could not make her break the habit.[24]

The European traders sought to outfit their women in civilized fashion and to inculcate in them the precepts of Christianity and proper womanly behaviour. Several Hudson's Bay Company officers were especially concerned that their children learn the English language so that they could stamp out what they considered to be immoral and superstitious Indian attitudes. By the 1790s, the number of mixed-blood children on the Bay had grown to such an extent that the London Committee was prepared to support a plan for the schooling of its employees' offspring. In 1794 it sent out from 50 to 100 spelling books and primers to each of the posts on Hudson Bay. The actual teaching was to be left to those parents with the time and inclination, but the Committee was hopeful that "much good will be the result of your care & Attention, to their Improvement."[25] The Committee was primarily concerned to provide the rudiments of education for sons who could now officially be employed in the lower ranks of the service, but it was considered important for daughters to be exposed to such British influences as well.

One of the most remarkable products of this early schooling was Jeanny, the wife of inland officer John Sutherland, who much impressed Nor'Westers Daniel Harmon and A. N. McLeod when they met her at an Hudson's Bay Company post on the Assiniboine River in 1800. Jeanny's parentage is unknown, but her father likely took an active part in her education at Albany, where she learned to speak English and to read and write a little. Harmon, who found Jeanny to be an interesting conversationalist, declared that she not only possessed good natural sense, but was far from being deficient in acquired knowledge. Skill at cribbage was among her accomplishments, for McLeod recorded that during a visit to his rival he had "had the Honor of playing Cribbage with Jeanny."[26] The Nor'Westers had much more respect for Jeanny than for her husband whom they considered a foolish drunkard.

By the early 1800s, the London Committee had recognized the need to send schoolmasters to the Bay to provide the children with more organized instruction in reading, writing and arithmetic and the basic principles of religion.[27] The officers, who responded most enthusiastically to this proposal, emphasized the necessity of educating girls as well as boys. They were particularly anxious to estrange their daughters from Indian influence. It was believed that the free manner in which Indian mothers discussed sexual matters made it impossible for them to inculcate in their daughters proper feminine virtues, especially chastity. John McNab at York Factory recommended that "a respectable Matron" be sent out to supervise the care of

Section of a page from the Albany Factory School Journal. Twenty-three children were in attendance in 1808-1809.

the children who should be boarded at a school where they
could be isolated from Indian women:

> . . . the female youth in particular should experience
> that delicacy & attention to their persons their
> particular situation requires — native women as
> attendants on these young persons seems improper —
> their society would keep alive the Indian language &
> with it, its native superstition which ought to be
> obliterated from the mind with all possible care.[28]

The Committee had difficulty in procuring suitable schoolmasters, or schoolmistresses, but in 1808 it succeeded in hiring
four schoolmasters who were sent out to the various posts on
the Bay. All children of the age of five and over could be
admitted to the schools "without discrimination", but they must
first be christened with a European name by the chief factor.[29]
Girls were well represented among the school pupils. At York
Factory, three out of the four children who began school in 1808
were the daughters of officers: Harriett, daughter of former
governor John Ballenden; Catherine, daughter of William

Geological Survey of Canada

School-age children at Albany, 1886.

Sinclair; and Mary, daughter of Thomas Bunn.[30] By 1811 at
Eastmain Factory, eight girls and seven boys were attending
school, representing a wide cross-section of the fur trade. Two of
the first pupils were Elizabeth Gladman, whose father was the
chief factor, and Margaret Moore, possibly a cousin, whose
father was a native-born canoe builder.[31] The largest school was
that at Albany run by William Harper; of the twenty-three
children listed in 1808-09, eight were girls between the ages of
six and fourteen. One of the most promising pupils was ten-
year-old Harriet Vincent, a daughter of officer Thomas Vincent
and his native wife Jane Renton. The importance placed on
religious training is shown in Harriet's schooling. In the fall she
was learning to read from Trimmer's *Sacred History*,
memorizing the Church Catechism and beginning to write. Her
progress was interrupted by a family hunting trip in December,
but Harriet and her sister returned to school in the new year.
During the "second term" Harriett learned selections from Dr
Watt's *Divine Songs for Children*, began arithmetic, and was
chosen along with four boys "to write Copy Books to go to
England".[32] But when Vincent moved his family to Moose

Factory the next year, prior to going on furlough, his daughters' education was curtailed, as the school at Moose had not proved very successful.

All of these first schools in Rupert's Land were short-lived because the schoolmasters showed considerably more interest in the fur trade than in their pupils. Ultimately, the extent to which mixed-blood children were exposed to civilizing influences depended upon the initiative of individual fathers. The efforts of some of the officers to teach European morality is evident in the orders for books sent to England; *Aesop's Fables* was a common request and *Duties of Woman* was ordered by John Best at Albany. Unfortunately, one is left to speculate on the influence its precepts may have had on Best's daughter, Catherine, who became the country wife of Chief Factor William Thomas.[33] Before he retired to England in 1815, George Taylor, the sloopmaster at York, evidently took pains to teach his Indian wife Jane and their family of eight children clean and industrious habits. Two of his daughters, Mary and Margaret, were widely admired, not only for their beauty, but for their "civilized" womanly qualities.[34] Chief Factor James Sutherland also devoted considerable time to instructing his children; in 1823 his daughter Sally was described by Reverend John West as "one of the best informed and most improved half-caste women" he had seen.[35] Captain Franklin noted that the children of the Orkney servants received a little education and showed a distinct improvement compared to those of the French-Canadian voyageurs who were left to grow up in ignorance.[36] While the North West Company never attempted to implement a plan of education for the children of its servants, a few concerned bourgeois such as Daniel Harmon and David Thompson endeavoured to teach their own children, and those of their colleagues, the basics of English and some simple prayers.[37]

Laudable as the efforts of the traders to civilize their daughters may have been, in effect, they were to place them in a vulnerable position by making them increasingly dependent upon white male protectors and the comforts of the fur-trade post. For a mixed-blood woman who lacked close ties to her Indian relations or was unaccustomed to the hardship of their existence, life was fraught with danger after the withdrawal of white male support through death or retirement. Hudson's Bay Company officer Edward Jarvis understood this when he pleaded with the London Committee to be allowed to bring home his native family in the 1780s; he was particularly concerned about his wife because she was "the daughter of an Englishman" and had few or no Indian friends.[38]

One of the most tragic illustrations of the fatal cycle of dependency that could be created was the case of Mary Norton, the daughter of Governor Moses Norton and an unidentified Cree woman. Norton lavished tender care and luxuries upon his daughter, and his will reveals great concern about her future welfare. Shortly before his death in December 1773, Norton, endeavouring to secure ample provision for Mary, added a codicil to his will instructing his executrix to raise his daughter's annuity to thirty pounds, five of which she was to give to her "aunt", Meo,See,tak,ka,pow. Norton's executrix, his English wife Sarah, was apparently able to ignore the codicil in favour of the less generous terms of the original will and only remitted ten pounds a year to the Committee to be divided equally between Mary and her "aunt".[39] Upon her father's death Mary did not have to go to live with her Indian relations, for Samuel Hearne was at last free to pursue his desire to make her his country wife. Hearne professed the utmost abhorrence for Norton; yet he idolized his daughter whom he extolled as an example of pure and virtuous womanhood. Mary's "benevolence, humanity, and scrupulous adherence to truth and honesty" he declared, "would have done honour to the most enlightened and devout Christian."[40] Unfortunately when Hearne surrendered Prince of Wales's Fort to the French and was taken prisoner in 1782, Mary was abandoned to her Indian relatives. During the bitter winter that followed she starved to death. Hearne charged that she had perished "a martyr to the principles of virtue", but the Indians would not willingly have let Mary die. Her helplessness likely imposed too heavy a burden upon them when starvation conditions prevailed and many other Indians died.[41]

Increasingly the fur traders began to acknowledge a kind of collective responsibility for the fate of their female offspring.

Concern for the welfare of their children led to the development
of an informal system of guardianship among the bourgeois of
the North West Company. When Roderick McKenzie retired
from the Indian Country in 1803 he entrusted the supervision of
his three mixed-blood children to his friend John Stuart. Then
when the eldest daughter Nancy married, her husband, J. G.
McTavish, took over responsibility for her younger sister until
she too found a husband.[42] Marriage was an important factor in
the future of a mixed-blood girl since her role would be
primarily defined within the framework of being a wife and
mother. The Indian custom of paying a bride price to the
parents of the girl was no longer operative; instead, in many
cases, fur-trade fathers began to provide their daughters with
dowries as was customary in their own country. The wealth of
some of the officers enabled them to dower their daughters
handsomely: each of the six daughters of retired Chief Factor
Thomas Thomas and his Cree wife brought one thousand
pounds to their marriage.[43]

In the Hudson's Bay Company, Committee policy had been
at least partially successful in restricting marital unions to the
upper ranks, and initially most of the marriageable mixed-blood
girls were the daughters of officers. Understandably, these
officers viewed incoming junior officers as the most promising
husbands for their daughters, and this pattern of intermarriage
was repeated many times over in the Company.[44] As the long-
time trader Charles McKenzie observed:

> . . . Chief Factors are in the way of portioning their
> daughters very high . . . They think their alliance is
> enough and they take care to monopolize all the most
> promising young men for Sons in law.[45]

Inevitably there were not enough incoming officers to go
around; younger daughters might just as often be married to
respectable servants or to the mixed-blood sons of officers.
Among the Nor'Westers, the 1806 ruling against marriage with
pure-blooded Indian women can be seen as an attempt to ensure
that the large number of marriageable mixed-blood girls now
available would find husbands within the fur trade to support
them. In the North West Company, there were few marriageable
daughters of the bourgeois in comparison with the large number

of mixed-blood women who were the daughters of the French-Canadian engagés. Numerous examples of bourgeois who married the daughters of voyageurs or freemen can be cited, one of the most famous being Daniel Harmon. In 1805, after refusing several offers of an Indian wife, the moralistic Harmon consented to marry Lisette Duval, the fourteen-year-old daughter of a French-Canadian.[46] The youthful age of Harmon's bride was not unusual; according to Captain Franklin: "The girls at the forts, particularly the daughters of Canadians, are given in marriage very young; they are very frequently wives at 12 years of age, and mothers at 14."[47]

Within the framework of the North West Company, the marriages between bourgeois and the daughters of the engagés cut across both class and racial lines; such unions may have served to foster the feeling of Company solidarity, "the North West spirit", which transcended distinctions of rank. It was a source of pride to more than one engagé that his comely daughters had become the wives of bourgeois. Ross Cox tells the story of a redoubtable old voyageur, Louis La Liberté, who felt he could address himself with familiarity to one of the Company's proprietors because he was father-in-law to three wintering partners.[48] A significant proportion of the bourgeois who were absorbed into the Hudson's Bay Company in 1821 — Peter Warren Dease, Thomas McMurray and William McIntosh — had country wives of French-Indian descent.[49]

Apart from the pressures that fathers exerted to secure advantageous matches for their daughters, there were many other reasons why incoming traders found young mixed-blood women desirable wives. A fur trader's daughter possessed the ideal qualifications to be a fur trader's wife. This child of the fur trade was a symbol of the fusion of European and Indian cultures; she knew no other way of life than that of the Indian country. If she was not as hardy as her Indian mother, the mixed-blood woman was still much better able to cope with the not inconsiderable rigours of life at a fur-trade post than a white woman would have been. Even in the late fur-trade period, it required considerable fortitude to be a trader's wife:

> They must follow them [their husbands] to the most savage and remote stations, and take part in all the

privations they encounter. . . . However, like the
wives of army subalterns they are mostly born to it,
have looked all their days to such a vagabond life as
their natural lot, and have no wishes beyond it.[50]

Throughout the fur-trade period, the women of the forts,
who were ultimately mostly mixed-bloods, remained an important element in the labour force. From their Indian mothers,
mixed-blood girls learned and in turn passed on those native
skills so necessary to the functioning of the trade: making
moccasins, netting snowshoes and preparing pemmican. They
were expert needlewomen, and their skill, in fashioning mittens,
caps and leggings, became increasingly useful. Governor
Simpson recorded, "it is the duty of the Women at the different
Posts to do all that is necessary in regard to Needle Work."
Mixed-blood women became renowned for their beautiful and
intricate bead and quill work.[51] The mixed-blood wife, skilled in
native ways, could be of great assistance to the running of her
husband's trading post. Charles McKenzie, who spent many
years in charge of a small post at Lac Seul, praised his
industrious wife Mary, a daughter of Nor'Wester William
McKay and Josette Latour. As late as the 1850s, McKenzie was
writing to his children:

> Your good Mother . . . is still as brisk as a Bee —She
> must take her hunting exercise. . . . I believe She
> snared upwards of 600 Rabbits this winter — merely to
> give them to the people — whose wives do not set a
> snare.[52]

McKenzie had such confidence in his wife that he left her in
charge of the post during his necessary summer absences.[53]

In addition to performing traditional Indian tasks, the
women at the forts took on a more "civilized" range of domestic
duties. They were responsible for at least an annual spring
cleaning of the fort buildings. Washing and scrubbing — two
domestic arts unknown to the fur-clad inhabitants of a dirt-
floored Indian tepee — became an integral part of their routine.
The clerk James Hargrave wrote to a friend: "the Dames" at
York Factory were kept "in Suds, Scrubbing & Scouring."[54]
The women also took an active part in planting and harvesting
potatoes which were the mainstay of the subsistence agriculture

practiced around many posts. At Moose Factory in 1830, the women with the aid of their children gathered in 196 bushels of potatoes.[55] At the posts along the Saskatchewan, the industry of the women was particularly essential. "The women here work very hard" declared Chief Factor John Rowand at Fort Edmonton, "if it was not so, I do not know how we would get on with the Company work."[56]

With her ties to the Indians and her familiarity with native customs and language, the mixed-blood wife was in a position to take over the role of intermediary or liaison between Indian and white without becoming a source of conflict as had been the case on occasion with Indian women. John Rowand's marriage to Louise Umfreville can be credited with increasing his influence among the Plains Indians. Mrs Rowand brought a band of horses to her marriage which over the years grew to the substantial number of over two hundred head. Since horses were a symbol of wealth and prestige among the Plains Indians, Rowand was understandably regarded as a considerable personage.[57] Métis girls were often excellent interpreters. The daughter of an old voyageur Cayenne Grogne could speak Cree, French and Mountainy (Chipewyan) fluently which made George Simpson desirous of securing a match between her and one of his clerks.[58] In writing of fur-trade life in the period after the union of the two companies, Isaac Cowie paid tribute to the mixed-blood wives of the Hudson's Bay Company men; many of the gentlemen owed much of their success in overcoming difficulties and maintaining the Company's influence over the natives to "the wisdom and good counsel of their wives."[59] Occasionally, a mixed-blood wife was known to have saved the life of her husband owing to her understanding of Indian characteristics. The Nor'Wester John Haldane was reputedly spared his scalp because of his country wife who had been able to intercede with some hostile Indians during an incident at Rat Portage.[60]

In April 1828 when stationed in New Caledonia, the young clerk James Douglas had wed à la façon du pays Amelia Connolly, the daughter of his superior, Chief Factor William Connolly, and his Cree wife. Only a few months later the timely action of Amelia and the interpreter's wife, Nancy Boucher,[61]

Amelia Douglas, the mixed-blood wife of James Douglas, who saved his life in the early months of their marriage, through her bravery and her knowledge of Carrier customs.

was to save Douglas during a potentially fatal confrontation with the Carrier Indians. That summer Douglas had discovered and rather brutally executed one of the perpetrators of the Fort George murders who had managed to escape detection. The Carriers, led by Chief Kwah, came to the fort demanding compensation for this cruel act and when Douglas refused they overpowered him and threatened his life. Hearing the commotion, Douglas's young bride rushed from her apartments, grabbed a dagger from one of the Indians and came to her husband's defense. She was quickly disarmed. With Kwah's nephew pointing a dagger at Douglas's breast and about to strike, Amelia and the interpreter's wife begged the chief to have mercy and to avoid bloodshed. She promised him and his followers ample restitution and then rushed upstairs and began throwing down trade goods to the crowd. This action diverted the Indians, and since the "throwing" of gifts was a mark of deference according to Carrier custom, the Indians were placated and departed.[62]

A mixed-blood woman did not have to struggle with a sense of divided loyalty; her interests were more closely identified with that of the traders. Governor Simpson commended the courage of Isabella, the mixed-blood wife of Charles Ross, in defending Fort McLoughlin, a coastal post in New Caledonia, during an incident in the early 1840s. While her husband was absent, some Indians who were trading with her son drew their knives on the young man. When she saw this, "the lady, pike in hand, chased the cowardly rascals from post to pillar, till she drove them out of the fort."[63]

On a personal level, the white man generally evinced a preference for a mixed-blood wife because her lighter skin and sharper features more closely approximated his concept of beauty. While this indicates that racial and colour prejudice were never very far below the surface, it is apparent that many mixed-blood girls were physically captivating with their delicacy of form, nimble movements and bright, penetrating black eyes.[64] An Englishman, John McNab, who accompanied a hunting party from Brandon House in 1816, found himself entranced by Janette, the sixteen-year-old daughter of an old French-Canadian freeman and his Indian wife:

She was neither bold, nor bashful, her behaviour was
free, unconstrain'd and remarkably modest. — She
was, with regard to her person, a handsome brunette,
fine black expressive eyes, arch'd eye brows, high
forehead, shaded with natural ringlets of black flowing
hair, an aquiline nose, pretty mouth, teeth exquisitely
beautiful, and the contour of her face of an oval form.
— She was tall & slender, well proportion'd but very
delicate . . .[65]

This unusually detailed description helps to explain why so
many of the Nor'Westers were enamoured of the daughters of
their engagés. Although fur-trade society showed relatively little
concern for degrees of race mixture, there is no doubt that the
fairness of some of the mixed-blood girls was considered a
highly desirable trait. Amelia Connolly looked remarkably
"unIndian", given the fact that her mother was a full-blooded
Cree. According to family tradition, James Douglas, who was
very proud of the light complexion of his "Little Snowbird",
was much disappointed when his wife arrived at Fort
Vancouver with a deep tan after a long summer trip from New
Caledonia.[66] The Nor'Wester Joseph Larocque was reputed to
be extremely jealous of his handsome mixed-blood wife, whose
grandmother had been a Cree: "though not a pure white, she
was fairer than many who are so called in Europe."[67] The
physical features of the mixed-blood woman were closer to the
white ideal; she was also considered more susceptible to
civilizing influences. Alexander Ross wrote that, "They have
also made considerable progress in refinement, and, with their
natural acuteness and singular talent for imitation, they soon
acquire all the ease and gracefulness of polished life."[68] Such
attributes were of particular concern to the officers who wanted
to inculcate in their families a sense of class-consciousness and
to acculturate them to English styles and values. Young men
coming into the service appreciated that it would do no harm to
their career prospects to form a connection with a well-
established fur-trade family.[69]

With the emergence of the mixed-blood wife, marriage à la
façon du pays evolved increasingly toward European concepts
of marriage. Most importantly, a union contracted after "the

custom of the country" was definitely coming to be regarded as a union for life. Fur-trade fathers were particularly anxious that a prospective husband make a lasting commitment. When Hudson's Bay Company officer J. E. Harriott espoused Elizabeth, a daughter of Chief Trader J. P. Pruden, he made "a solemn promise to her father to live with her and treat her as my wife as long as we both lived."[70] It was not only Company officers who displayed fatherly concern. The agreement that follows was recorded by the father of Charlet Turner when she married James Harper at Martins Fall in 1841. Turner, a mixed-blood and possibly a descendant of a prominent Hudson's Bay Company inland officer of that name, wrote:

> James harper I this day consent to be your father in law and by the blessings of the ald mite god join you to my beloved Daughter Charlet Turner hoping that you will consider your self well married to her as if you were joined by a minister.[71]

At the fur-trade posts, country marriages were accorded public recognition similar to that found at European weddings. The couple would exchange brief vows before witnesses, usually the officer in charge of the post, and the union would be celebrated with a dram to all hands and a dance which might keep the engagés jigging till morning. Marriages were quite in vogue at Fort Alexander in 1808 according to George Nelson: "we were obliged to leave off and prepare for a dance (which is now the third) in honour to Mr. Seraphim's wedding — Mr. McDonald played the violin for us."[72] When the young clerk Robert Miles took Betsey Sinclair, daughter of Chief Factor William Sinclair and his native wife Nahovway, as "a Femme du Pays" at York Factory in the fall of 1822, a friend recorded that "we had a Dance & supper on the occasion, when no one but the happy Swain was allowed to go sober to bed."[73]

Significantly, those deviations from European marriage customs which had been noticeable in both companies showed a marked decrease. As the case of Chief Factor W. H. Cook shows, however, it was not unknown for Hudson's Bay Company officers to continue to practise polygamy even when their wives were mixed-bloods. The two daughters of Matthew Cocking apparently saw nothing amiss in sharing Cook, but other mixed-blood women had learned enough of English custom to protest against such treatment. Jane Renton who had been the country wife of Albany officer Thomas Vincent for many years was deeply wounded when, around 1817, her husband decided to take a second wife, a young widow named Jane Sutherland. The response of the first wife, whose family was now grown up, was to promptly leave Vincent and go to live with her relatives at Moose Factory. The censure of some of Vincent's colleagues was not enough to make him repent his action, but he did have enough sense of moral responsibility to make financial provision for both of his wives.[74] Among the Nor'Westers, the trend toward serial monogamy diminished considerably. Numerous examples can be cited of bourgeois who remained faithful to their mixed-blood wives, even to the extent of taking them along when they retired from the Indian Country.

In its hey-day, marriage *à la façon du pays* was certainly considered the equivalent of a valid marriage. As J. E. Harriott maintained:

> It was not customary for an European to take one wife and discard her, and then take another. The marriage according to the custom [of the country] was considered a marriage for life . . . I know of hundreds of people living and dying with the woman they took in that way without any other formalities.[75]

His sentiments were echoed by the old voyageur, Pierre Marois, who declared that the custom of the country was regarded "comme union de mari et femme . . . et union aussi sacrée."[76] Both men went on to claim that if they left the Indian Country, they would go through the formality of a church marriage, but they would regard this ceremony as merely "une bénédiction" and not an admission that no marriage had existed before. Harriott emphasized that he would submit to "the civilized form of solemnizing marriage . . . to please people and to conform to the custom of society. I would not consider myself more strongly bound to the woman than before." Whatever the views of the fur traders, however, it is understandable that the outside world might question the validity of these unions.

In a number of cases dealing with the settlement of estates, selfish, self-righteous relatives, notably those of Chief Factor Peter Skene Ogden and Chief Trader Samuel Black, tried to disinherit the traders' families on the grounds that their unions had been unlawful and the children illegitimate.[77] Fortunately for the native families, the executors of these estates were usually fur traders who fought hard to protect their rights, and initially English law was inclined to a favourable interpretation of "the custom of the country". In 1832, after the death of Chief Trader Joseph McGillivray, the authorities decided that his country wife Françoise Boucher was fully entitled to be considered his widow because she and McGillivray had lived together "as Man & Wife in the Indian territories, according to the customs of that Country & acknowledged as such & further that there were not any resident Clergy within some hundred miles of the places at which they resided."[78] Had the marital relationship been denied, "McGillivray's Lady" would have had the status of spinster, and the ten per cent duty applied to "strangers in blood" would have been levied upon her inheritance. In his will, Chief Trader Alexander Roderick McLeod had specifically stated that he considered the mother of his children to be his "legitimate wife" and emphasized that it was his "serious determination that no plea be adduced in any shape to alter my views." After his death in 1840, two English lawyers gave their opinion that his union constituted a valid marriage: "This marriage took place in a remote part of the Colony, where there were no Established Clergymen, and was solemnized in Conformity with the Customs of the Country."[79]

After the North West Company was absorbed into the Hudson's Bay Company in 1821, the new Company took steps to standardize the social customs which had evolved in the Indian Country. In order to regularize marriage à la façon du pays, a marriage contract was introduced which emphasized the husband's economic responsibilities. By the general terms of the certificates, both parties, in the presence of the chief factor and other witnesses, affixed their signature or mark to a declaration which gave the woman the status of legal wife. The following contract executed at Oxford House in 1830 is representative:

This is to certify that I, Magnus Harper, Native of

1859 316

Hudson's Bay Co's Territory
Lac Seul Post
5th September 1859

I "John Moar" Half Breed born in the Hudson's Bay Company's Territory and in the Service of the Hudson's Bay Company in the Capacity of Bowsman do agree to take unto me "Matilda Morriseau" for my lawful Wife she being also a Half Breed born in the Hudson's Bay Company's Territory and agreeable to the Union, and I John Moar promise to have the ceremony of marriage performed by a Clergyman on the first opportunity that presents itself

Witnesses —

John x Moar   } Father & Mother   John Moar
Nancy x Thomas   } of the Bridegroom

Antoine x Morriseau   } Father & Mother   I the undersigned
Marry x Daniel   } of the Bride   agree to the above
John Morcille   } Honble   Her
Murdoch McÑel   } Hudson's   Matilda x Morriseau
John x Cromarty   } Bay   Mark
James x Twain   } Company's Servants

A. Belanger
Clerk for the Honble
Hudson's Bay Company

Marriage contract of John Moar and Matilda Morriseau. Dated Lac Seul Post, 5 September 1859.

Hudson's Bay, North America, have taken to Wife, for better or for worse Peggy La Pierre, Native of Hudson's Bay, North America, and I by this document do hereby bind & promise to cherish and support the said Peggy La Pierre as my lawful married Wife, during the term of her natural life . . .[80]

Numerous contracts, especially those drawn up between the French-Canadian engagés and the father or guardian of their intended, contained the proviso that the wife would receive financial compensation if the husband failed to fulfil his marital obligations.[81] The Company also began to take stern measures with any servants who attempted to desert their wives. At Fort Vancouver, it was reported, a man could be "arrested" and forced to give security that he would not abandon his family.[82]

With the arrival of the missionaries in the post-union period and their insistence that it was the prerogative of the church alone to perform marriages, a clause stating that the couple would seek the sanction of the church at the first possible opportunity was added to many of the Company contracts. The slow spread of missionary activity into more remote areas, however, meant that for many fur-trade couples this opportunity never arose, and marriages continued to be performed under the civil authority of the Hudson's Bay Company. Many chief factors were, in fact, Justices of the Peace who, by a law passed in both England and in Canada in 1836, were empowered to perform marriages. In the 1830s Chief Factor Peter Skene Ogden used his authority as a Justice of the Peace to marry couples in the remote district of New Caledonia. When his marrying of the young clerk A. C. Anderson to the daughter of Chief Factor James Birnie was questioned by an over-zealous missionary far away at Fort Vancouver, Anderson himself made a learned and thorough defense of his action. A long tradition of European marriage law, he claimed, acknowledged that marriage was essentially a civil contract; the religious ceremony was merely a desirable but unnecessary social convention.[83] In 1845, the Council of the Northern Department clarified the Company's position on marriage: in the absence of a clergyman, chief factors *only* could solemnize marriages, and no person could take a wife without the sanction of the gentleman in charge of the district.[84]

While it is true that a sense of social responsibility for the fate of fur traders' daughters had created an increasing stability for marriage à la façon du pays, some men, even as in white society, had no scruples about shirking their marital obligations. Abandonment appears to have been a very real fear for a mixed-blood wife because the alternatives open to an Indian wife were no longer feasible for her. On occasion, the fear of abandonment seems to have manifested itself in the desperate action of infanticide. One of the daughters of Hudson's Bay Company Governor Thomas Thomas, who became the country wife of Nor'Wester John George McTavish during his sojourn at Moose Factory, reputedly smothered two children when McTavish abandoned her. Another, Jane Auld, the mixed-blood wife of Chief Factor John Charles, took the life of her infant, fearing (erroneously) that she had been forsaken when her husband went on furlough to England.[85] Furlough was a time of severe anxiety for mixed-blood wives, for they could never be sure that their husbands were coming back; sometimes, indeed, the men were posted to other districts and reunion was difficult.[86] While most traders endeavoured to make adequate provision for their wives in the event of death or retirement, some callously did not. Chief Factor John Haldane earned the disapproval of his colleagues for reneging on his promise of a sixty-dollar annuity for his faithful country wife Josette Latour when he retired to Scotland; she was left to eke out a penurious existence at Moose Factory.[87]

For a woman to be left without a male protector was deemed undesirable and accounts for the incessant pressure that mixed-blood women felt to remarry. Those who were recently widowed, unless too old, were expected to marry again, while the custom of "turning off" may have remained a means of, at least, ensuring that mixed-blood wives, whose husbands were leaving them in the Indian Country, would continue to be maintained at a fur-trade post. The exigencies of fur-trade life were such that it was not uncommon for a mixed-blood woman to have two or three husbands in her lifetime. Ke-che-cow-e-com-coot, Matthew Cocking's daughter, became the wife of John Pocock Holmes after her former partner, Chief Factor

Thomas Stayner, retired to Britain in the early 1800s. Marguerite Wadin was apparently abandoned by Nor'Wester Alexander McKay when he left the Indian Country in 1808, but she later entered into what proved to be a long and happy marriage with John McLoughlin, who was destined to have a prominent career in the Columbia District.[88] The case of Françoise Boucher, a daughter of a French-Canadian guide, is particularly illustrative. Françoise became the wife of an interpreter at the age of fourteen and lived with her husband until he was killed by Indians three years later. Shortly afterward, the young widow, reputedly good-looking, even-tempered and clever, was taken by a bourgeois, possibly John Clarke. Although they lived together for eight years, Clarke, on leaving the country turned off his wife who was childless, to the mixed-blood clerk Joseph McGillivray. McGillivray, whose father had warned him to avoid the encumbrance of a family, was soon "lamenting" his wife's new-found ability to produce sons. Their relationship became a devoted one and McGillivray rewarded Françoise for her "constant attachment and affection" in his will.[89]

Although the story of Françoise Boucher had a happy ending, her experience reveals that mixed-blood women were basically locked into a marital structure, adapted by the traders from European society to serve patriarchal needs. The mixed-blood woman was increasingly deprived of the autonomy which the Indian woman had enjoyed with regard to marriage and divorce. She was given in marriage when very young, and her wishes were often not considered. Fortunately few fur-trade marriages were as unhappy as Harriet Vincent's first one. When only twelve years old, she was given by her father to D. R. Stewart who was employed in the timber trade at Moose Factory. A most reluctant bride, Harriet was dragged forcibly from her mother's room. After nine miserable years Harriet, when expecting her third child, was summarily abandoned by Stewart who returned to Canada. Soon after the young woman found a suitor much more to her liking, and her marriage to George Gladman Jr proved a lasting and happy one.[90] Cases of mixed-blood women attempting to leave their husbands were rare, although on occasion, a strong-willed woman could manipulate the flexibility of the "custom of the country" to alleviate her lot.

The behaviour of the Métis woman Françoise Laurain suggests that the pressure put upon women in fur-trade society to remarry was not entirely welcome. In November 1823, Françoise had been formally married in Red River to the Orkney clerk Joshua Halcro. Bad health forced Halcro to return to Britain in the fall of 1824, but he arranged for his wife to stay at York Factory, hoping to return the following summer.[91] When Halcro died in Britain and news of his death was sent to York, his widow was given to understand that her only options were to go with the Indians or become the country wife of Chief Factor John Stuart. Françoise reluctantly chose the lesser of two evils. A "Grand Ball" was held to celebrate the nuptials,[92] but the marriage proved an immediate disaster. Stuart was forced to leave his new bride at Norway House instead of taking her to his post, for she had never ceased wailing and crying and begged to be allowed to go to spend the winter with her mother. She told Stuart that she had no particular aversion to him personally but that she wanted "simply to be for a time alone." Stuart hoped for a reunion in the spring but this never materialized.[93]

In the final analysis, the cases in which the traders endeavoured to do their best by their wives outnumbered those in which mixed-blood women were maltreated. With the emergence of the mixed-blood wife, the trend was the formation of lasting and devoted marital relationships. The growth of widespread intermarriage between the men of both companies and the "daughters of the country" had important implications for fur-trade society. The complex kinship network which developed gave a unique cohesiveness to this early Western Canadian society, a society characterized by its own indigenous customs. As the mixed-blood wife replaced the Indian wife, fur-trade custom became less subject to Indian influence and evolved more in accord with European practices. What is particularly striking about fur-trade life was the extent to which a concern for women and family influenced the development of social custom in a world where both initially were supposed to have been absent.

6

MY ONLY CONSOLATION

The fur-trade posts had never been planned to accommodate large numbers of women and children. The traders' families therefore were housed and fitted into the daily life at the posts in a makeshift manner. Owing to the quasi-military routine at the forts, and perhaps influenced by Indian custom, a kind of ritualized segregation evolved with regard to the women's participation at mealtimes and holiday celebrations. Nevertheless, in an environment where home and work were never far apart, family considerations were an important aspect of the traders' existence. After the union of the rival companies in 1821, the reconstituted Hudson's Bay Company drew up a new set of rules designed to make family life at its posts conform to British standards. Many of the chief factors, however, opposed the strict economy measures which the London Committee and Governor Simpson intended to impose on the maintenance of families. Simpson, a newcomer who was unsympathetic to fur-trade ways, lamented that his Council were nearly "all Family Men" and too much influenced by the "Sapient Councils of their Squaws".[1]

In the post-union period with the turmoil of competition passed, many traders found in their families a particular source of interest and consolation in a life that was often monotonous and unrewarding. The voluminous private correspondence of the Hudson's Bay Company officers which has survived from this period reveals much about what Douglas meant by "the many tender ties which find a way to the heart"; the concern and affection which many fur traders expressed toward their wives and children provide valuable insight into Canadian family life in the first half of the nineteenth century.

*The stone house, the first building to be erected at Lower Fort Garry.
Governor George Simpson and his wife Frances moved into this house
in the fall of 1832. Photograph by H. L. Hime, 1858.*

Life in a fur-trade post, especially from the twentieth
century point of view, was primitive and cramped, with little
room for privacy. The domestic arrangements at Fort Vermilion
on the Saskatchewan River in 1809 (where the population
numbered 36 men, 27 women and 67 children) were probably
typical of the accommodations provided at a North West
Company post. Unmarried voyageurs shared the same quarters
as family men, four or five families, numbering between ten and
eighteen people, being lodged in one "house". Only the officers
were provided with separate houses.[2] In later posts, there was
usually a bachelors' hall for the unmarried men, and living
quarters for the families were partitioned so that each family
had a separate unit. Still, true privacy and luxury were reserved
for the officers. Some of the houses built for the chief factors in
the nineteenth century, including John Rowand's "Big House"
at Fort Edmonton and the stone house at Lower Fort Garry,
were relatively grand and privately furnished to suit the tastes of
the gentlemen of the fur trade.

Not much actual living was done in the private quarters, for
nearly all the posts had communal dining-rooms for officers'
and servants' messes. In keeping with both military tradition
and Indian practice, however, it was customary for the women
and children to eat separately from the men. According to Ross
Cox, in the early nineteenth century native women could be
found at some of the Nor'Westers' posts continuing in "the
savage fashion of squatting on the ground at their meals, at
which their fingers supply the place of forks."[3] Hudson's Bay
Company officers were evidently quicker to introduce their
wives to British table manners, for among the items imported
privately from England were "handsome" table knives and
forks, monogrammed silver teaspoons, and cups and saucers.[4]
Yet even at the English posts the women usually ate after the
men. Arrangements at Fort Vancouver, the headquarters of the
Columbia District, seem to have been especially male-oriented.
At a banquet held in his honour in 1842, Captain Charles
Wilkes, an American, noted critically that not even the wives of
the chief officers were present. Wilkes, like other outside
observers of fur-trade society, felt that the wives should not be
treated in such a demeaning fashion and that the exclusion of

the women would "tend to prevent improvement, and retard the advancement of civilization."[5]

The gentlemen of the fur trade were sensitive to any suggestion that they might be behaving in an uncivilized manner and, by the 1840s, a number of officers had begun introducing their mixed-blood wives to table. Jane Lee Lewes dined with her husband and the other officers at Fort Simpson, and at Fort Colvile the warm family atmosphere created by Archibald McDonald and his wife Jane enhanced the post's reputation for hospitality and good cheer. One visiting trader enthused: ". . . when seated at table with Mr & Mrs McDonald and their family, one cannot help thinking himself once more at home enjoying a tête-a-tête in some domestic circle".[6] An attempt to introduce the mixed-blood wives of Nicol Finlayson and George Gladman to the officers' mess at York Factory in 1840 was less successful; the women themselves soon withdrew because they were afraid of being ridiculed.[7] Ten years later, however, it had become routine for the mixed-blood wives of officers to take places at the mess table at Upper Fort Garry.

The traditional means of celebrating New Year's Day, the most important holiday, especially in the Nor'Westers' calendar, also reveals a ritual segregation of the sexes. Early in the morning after firing a salute to honour the bourgeois, the men came in to wish him the compliments of the season and receive a regale; after they were dismissed, their wives, decked out in their finest garments, were allowed in to receive a similar treat. This time-honoured custom of the Nor'Westers' was carried over to the Hudson's Bay Company posts after the union. Chief Factor John Stuart described the scene at Carlton House on 1 January 1825:

> New Years Day was [brought] in by a Salute of Musketry fired at our doors and windows after which the people came into the Hall to wish us the Compliments of the season. . . . they were liberally treated with Shrub, Rum and Cakes to all of which they did justice . . . on retiring they fired another salute, after which the Ladies paid us a visit and having first Kissed them a la mode de pays we treated them in much the same manner as we had done their husbands

Jane Klyne McDonald, widow of Chief Factor Archibald McDonald, with her sons Angus (born in Montreal, 1846) and John (born at Fort Colvile, 1837). c. 1856, at St Andrews East, Lower Canada.

and it is but common justice to remark that though
they had shrub at discretion they comported themselves decently and soon retired to the society of their
Husbands in their own Houses . . .[8]

At four in the afternoon, the men assembled for a special
feast, complete with plum pudding, and then amused themselves
singing songs in Gaelic and French, while the table was laid
again and the women took their turn. Segregation came to an
abrupt end in the dance which followed.

Dancing was the favourite pastime of the fur traders, who
found it a welcome break from the monotony of the daily
routine, even though the only music might be a squeaky old
fiddle. In the hey-day of the Nor'Westers, any excuse for having
a ball was seized upon, be it a wedding or the arrival of the
annual brigade. At Fort Alexander in 1801, the bourgeois gave
a ball to celebrate the end of pemmican making for the year:
"The men & women danced till twelve oClock at night", he
recorded.[9] The women enjoyed the balls as much as the men,
but curiously, they often did not follow the same dance steps as
their male partners. Perhaps mixed-blood women who adopted
a grave countenance and slower step were influenced by the
solemn ritual of the dances performed by the Indian women.
As Captain Franklin observed: "The half-breed women are
passionately fond of this entertainment, but a stranger would
imagine the contrary on witnessing their apparent want of
animation."[10] When J. H. Lefroy participated in the holiday
festivities at Fort Chipewyan in the 1840s, he made note of one
particular dance called "Belle Rosalie". In this round dance, all
joined hands, and one man led the song which the rest repeated
in unison. At the last two lines, "Embracez que vous voudrez,
Car j'aurai la moitée", the leader put the lady on his right (Belle
Rosalie) into the ring; at the first pause she then gave a kiss to
someone and rejoined the circle on the left of the leader and so it
went round. When a man was in the centre, he was called Beau
Rosier.[11]

Kissing à la mode du pays, a symbolic gesture of gallantry
toward the ladies, was a widespread custom in fur-trade society.
In the North West Company, one of the oaths that the young
mangeur de lard took when he was initiated as a true homme du

nord after crossing the Grand Portage was that he would never kiss a voyageur's wife against her will.[12] As has been seen, a customary part of any festive ceremony was for the officer in charge to bestow a kiss *à la mode du pays* (apparently on the mouth) on each of the women at the post. This salute was also performed at the departure of the transport brigades. J. H. Lefroy, on leaving Fort Dunvegan, was "much interested to see my men, each cap in hand, and with the manner of a courtier", respectfully approach the wife of the chief factor and the other mixed-blood women, "and one after another bid these ladies farewell with a kiss."[13] This kissing custom was one which George Simpson was evidently quick to learn; the new governor was much less enthusiastic about the fur traders' love of entertainment, believing that it interrupted post discipline and routine. Part of the strict new regime that was introduced after the union of the two companies in 1821 was the curtailing of the men's passion for dancing; now balls would only be allowed in the Christmas holiday season.

The London Committee and Governor Simpson, in embarking on a policy of economy and consolidation after the union, wished to divest the Company of any further responsibility for the maintenance of the families of its active employees. While raising salaries, the Committee proposed to require each man to clothe his family on his own private account and to impose a proportional tax to cover the cost of provisions. The officers of the Council of the Northern Department, many of whom were former Nor'Westers, opposed this plan. In 1822, a long list of officers petitioned the Governor, claiming that most servants could not possibly afford to pay for the support of their families and emphasizing that the services performed by the women paid for their keep.[14] The women too protested; the wives at Fort Chipewyan staged a small "strike" by refusing to attend to their Saturday duty of cleaning out the fort. One observer noted that the ladies held an animated debate over whether their husbands should have to pay for their support and resolved "that such treatment was repugnant to former usage & held to be unfair."[15] Although Simpson was persuaded to change his mind and argue the case of his Council, it took several years before the London Committee would agree to compromise on this issue. The imposition of specific charges for the support of families was dropped in favour of a vaguely worded resolution passed by the Council in 1824:

> That no Officer or Servant in the companys service be hereafter allowed to take a woman without binding himself down to such reasonable provision for the maintenance of the woman and children as on a fair and equitable principle may be considered necessary not only during their residence in the country but after their departure hence.[16]

According to Simpson, another source of waste and inefficiency was the old practice of allowing families, particularly those of officers, to accompany the brigades on the long summer journey to and from the main depot. Chief Factor John Clarke infuriated Simpson because of his tendency to let domestic affairs interfere with sound business management. In 1820, Clarke had abandoned en route some of the goods destined for Athabasca in order to make a light canoe for the better accommodation of his mixed-blood wife and her servant. This extravagance, Simpson estimated, had cost the Company five hundred pounds![17] Too often delays were caused by canoes being diverted to carry women and children with "their Baggage Pots Pans Kettles & Bags of Moss."[18] The Governor's 1824 trip to the Columbia convinced him that it was most inexpedient to allow families to accompany the brigades across the Rockies:

> We must really put a stop to the practise of Gentlemen bringing their Women & Children from the East to the West side of the mountain, it is attended with much expense and inconvenience on the Voyage, business itself must give way to domestick considerations, the Gentlemen became drones and are not disposable in short the evil is more serious than I am well able to describe.[19]

In this case, the Council acquiesced and the following year passed a resolution stating that Gentlemen appointed to the two districts across the Rockies were not to encumber themselves with families.[20]

These issues indicate the conflict that was inherent in the profit-oriented concerns of the Company and the private concerns of its employees. There was wider agreement about the desirability of acculturating native families to British standards. Thus, in 1823, a new series of regulations was passed by the Council of the Northern Department designed to achieve "the more effectual civilization and moral improvement" of families attached to Company establishments.[21] Generally, the fur traders considered an introduction to the precepts of Christianity a necessary prerequisite to the civilization of their wives and children. Certainly individual traders took pains to teach their families the basic principles of religion. Daniel Harmon was much gratified that "through the merciful agency of the Holy Spirit" he was able to share with his wife Lisette "the consolations and hopes of the gospel".[22] Chief Factor John Work, like many others, was anxious that his children be brought up in "the fear of God".[23] The holding of Sunday services at Hudson's Bay Company posts had always been encouraged, but by the new rules it was made compulsory for every man, woman and child at a post to attend religious observances, either Catholic or Protestant, to be conducted by the chief factor or another officer. Fathers were instructed to teach their children some short prayers to be repeated "punctually" at bedtime.

The officers were also concerned to curb the widespread use of the Indian tongue among fur-trade families, although this was the language in which most of the women had the greatest facility. Daniel Harmon revealed that he spoke Cree to his children, as this was the language that their mother was most at home in — though she could speak some French.[24] But the Council, considering that the perpetuation of the Indian tongue would hinder the enlightenment of native families, ruled that "mother & children always be addressed and habituated to converse in the vernacular dialect (whether English or French) of the Father." In the later period, it appears that French was more commonly to be heard at the fur-trade posts than English. When George Keith took his part-Indian wife Nanette to live in Scotland in the 1840s, she could scarcely speak a word of that language. Similarly, part of Amelia Douglas's reluctance to play an active role as "Governor's lady" in the colony of British Columbia stemmed from the fact that she was more fluent in the

French and Indian languages, than English.[25]

Since formal schooling in the post-union period was to be centered in the Red River Colony, placing it beyond the reach of many, fathers were instructed to devote their leisure time to teaching their children to read and write. Company men were to take a firm hand in encouraging their families to adopt habits of industry, cleanliness and decency; the mothers' role was to be diminished, as Indian and mixed-blood women were considered to be hopelessly lax disciplinarians and lacking in propriety.

The extent to which these regulations were successfully implemented depended largely upon the effectiveness of the chief factor at each post. Chief Factor James Keith, perhaps the most moralistic of all the traders, played an important part in formulating these rules and worked hard to improve standards at Fort Severn and Fort Chipewyan in the 1820s. [26] In the same way at Fort Edmonton, Chief Factor John Rowand ruled with an iron hand and was praised by Alexander Ross for the fort's well-regulated domestic life:

> I had seen very few places in the country where domestic arrangements, either within doors or without, were conducted with so much propriety as at this place. At almost every other post, men and women are to be seen congregating together during the sports and amusements of the men, and the women are often seen flirting idly about the establishments, mixing among the men at their several duties. But it is not so here; I did not notice a woman, old or young, going about the place idle; all seemed to keep at home and to be employed about their own affairs. The moral and pleasing effect was such as might be expected, and reflects great credit on Mr. Rowand and on his family.[27]

Ross's comments about the laxness at the other posts seem to have soon become outdated. Other chief factors — John McLoughlin and James Douglas at Fort Vancouver, John Work at Fort Simpson and Archibald McDonald at Fort Colvile — endeavoured to run their posts in accordance with Victorian morality and industry.

Indeed, many of the Hudson's Bay Company officers of the

Royal Ontario Museum

Chief Factor John Rowand was praised for Fort Edmonton's well-regulated domestic life where no women were idle. 'Fort Edmonton' by Emile Petitot. c. 1867.

nineteenth century appear to have been typical Victorian patriarchs; but if they tended to be rather autocratic, they were not unloving. A genuine affection for their native wives and children shines through their private correspondence. Many fur traders came to realize that their native wives possessed sterling qualities which more than compensated for their lack of "civilized grace and polish". In writing to his relatives, Charles Ross said of his wife Isabella Mainville, whose mother had been an Ojibwa:

> I have as yet said nothing about my wife, whence you will probably infer that I am rather ashamed of her —in this, however, you would be wrong. She is not indeed exactly fitted to shine at the head of a nobleman's table, but she suits the sphere she has to move in better than any such toy . . . as to beauty [she

Provincial Archives of British Columbia

Chief Factor John Work. Undated.

is] quite as comely as her husband.[28]

Chief Factor John Work frequently expressed his esteem for his Métis wife Josette Legacé, the daughter of a voyageur and a Spokan woman. Always a courageous helpmate, Josette, in spite of a growing family, accompanied Work on most of his trading expeditions including those into the difficult Snake Country. In the 1830s, Work was relieved to be able to establish a more permanent if remote home at Fort Simpson on the Nass River, the headquarters of the Pacific coastal trade. Here Mrs Work is reputed to have introduced rudiments of domestic husbandry among the Tsimshian women of the area and to have exerted a moderating influence over the practice of slavery

Mrs John Work, née Josette Legacé, with daughter Suzette and son David. Undated.

among that tribe.[29] Work felt he had been fortunate in his choice of a wife; she had been but a girl of fifteen when he wed her *à la façon du pays* at Fort Colvile:

> The little Wife and I get on very well. She is to me an affectionate partner simple and uninstructed as she is and takes good care of my children & myself.[30]

Charles McKenzie remained devoted to his capable wife: "I have to thank the Goodness of God that your mother keeps her usual good health" he wrote to his son, "I would be the most miserable being without her."[31] Chief Trader Nicol Finlayson was reduced to such a state when his wife Betsey died of dropsy in the fall of 1841. Deeply touched by the fortitude his wife had

shown in bearing the hardships of his posting to the distant
Ungava region, he was sorry that she did not long enjoy the
comparative comfort of Red River. He lamented to his friend
James Hargrave:

> . . . my heart is desolate . . . you have seen my
> departed for a short time and no doubt formed your
> own opinion of her, but no one knew her worth so well
> as I did — she died too when I was absent at Lac la
> Pluie, I had not even the Cold Consolation of closing
> her eyes.[32]

Shortly after his posting to the Columbia District, George
Barnston married Ellen Matthews, whose father had been a
clerk in the Pacific Fur Company and whose mother Kilakotah
was a relative of Chief Concomely. It was a decision he never
regretted, even though it meant breaking a pledge he had made
with another young clerk that they would never take a wife in
the Indian Country.[33] In 1831, after a disagreement with
Governor Simpson, Barnston determined to quit the Company,
taking "his Chinook beauty" and little son east across the
mountains. Although he soon re-entered the service, his career
was slow to prosper and he spent many years at an obscure post
in the Albany District. Yet Barnston found much comfort in his
wife and children, reflecting the growing nineteenth-century
view that a man's family was his refuge from the hard knocks of
the world. "There is Love . . . within Doors" he wrote "and
while that is the Case many a bitter blast may be born from
without."[34] His wife Ellen adapted without complaint to a life
far removed from the populous Chinook village where she had
grown up. Barnston described her as "a perfect mine of
happiness" and he also derived much joy from his growing
"tribe of Biennials" whom, with their mother, he attempted to
imbue with the basic principles of religion and education.[35]

Barnston shared the fate of many of his contemporaries in
having a large family; both he and John Work had eleven
children, while Archibald McDonald and Alexander Ross each
had thirteen. The problems of how to support and educate so
many caused considerable anxiety, yet it is evident that fur-
trade fathers found considerable happiness in their children and
were intimately involved in their upbringing. John Work

Jean Murray Cole Collection

Mary Anne Barnston, only daughter of Chief
Factor Archibald McDonald, with her infant
daughter Helena. She married Dr James Barnston,
son of Chief Trader George Barnston. c. 1860.

declared that his children were "almost the only pleasure I have"
and, typically, he was delighted when his first son was born in
1839.[36] Archibald McDonald's pride in his children was clearly
revealed in this account of family life, written from Fort Colvile
in 1842:

> Our last, another Boy, is now about 6 months old. His
> twin brothers are very fine little fellows, now that they
> begin to speak becoming exceedingly interesting. In
> features, voice, height & colour of hair they are so alike
> as scarcely to know the difference; & to mend the
> matter the mother to a thread, keeps them in the same
> kind of garb. Were you at this moment to see them,
> assisted by an elder brother going five years, who
> thinks himself amazingly wise with tables, chairs,
> sofas, cushions, tongs, broomsticks, cats, dogs & all
> other imaginable things they can lay their hands on
> strewed around me, you would say 'twas a delightful
> confusion & then exclaim "McDonald, how the deuce

can you write with such a racket about you."[37]
The McDonalds were grief-stricken when several years later,
while the entire family was on its way east, the adored little
twins and their younger brother died in a scarlet fever epidemic
at Fort Edmonton.[38]

Infant mortality was high in the Indian Country as it was
elsewhere in the nineteenth century, but that did not make the
loss of a child any easier to bear. Ellen Barnston was so
distraught over the deaths of two of her daughters that her
husband feared for her reason, but he himself was scarcely less
affected. Sorrowing over the death of his daughter Mary, whom
he had personally taken to school in Scotland, he grieved, "God
has surely shown me, we belong not to each other, but to him,
may he pardon me, my regret, my sorrow and my
Lamentations."[39]

It was as much a desire to see their children educated in a
Christian manner as to enjoy the fruits of civilization that made
many fur traders anxious to retire from the Indian Country.
Previously it had been customary, particularly for the
Nor'Westers, to leave their Indian wives behind, even though
they might take their children with them. Most bourgeois who
married mixed-blood women, however, did not follow this
course but took their entire family with them when they
returned to Eastern Canada. David Thompson brought his
mixed-blood wife Charlotte, who had accompanied him on
most of his far-flung journeys, to settle down with him in
Terrebonne in Lower Canada in 1812.[40] Other bourgeois, such
as John "Le Prêtre" Macdonell and Daniel Harmon, found that
the bonds of duty and affection had grown too strong to allow
them to "turn off" their country wives when the time came.
After retiring from the trade in 1814, Macdonell built a large
stone villa at Point Fortune near Vaudreuil for his Métis wife
Magdeleine Poitras and their six children. It would have been
too cruel, he declared, to leave the mother of his children in the
Indian Country, she who had been his "constant companion"
for eighteen years ever since she was twelve years old.[41] Daniel
Harmon had intended to turn off Lisette some day, but when
in 1819 he decided that he must take his children from the wilds
of New Caledonia, he found the idea unthinkable. Religion and

humanity, he believed, left him no other choice but to take his
wife along with the children back to his home in Vermont:

> Having lived with this woman as my wife, though we
> were never formally contracted to each other, . . . and
> having children by her, I consider that I am under a
> moral obligation not to dissolve the connexion, if she is
> willing to continue it. The union which had been
> formed between us, in the providence of God, has not
> only been cemented by a long and mutual performance
> of kind offices, but, also, by a more sacred
> consideration. . . . I consider it to be my duty to take
> her to a christian land, where she may enjoy Divine
> ordinances, grow in grace, and ripen for glory. We
> have wept together over the early departure of several
> children, and especially, over the death of a beloved
> son. We have children still living, who are equally dear
> to us both. How could I spend my days in the civilized
> world, and leave my beloved children in the
> wilderness? The thought has in it the bitterness of
> death. How could I tear them from a mother's love,
> and leave her to mourn over their absence, to the day
> of her death? Possessing only the common feelings of
> humanity, how could I think of her, in such
> circumstances, without anguish?[42]

Laudable as it was to keep mother and children together,
the transition to the civilized world was not an easy one for
many fur-trade families. Ross Cox noted that those Nor'Westers
who purchased estates in Eastern Canada lived in "a kind of
half-Indian, half-civilized manner, constantly smoking their
calumet and railing at the fashionable frivolities of the great
world."[43] It was observed that "Indian Traders" who brought
their families out with the intention of turning gentlemen
farmers were seldom ever successful.[44] A notable exception to
this pattern was the former Nor'Wester J. D. Cameron, who
settled near Grafton, Upper Canada, in 1846. His wife Mary,
one of the few Indian women to have been brought east, appears
to have made a remarkable adjustment to pioneering life. She
took an active interest in the farming operations of her son
Ranald who lived not far away; in fact, Cameron wrote to

Governor Simpson in 1848:

> The Old Squaw had she control over the Farm would
> conduct it much better than her son — she is now
> actually engaged in the woods making a new road for
> hawling out wood.[45]

Chief Factor Peter Warren Dease settled his family on a
country property near Montreal in the 1840s, but a
contemporary lamented that like other old Nor'Westers, Dease
was careless about his finances and too much under the thumb
of his Métis wife Elizabeth:

> [he] allows himself to be entirely governed & dictated
> to in his own house by his Old Squaw & Sons She
> holding the Purse strings & they spending the Contents
> par la Porte et par les fenetres. — This state of
> nothingness however does not seem to annoy him.[46]

Nevertheless, Mrs Dease seems to have made a more
successful adjustment to life in the Montreal area than many of
the mixed-blood wives of former Nor'Westers who settled there
in the 1830s and 1840s. Chief Factor Allan McDonell had
reason to be proud of his stylish establishment in Montreal,
but his poor native wife Margaret appeared to be "quite out of
her element amongst so much that must excite her
admiration."[47] The strangeness and homesickness experienced
by native wives was somewhat alleviated if friends and relatives
could be persuaded to settle near by. Pockets of retired
Hudson's Bay Company officers grew up in several places in
Ontario, especially in the Cobourg area. Jacob Corrigal retired
there in the early 1840s and was later followed by his daughter
Ann and her husband William Nourse. Evidently Thomas
McMurray's wife and daughter were quite unhappy when he
first settled them in the area, but they became reconciled to their
"new mode of life", especially when old Cuthbert Cumming who
had married Jane McMurray retired near them in 1842.[48]

While some mixed-blood wives found it difficult to adapt
to life in Eastern Canada, others endured the shock of being
transported thousands of miles across the Atlantic to Great
Britain. In a marked change of policy, the Hudson's Bay
Company, after the union of 1821, lifted its ban on employees
taking their native wives to Britain provided they had adequate

means to support their families.[49] This option never proved to be popular, but there were a few officers whose strong attachment to both family and land of their birth resulted in their retiring to Scotland with their mixed-blood wives. In 1844, Chief Factor George Keith took "his Duchess" Nanette Sutherland out to Lachine where they were formally married prior to sailing for Scotland. Keith's brother and Governor Simpson had both tried to dissuade him from this course, but the old trader felt he could not in conscience part with his wife, particularly because of his responsibility for their youngest daughter who had been born mentally retarded. Mrs Keith suffered badly from seasickness for almost the entire ocean voyage, but at length the family was safely settled in Aberdeen for the winter. It soon became apparent to Keith, however, that town life would be too difficult an adjustment for his wife so he bought a pleasant cottage with a nice garden and an acre of land a few miles outside the city.[50] Initially given to longing for "scenes & associations left behind", Nanette gradually became reconciled to her new home. She enjoyed tending her garden and began selling fresh produce and eggs from her flock of chickens; her native craft work also attracted much interest. Keith was thankful to find friends who would make allowances for his wife's social deficiencies and was gratified by her continuing improvement:

> . . . the Gud-wife . . . has acquired a considerable smattering of the English language, together with some comparative degree of civilized polish. . . . all things considered I think she deserves some credit for . . . playing her part so well as she does.[51]

The Keiths were joined several years later by Chief Factor Alexander Christie, the retired governor of Assiniboia. His wife Ann, the half-Cree daughter of Hudson's Bay Company officer John Thomas, had been reluctant to leave Red River which, in her view, possessed "all the advantages desirable in a residence."[52] Mrs Christie was most homesick during her first winter in Britain which was spent in London. She suffered from the damp changeable climate and was terrified by the noise and bustle of the metropolis; "no argument would induce her to venture out on the streets, for fear of being crushed by the

crowd."[53] Things improved somewhat when the Christies settled
on a comfortable property outside Aberdeen not far from the
Keiths. In 1852, Letitia Hargrave, the Scottish wife of the chief
factor at York Factory, was warmly welcomed when she paid a
visit to both of these families. She described Mrs Christie as
"more than agreeable", noting that she was accepted by a circle
of friends who were respectable if not genteel. The Scottish
woman was somewhat nonplussed, however, by the "Indianisms"
of old Mrs Keith and her married daughter who was visiting
from Canada:

> Mrs. Keith & Mrs. Swanston came to call for me.
> . . . The Duchess is splendid in her own way & they
> both precipitated themselves upon me & declared
> themselves my friends. . . . The old lady . . . is
> hideously black & ugly but is wonderfully lively, even
> hilarious in her manner. Old Squirly gives utterance to
> the most fearful Indian yell & her daughter & she are
> too much for a small room when they express
> astonishment.[54]

Undoubtedly, both Mrs Keith and Mrs Christie would
have found it much more satisfactory if their husbands'
devotion to them had extended to their ultimately settling in
Rupert's Land. This had become an option with the creation of
the Red River Colony in 1811, but for many years conditions
were so primitive, that few bourgeois were tempted to settle in
what was described as "the antipodes of a paradise".[55] Quite a
number of Hudson's Bay Company officers, however, especially
those with Indian wives, were anxious to retire to the new
settlement. With the prospect of churches and schools being
established, Red River would provide a place where their
children could be maintained in "the Habits and Duties of
Civilized Life" without being divorced from a familiar
environment.[56] Retired Chief Factors James Bird, Thomas
Thomas and Robert Logan automatically became the social
leaders of the colony. In 1825, they were joined by Alexander
Ross who, with the intent of providing his offspring with a
Christian education, arranged for his Okanagan wife and young
children to be transported in the Company canoes from the
Columbia.[57] Red River also became home to many of the

servants of both companies; to employees made redundant by the union of 1821, the Hudson's Bay Company gave small allotments of land and assistance to start life anew as settlers.[58]

In the late fur-trade period, the colony of Vancouver Island provided another place of retirement; officers James Douglas, James Murray Yale and John Work found much to recommend it. John Work built a commodious house near Fort Victoria, where he died in 1861. His Métis wife, Josette, survived him by over thirty years, a respected and remarkably youthful-looking matriarch. John Tod, an old family friend who was invited to the widow's home for Christmas 1868, was much impressed by the closeness of the family:

> It was a joyful sight to behold. Thirty two of our late friend's descendents all seated at the same table. . . . my heart warmed with a glow it has seldom felt, to see them all in the full bloom of health, and so happy.[59]

Josette Work was evidently able to cope with the rapid changes brought about by the settlement of British Columbia. The oldest resident of the province upon her death in 1896, she was remembered in a tribute by the Legislature for her "usefulness in pioneer work and many good deeds."[60]

Given the cultural gap between the traders, especially the officers, and their native wives, the strong family ties which developed in fur-trade society appear all the more remarkable. While the caring and concern of many fathers were undoubtedly genuine, much credit, as George Keith acknowledged, was due to the mothers on whom the double burden of personal sacrifice and cultural adjustment mostly fell. The fur-trade officers were particularly anxious for native women to become acculturated to European ideals of womanhood; what the men often failed to realize was the psychological stress and dislocation that such a process of acculturation could engender. If the founding of the Red River Settlement solved for many fur-trade fathers the dilemma of what to do with their families in retirement, it was also welcomed because it offered the "prospect of Civilization diffusing itself among us".[61] As a result, younger generations of mixed-blood girls were increasingly subjected to the pressures of English customs.

St John's Church and the Red River Academy. By J. Fleming,
September 1857.

145

7

"QUITE ENGLISH IN HER MANNER"

The coming of settlement to Rupert's Land was to have a profound effect upon fur-trade society, for it created a base for the introduction of the basic tenets of civilization — agriculture, Christianity and education. Significantly, a new and powerful agent for social change appeared in the person of the missionary. In 1818, a Roman Catholic mission had been established in Red River under the auspices of Lord Selkirk to minister to the growing French-Canadian and Métis population. Two years later the Hudson's Bay Company, with the help of the Church Missionary Society, sent the Reverend John West to the colony to attend to the spiritual needs of the Protestants. The attitudes brought by the clergy, who viewed themselves as the upholders of civilization, were to have a far-reaching impact upon the women in fur-trade society, especially the rising mixed-blood generation. Fur-trade officers, most of whom were Protestant, looked to the Church of England missionaries to assist them in providing the education needed to equip their daughters with the manners and morals of young Victorian ladies. A number of mixed-blood girls were to receive praise for becoming "quite English". This process, however, had the unfortunate consequence of making them, like their white counterparts, increasingly vulnerable and dependent upon male protectors. In reality, the more acculturated a mixed-blood woman became the more she lost that sphere of autonomy and purpose which native women had been able to maintain.

In the changing social climate of nineteenth-century Rupert's Land, with the old customs of fur-trade society coming under attack, mixed-blood women became increasingly exposed to sexual exploitation. In the name of morality, the missionaries denounced marriage *à la façon du pays* as being sinful and debased, but while they eventually succeeded in gaining wide-spread recognition for the necessity of church marriage, this attack on fur-trade custom ironically had a detrimental effect on the position of native women. The double standard arrived with a vengeance. Incoming traders, feeling free to ignore the marital obligations implied by the "custom of the country", increasingly looked upon native women as objects for temporary sexual gratification, not as wives. The women, on the other hand, now found themselves being judged according to strict Victorian standards of female propriety. It was they, not the traders, who were to be held responsible for the perpetuation of immorality in Rupert's Land because promiscuous tendencies were supposedly inherent in their Indian blood! Racism now began to pose a serious threat even to the acculturated mixed-blood woman.

The arrival of the missionaries placed the question of schooling in Rupert's Land upon a whole new footing, and the Colony of Red River provided the centre for their educational activities. The missionaries considered a sound Christian education to be the key to the salvation of the rising generation —a means of erasing barbaric and heathen notions from the minds of the children.[1] With regard to the native female population, it was considered essential that they should be acculturated to the ways of civilized women. But the lack of suitable female educators meant schools for girls — the separate education of the sexes being deemed essential — were slow in being established in Red River. In 1824, Miss Mary Allez, a recent immigrant from Guernsey, made a start at a boarding school for girls, but this project was curtailed within the year by her marriage to a Company clerk.[2] Little real progress was made in Protestant female education until the arrival of the Church of England missionary William Cockran and his English wife Ann. In the summer of 1827, Mrs Cockran set up a boarding school for girls to which quite a number of Company officers sent their daughters.[3] Catholic education for girls began in January 1829 when Bishop Provencher prevailed upon Angélique and Marguerite Nolin, the educated mixed-blood daughters of Jean-Baptiste Nolin, who had come from Sault Ste Marie to open a school.[4]

The Protestant missionaries, in particular, expressed much optimism about the beneficial effects of Christianity on mixed-blood girls:

> Experience has taught the [Church Missionary] Society the influence which female education is calculated to produce in an uncivilized country . . . The females in question are never likely to see any country but this; in the course of time they will be disposed of in marriage to persons in the service and thus stationed in different parts of the country, and may we not hope that thus we shall have female missionaries by & bye throughout the Indian territories.[5]

Although spiritual training was considered of the utmost importance, the clergy also recognized that the education of native females must have a strong practical element. As one observer lamented, "the household duties performed to the wishes of the labouring classes elsewhere are almost unknown among the half breed caste of this land."[6] In the early 1830s, the Cockrans endeavoured to meet this need by establishing a day school where Mrs Cockran would be able to teach the mixed-blood girls of Red River how to be good housewives. This process would involve training in domestic skills such as cooking and sewing, and the inculcating of proper wifely attitudes. A good wife must be cleanly and industrious in her habits and docile and obedient to her husband. Above all she must be sexually pure. Every vestige of the sexual freedom to which Indian women had been accustomed was to be stamped out; chastity, it was impressed upon young mixed-blood women, was their greatest virtue and responsibility. According to contemporary British sentiment: "A woman who has once lost chastity has lost every good quality. She has from that moment all the vices."[7]

While many Company officers applauded the missionaries' efforts to acculturate their mixed-blood offspring, they objected to *their* daughters being educated in the same style as daughters of Company servants. The officers were not interested in having their daughters learn menial domestic skills; they wanted them to acquire the accomplishments of ladies as befitted their status as daughters of the fur-trade gentry. Ever concerned to maintain the distinction in rank between themselves and Company servants, the officers had been painfully aware that in the past their native wives had not possessed the attributes which they considered appropriate to women of their station.[8] Their desire to raise their daughters in the English manner was accentuated by the founding of Red River itself; in a colony which envisioned itself as being "a little Britain in the wilderness", class distinctions would become increasingly important. Company officers were anxious that their families be equipped to retain their social positions in Rupert's Land. Giving their daughters a refined English education, they hoped, would be sufficient to overcome the taint of their mixed blood.

William Cockran despaired of the officers' wish to make their daughters "ladies all at once"[9], but the other Church of England missionary, David Jones, whose English wife Mary had come out to join him in 1829, was more prepared to cater to their class aspirations. In 1832, the Joneses founded the Red River Academy, a boarding school for boys and girls where a superior education could be obtained for the cost of thirty pounds per annum. A governess from England was to be imported to teach the girls, and the discussion over her qualifications underscored the officers' desire to turn their daughters into British ladies. Jones would have been satisfied with a woman of "matured Christian experience", but the officers insisted that she should be able to teach "the ornamental as well as the useful branches of Education; in short an accomplished well-bred lady, capable of teaching music, drawing, &c &c, of conciliating disposition and mild temper." Governor Simpson also recommended that two respectable English women servants be sent out "as we consider it very desirable that the young ladies should have as little discourse with the native women in this country as possible."[10]

The history of the girls' section of the Red River Academy was a chequered one. Almost before it got started, a scandal caused by one of its pupils threatened to throw the project into disrepute. In the summer of 1832, Jones and his wife were distraught to discover that one of their charges, a daughter of Chief Trader Roderick McKenzie, Jr, was pregnant and that it was she who had seduced the young Indian responsible. It was feared that the reputation of the school would be damaged by this occurrence, but Governor Simpson did his best to assure his fellow officers that the Joneses were in no way guilty of neglect. The girl, who was described as "a poor silly stupid creature", was quietly married off.[11] Although the incident was allowed to pass, several officers, especially Chief Trader Donald Ross who had a whole bevy of daughters, emphasized that the affair pointed up the pressing need for vigilance:

> . . . in matters touching the fame of the female sex in particular, a parent has not only his own feelings, but the prejudices and censures of the multitude to consult — how unreasonable or ill founded so ever these may prove to be.[12]

This lesson was apparently taken to heart, for subsequently the girls at the school were strictly chaperoned; according to a later observer: "The ladies of this Academy are as strictly guarded . . . as the inmates of a Turkish Seraglio."[13]

By the fall of 1833, the prospects for the school appeared very promising. Over forty children had been enrolled and the new governess, the widowed Mrs Mary Lowman, was praised as a "clever unsurpassed woman." Old Chief Factor J. D. Cameron, on bringing his daughter to the school, was especially impressed with the attitude of Mrs Lowman:

> She spares no pains with her pupils — she learns them to sit, to stand, to walk, and perhaps, to lie down. She appears to have their improvement very much at heart — when she reprimands them, she does it in the Kind affectionate terms of a Mother.[14]

The stability of the school was soon shaken by the marriage of the governess in January 1835 to one of the "nobs" of the settlement, retired Chief Factor James Bird. The girls were abandoned to the harsh discipline of the boys' teacher, John Macallum, until a replacement could be found. A Miss Anne Armstrong, who arrived the following autumn, was to have been the new governess, but the officers opposed her appointment because she was not qualified to teach "the ornamental subjects" which were deemed so necessary to their daughters' education.[15] The girls' school was further deranged

Mrs Mary Lowman, governess of the girls' section of the Red River Academy until her marriage in January 1835 to Chief Factor James Bird.

by the death in October 1836 of Mary Jones who had generally supervised the welfare of the female pupils. So grieved were many of the Company officers by the loss of one who had been "the friend & benefactress of the half-caste females" of Rupert's Land that they arranged for a memorial tablet to be erected over Mrs Jones's pew at the Upper Church.[16]

In an effort to fill the gap, Mrs Sarah Ingham, who had come out to the colony as a companion-servant to Mrs Lowman, endeavoured to establish an auxiliary school for girls under the patronage of several prominent settlers. It is unlikely that many of the active officers would have sent their daughters to Mrs Ingham, but they were given little opportunity, for she soon married Robert Logan, one of her patrons.[17] In the meantime, the Academy staggered on under the direction of Macallum. Another governess, a pernickety, aging spinster named Miss Allan, was eventually secured in 1840, but her performance did not at all accord with Macallum's ideas of pedagogy. He finally dismissed her in 1845 on the grounds that:

> she was careless & lazy, had extraordinary peculiarities
> of manner wch made her the laugh of her school girls &
> was not sufficiently accomplished to carry on the
> education of young ladies.[18]

In spite of these difficulties, many mixed-blood girls who attended the Red River Academy made considerable progress in acquiring the grace and polish expected of young Victorian ladies. Betsey Charles, the daughter of wealthy Chief Factor John Charles, was described as "a fine clever and accomplished girl . . . quite English in her manner."[19] James Hargrave, no easy critic, had special praise for a daughter of Andrew McDermot, a prominent Red River merchant: "in good sense, instinct and . . . self possession in company she reminds me more of our British Ladies than any other I have met in this land."[20] It is certainly significant that by the time of Miss Allan's dismissal, Macallum considered one of the Academy's own former pupils, Miss Jane McKenzie, sufficiently accomplished to take her place. Some of the more fastidious officers expressed reservations about this young mixed-blood woman's qualifications and her romantic preoccupations, but her appointment as schoolmistress indicates the progress which many of the daughters of Company officers had made in their education.[21]

The missionaries were not to be entirely disappointed in their hopes that well-educated mixed-blood women would be of service to the cause of Christianity. Sophia, the youngest daughter of former governor Thomas Thomas, had been placed in the care of the Church of England missionaries at an early age. An apt pupil and "a good pious girl", she grew up a devout Christian.[22] In 1843, she married the Reverend William Mason and, with her knowledge of Cree and her sincere interest in the welfare of the Indians, was of great help to her husband's ministry at Norway House. Although she had a delicate constitution, Sophia was reputed to have devoted herself unceasingly to the operation of the Indian day school, visiting the sick, and translating hymns and scripture. Her lasting work was the production of a Cree Bible. In 1858, the Masons went to England, but Sophia's health deteriorated rapidly in the damp climate. In 1861, a few months after giving birth to her ninth child, Sophia Mason died of tuberculosis. Her husband's journal entry for 10 October provides a touching tribute:

> This morning, after uttering the word 'heaven', my dear wife passed into the presence of her Saviour, at a quarter before ten o'clock, without a single struggle, or even a groan.
>
> Oh how great is my loss and that of the nine poor orphan children. May 'the Lord take them up'. Yet, in the midst of all, we have much to be thankful for. She has been spared to accomplish a great work, the Cree Bible; and to bear such a testimony for Jesus amongst the heathen, by the patience with which she suffered, and her zeal and persevering labours to make known the glorious Gospel of salvation . . .[23]

Both missionaries and fur-trade fathers undoubtedly viewed the rapid acculturation of mixed-blood girls as being in the best interests of the young women themselves. Hudson's Bay Company fathers had for a long time been concerned to save their daughters from the hardships of the "savage" life where they would experience little of "those tender Attentions which Europeans bestow on the Sex."[24] However, the white male attitude also involved pressing mixed-blood girls into the

The Reverend John West denounced the 'custom of the country' as immoral. This drawing entitled "Visit to an Encampment of Indians" is from his journal published in 1824.

increasingly passive and dependent mould that was deemed appropriate to the function of women in nineteenth-century European society. In cultivating the civilized graces of the British lady, the young mixed-blood woman was also in danger of assuming the relative uselessness and excessive dependency of her white sister, which contrasted sharply with the autonomy and self-reliance of the Indian woman. And what would be their fate should they fail to secure appropriate husbands? It is true that many newcomers found admirable wives among young mixed-blood women. Yet social changes in the post-union period brought the status of mixed marriages into question in Rupert's Land and placed native women in an increasingly vulnerable position.

One of the most serious conflicts in nineteenth-century fur-trade society resulted from the missionaries' attack on the old custom of marriage *à la façon du pays*. The Church of England clergy, in particular, denounced "the custom of the country" as immoral and living in sin. Little progress toward civilized living could be made, declared John West, until couples had been married according to the rites of the Church of England; Christian marriage constituted "the parent not the child of civil society".[25] West's excessive zeal on this subject made his ministry in Red River quite unpopular. Many retired Company officers felt that the pronouncements of a clergyman could not add more legality or sanctity to unions which had already lasted for decades. Nevertheless, West persisted, being particularly anxious that retired Chief Factors James Bird and Thomas Thomas formalize their unions with their Indian wives. These "Gentlemen" were prominent in the colony and should set an example for the rest of its citizens.[26] When West left Rupert's Land in 1823, he had performed a total of sixty-five marriages, including a number of couples who lived at the posts along the route to York Factory.[27] His successors, David Jones and William Cockran, continued to rail against the immoral habits of the fur traders. Jones's dogmatic stance was hardly conciliating. It had been West's custom to baptize traders' wives immediately before the marriage ceremony, but Jones was adamant that it would be a sacrilege to pronounce "our excellent Liturgy" over persons entirely ignorant of its meaning. When several traders maintained that there would be little point in having a church marriage since their wives would still be regarded as "heathens" unless baptized, Jones declared that they were merely looking for an excuse to continue "living in sin".[28]

The most bitter feud over the issue of marriage *à la façon du pays* erupted at Fort Vancouver, the headquarters of the Columbia District. As early as 1824 when the possibility of establishing a mission in this area was broached, Governor Simpson had given a prophetic warning:

> The Missionaries . . . ought to understand in the outset that nearly all the Gentlemen & Servants have Families altho' Marriage ceremonies are unknown in the Country and that it would be all in vain to attempt breaking through this uncivilised custom.[29]

But the post's first clergyman, the Reverend Herbert Beaver, was totally unsympathetic to fur-trade custom, in spite of his appropriate name. Arriving in the fall of 1836 with his English wife, Jane, he denounced Fort Vancouver as a

An unsigned, undated water-colour of Fort Vancouver, believed to be the early 1850s. The house of the chief factor is at the right, behind the cannon.

"deplorable scene of vice and ignorance". He refused to give any credence to "the custom of the country", styling the traders' wives as concubines and chastising the men for indulging in fornication.[30] This most insulting and unfair assessment of the well-regulated domestic situation at the fort understandably outraged fiery-tempered Chief Factor John McLoughlin. McLoughlin himself had remained devoted to his mixed-blood wife Marguerite Wadin McKay[31] whom he had wed *à la façon du pays* in the Rainy Lake area in 1811 when he was a young Nor'Wester. He had taken his wife and family with him upon being given charge of the Columbia District in 1824, and according to contemporaries, Marguerite McLoughlin was a most respectable first lady of Fort Vancouver. She was noted for "her numerous charities and many excellent qualities of heart" —"one of the kindest women in the world."[32] But to Beaver, good Mrs McLoughlin was only a "kept Mistress" who could not be allowed to associate with properly married females such as his own wife. "Shall the man, who has raised his partner by marriage to his own level" raged the parson, "degrade himself and her, by suffering her to be put on an equality with other men's paramours?"[33]

McLoughlin, who had Catholic predilections, deeply resented these slanders against his wife and stoutly refused to give in to Beaver's demand that he submit to a Church of England marriage ceremony. In order to silence any charge of illegality against his union, he asked James Douglas, acting in his capacity of Justice of the Peace, to perform a civil ceremony. When Beaver and his wife continued to heap invective upon Mrs McLoughlin, her husband's anger reached such a pitch that on one occasion he could not refrain from giving the missionary a sound drubbing with his own cane.[34]

Chief Trader James Douglas, on the other hand, was more prepared to concede to Beaver's wishes, believing that it was proper for a couple to have their union blessed by the church when the opportunity arose. On 28 February 1837, Douglas and his wife Amelia were wed according to the rites of the Church of England, this being one of the few marriages which Beaver managed to perform during his stay at the fort.[35] Douglas, however, soon became alienated by Beaver's cutting remarks about native women. In 1838, when left in temporary command of the fort, Douglas was provoked to take a stand against Beaver's accusation that the factor's house was "a common receptacle for every mistress of an officer in the service, who may take a fancy to visit the Fort". Only the *wives* of officers, Douglas sharply informed Beaver, were allowed to accompany their husbands on brigade business. The wife taken according to "the custom of the country", he emphasized, bore no resemblance to a "loose woman":

> The woman who is not sensible of violating and [sic] law, who lives chastely with the husband of her choice, in a state approved by friends and sanctioned by immemorial custom, which she believes strictly honourable, forms a perfect contrast to the degraded creature who has sacrificed the great principle which from infancy she is taught to revere as the ground work of female virtue; who lives a disgrace to friends and an outcast from society.[36]

Indeed, Beaver and his wife created such friction that all were gratified when he was relieved of his post, and the couple departed in the fall of 1838.

The dismal failure of Beaver was in sharp contrast to the success of the Pacific Mission established by the Roman Catholic priests, François N. Blanchet and Modeste Demers, who travelled overland to the Columbia in the same year. Although the majority of the populace at Fort Vancouver were Roman Catholic, the priests' conciliatory attitude toward the custom of the country also contributed to their welcome. The Roman Catholic Church did not recognize the sanctity of a country marriage, but the priests did acknowledge the existence of a marital bond by considering that a cohabiting couple was living in a state of "natural marriage". The only children stigmatized with illegitimacy were those whose father could not be identified. The general tenor of the Roman Catholic rite was that the parties were "renewing and ratifying their mutal consent of marriage" and formally recognizing the legitimacy of their children. To such a ceremony Chief Factor McLoughlin and "his legitimate wife" Marguerite consented on 19 November 1842.[37]

On their way across Rupert's Land, Blanchet and Demers performed numerous marriage ceremonies for couples who had previously been married *à la façon du pays*. Having received special Papal dispensation to marry persons of different faiths, quite a number of the ceremonies they performed were between Catholics and Protestants.[38] By this time, the missionaries had wrought a general change in attitude toward the question of church marriage. Even the Church of England clergy were enthusiastic about the progress being made. By the late 1820s Cockran wrote of the improved moral climate of Red River:

> Many that could not be prevailed upon formerly to marry their women have now seen the sin of despising the ordinance, and have felt truly sorry for the contempt and neglect of it.[39]

It also became customary for traders, if they happened to have an opportunity of visiting the settlement with their wives, to seek religious sanction for their unions.[40] In June 1835 Archibald McDonald and his mixed-blood wife Jane Klyne were formally married when they came to Red River to bring four of their children to school there. In a letter to his friend

Edward Ermatinger, McDonald commented on his fellow officers' changing point of view:

> All my colleagues are now about following the example, & it is my full conviction few of them can do no better —the great mistake is in flattering themselves with a different notion too long — nothing is gained by procrastination, but much is lost by it.

Yet McDonald could not refrain from pointing out the irony of the solemn pronouncements of the clergy, for he and his beloved Jane had lived in most exemplary domestic fashion ever since he had wed her *à la façon du pays* ten years before:

> . . . [we] were joined in Holy wedlock & of course declared at full liberty to live together as man & wife & to increase & multiply as to them might seem fit —And I hope the validity of this ceremony is not to be questioned though it has not the further advantage of a Newspaper Confirmation.[41]

There were a number of older fur traders who still stubbornly clung to the old ways. Not until 1838 was former Hudson's Bay Company officer William Hemmings Cook persuaded to have his thirty-five-year-old union with Mary (Agathas) Cocking blest by the church, although the couple had lived in Red River since the early 1820s.[42] A few traders — Chief Factors Peter Skene Ogden and John Rowand — eschewed the religious ceremony until the end. John Rowand could have formally wed Louise Umfreville when the Catholic priests passed through Fort Edmonton in 1838, but he apparently deemed this unnecessary for a relationship which had lasted almost three decades. He was to remain loyal to "my old friend the Mother of all my children" until her death in 1849.[43] Significantly, Rowand did not intend that his children follow his example. His four daughters were baptized by the priests, and Rowand acted as the chief witness to the marriage of his eldest daughter Nancy to Chief Trader J. E. Harriott.[44] Clearly, while the old order might linger, especially in remote areas, the younger generation was increasingly expected to obey the dictates of the clergy.

It was as well that the missionaries succeeded in establishing the necessity of church marriage because in the post-union society of the fur trade, traditional processes were so undercut that "the custom of the country" no longer afforded native women any guarantee of security. Paradoxically, the attitude of the church contributed to the vulnerability of the native women's position during this period of changing customs. According to old fur-trade custom, if a man formed a liaison with a woman she was considered to be his wife, entitled to the recognition and support that a marital relationship implied. Now, with the insistence of the missionary that only a church marriage had validity, the woman taken *à la façon du pays* could easily be denied wifely status; she was merely someone with whom to gratify one's passions but never actually marry. The presence of the missionaries helped to block the traditional socializing process which had conditioned incoming whites to a responsible view of the custom of the country. Certainly some of the nineteenth-century attitudes toward sex and marriage that were imported with the young British gentlemen being recruited into the Company's service did little to enhance the status of native women.

Many of the well-educated young men who became Company officers in the post-union period were imbued with the Victorian middle-class desire for respectability and success.[45] Their position on marriage, well articulated in the writings of the clerk James Hargrave, was to postpone wedded bliss until one had secured a sizeable competence and could maintain a family in comfortable circumstances. In choosing a wife, love was expected to play a part, but the wise man would bestow his affection upon a woman capable of adorning his station in life and, if possible, with the connections to advance his career. She would be of spotless character, but if in the meantime, he himself found sexual abstinence to be impossible (it seems to have been assumed that in young men it was) then there was a certain class of woman to whom one could resort. The secret was to be discreet.

The transference of this attitude to fur-trade society had serious consequences for native women because in this setting the double standard was exacerbated by racial prejudice. Men such as Hargrave dreamed of one day winning the hand of some fair Scottish damsel and settling in the civilized world, but during their sojourn in Rupert's Land, what harm in a little indulgence in "the fascinations of dark-eyed beauty?"[46] In well-settled areas in the post-union period, there was a growing tendency for Indian women to be reduced to the state of prostitutes, a situation conveniently blamed upon the supposed immoral leanings of their race. Evidently by the 1840s, prostitution had become a serious problem at York Factory; even Hargrave, who stoutly maintained that he was the epitome of the abstemious bachelor, revealed in a private letter to a servant at York that he had been "obliged" by an Indian woman at the fort ("any port in a storm").[47] For an officer to actually marry an Indian woman was now completely out of the question. Hargrave declared: "a young Gent[n] from Britain would as soon think of matching himself with the contemporary of his grandmother as with a pure Squaw."[48] When in 1837 former Nor'Wester Richard Grant endeavoured to continue in the old ways and took an Indian wife *à la façon du pays* at Oxford House, Hargrave was appalled. Considering the woman to be totally unsuitable to Grant's station, Hargrave applied considerable pressure to bring about their separation and was much relieved when "the erring fellow" was posted to the Columbia in 1842:

> . . . for his own sake I am truly glad he is gone, for his ideas about love and the sex were too primitive to suit the atmosphere of the world as it is _now_ about Oxford and Norway House.[49]

Even young mixed-blood girls, raised with the expectation of becoming the wives of officers, could find themselves reduced to the status of mistresses, a situation which must have caused them considerable grief and confusion. The swashbuckling Governor William Williams, appointed to superintend the affairs of the Hudson's Bay Company in 1818, formed a liaison with Sally, a daughter of Peter Fidler, soon after his arrival in the Indian Country. Sally, and undoubtedly fur-trade society at large, considered that she was Williams's wife. In his view she was only a pleasurable mistress, for he already had a wife in England. Two children were born to Sally, but Williams abruptly severed his connection with his native dependants when he was transferred to the Southern Department and his wife came out to join him in 1822.[50] The classic practitioner of this new exploitative attitude toward native women was Williams's successor, George Simpson, the most important personage in the nineteenth-century fur trade. Having never served a real apprenticeship in Rupert's Land, Simpson had not been subjected to the traditional socialization process, and he showed a distinct lack of sympathy for the marital concerns of his associates. To him, Chief Factor John Clarke's half-breed wife Sapphira Spence was merely "an Indian mistress", but to most traders, she was "Madame Clarke", having been ceremoniously wed *à la façon du pays*.[51] The Governor's reputation for having a woman at every post is exaggerated, but he showed a flagrant disregard for fur-trade custom and formed a series of liaisons with young mixed-blood women whom he treated in a most callous manner.[52]

Sometime in 1821 during his first year in Rupert's Land, Simpson formed a union with Betsey Sinclair, the daughter of a former Hudson's Bay Company officer. From Betsey's point of view, the prospect of having such an important husband was undoubtedly attractive, and again fur-trade society assumed that Simpson would treat her as a country wife. In a York Fort journal on 10 February 1822, the writer saw fit to record that "Mrs. Simpson was delivered of a daughter."[53] Simpson did not regard Betsey in this light; to him, she was "his article", "an unnecessary & expensive appendage" for whom he had little time since he was kept busy with extensive tours of the Company's operations. When Simpson set off from York Factory that fall, he left it to his friend John G. McTavish to dispose of Betsey as he saw fit, with the proviso that she should not become "a general accommodation shop".[54]

Simpson does not appear to have taken up with another mistress until his return from furlough in Britain in 1825-26. Initially his attitude toward Margaret Taylor, whose brother Thomas was his personal servant at this time, shows that the Governor regarded mixed-blood women primarily as objects for sexual gratification. Upon his departure on another long tour in the fall of 1826, he left Margaret at York Factory under the surveillance of McTavish:

> Pray keep an Eye on the commodity if she bring forth

Mary Keith, daughter of Chief Factor James Keith. Her marriage to Thomas Taylor, personal servant to George Simpson was arranged by Simpson and her uncle, Chief Factor George Keith.

> anything in proper time & of the right colour let them
> be taken care of but if any thing be amiss let the whole
> be bundled about their business . . .[55]

Margaret herself did not warrant such suspicion, and early in 1827 a son, named George after his father, was born.[56]

Simpson did provide support for this woman and her child whom he maintained at York Factory; at the same time he appears to have kept another mistress at Lachine. Her identity is not certain, but it is likely that Simpson's son James Keith Simpson was born of this relationship.[57] By this time the Governor's relatives began to think his liaisons were unseemly; his cousin Aemileus chided him: "I do not think it improves the arrangements of your domestic economy to have a mistress attached to your Establishment — rather have her Elsewhere."[58] Simpson may have severed this connection because after 1828 his relationship with Margaret Taylor began to approximate a traditional country marriage. The Governor took her with him on his journey to New Caledonia that fall and he valued her company. "The commodity" he confided to McTavish, "has been a great consolation to me."[59] He even went so far as to refer to Thomas Taylor as his brother-in-law. In the summer of 1829, he made arrangements for Margaret, now far advanced in her second pregnancy, to stay at Bas de la Rivière until his return from another furlough. But within the year, Margaret Taylor was to be callously cast aside when Simpson married his young British cousin!

Mixed-blood women were particularly vulnerable to such treatment and in the conflict of changing customs could easily be victimized. Mary Taylor, the sister of Margaret, found the behaviour of incoming young clerks difficult to comprehend. In the mid-1820s, James Hargrave, then a clerk, had shown more than a passing interest in this attractive young woman; indeed, he had given her the impression that he intended to marry her and she had refused another offer. But when Hargrave heard that Mary was waiting at Norway House for him to send for her, he immediately enlisted the aid of a friend to "undeceive" her. He had no intention of marrying a mixed-blood, although he did admit that he had scarcely seen a young woman "of her caste" whom he would have preferred before pretty Miss

Taylor.[60] The Taylor girls may have suffered from the lack of a father's protection, for their father, the sloopmaster George Taylor, had retired to England in the early 1800s.

Indeed many fathers in Rupert's Land worried about the safety of their adolescent daughters, as they were all too aware of the liberties which some young men felt free to take with native girls. Ironically even Simpson was to feel a father's anxiety when his daughter Maria, by Betsey Sinclair, came of marriageable age. When Maria was sent to Norway House in 1838, the Governor asked Donald Ross to be on the lookout for a respectable husband for her. If none could be found, the girl was to be settled some place off the main voyageur route, as her father did not wish "to keep her conspicuous on the communication". Other officers had expressed concern that young ladies were housed too close to young bachelors at Norway House, and when Maria soon attracted the rapt admiration of a visiting English botanist, Robert Wallace, it was decided that the most honourable course would be to unite the young lovers *à la façon du pays*, there being no clergyman available.[61] The fate of other young mixed-blood girls, who were increasingly being charged to guard their virtue, was not so happy. When Margaret Sinclair was awaiting an intended husband at York Factory in the summer of 1845, she was heard talking in her sleep about having been raped. Her graphic description ended with the observation that it was "a common thing". Some of her friends and even her sister had experienced a similar misfortune.[62]

Despite the increased sexual exploitation of native women, it was the women themselves who were more likely to be held responsible and penalized for any immorality. The introduction of British morality brought with it the invidious "double standard".[63] Because Victorian society placed such a premium on feminine purity, European males could excuse themselves by emphasizing the moral failings of native women for their lack of concern about such matters. "Absolute purity" piously intoned James Hargrave, "could not be attained in one generation, — much time and long continued care will . . . be required to raise even their youngest children to an equality with their fairer sisterhood".[64] Yet while the women were increasingly being judged by strict standards of Victorian propriety, the clergy were prepared to overlook men's sexual indulgences. At Fort Vancouver, the Reverend Beaver declared that in order to introduce a degree of respectability all "loose females" — by which he meant women who had not been married by church rite — should be barred from the fort. They might be maintained outside the walls where the men could visit them on the sly to at least conform with the "outward decorum" which men in civilized countries observed toward their mistresses.[65]

The clergy were particularly prone to applying the double standard against native women. Those of the Church of England would accord no recognition to native wives who had not received the rites of baptism and marriage; although their identities would have been known, they were recorded in the registers merely as "Indian, Half-Breed or Half-Caste" women.[66] Beaver even went so far as to propose punishing the women directly for "living in sin" by denying them rations and medical attention to bring them to a sense of their shame.[67] When church marriages became the custom, wives who could not claim "benefit of clergy" were looked upon as most debased creatures. This attitude was carried to cruel lengths in Red River by the schoolmaster John Macallum who, in his zeal for social propriety, forbade his pupils to have any contact with their mothers if they had been guilty of "living in sin" with their fathers. A tragic victim of this situation was the destitute Indian wife of a trader Kenneth McKenzie, who had gone off to join the American Fur Company. She never saw her two daughters who had been placed in the Academy, except when they, at the risk of severe punishment, would sneak out to visit her. The hypocrisy of Macallum's stance was obvious; even Letitia Hargrave, a well-bred Scottish woman, was moved to comment:

> This may be all very right, but it is fearfully cruel for the poor unfortunate mothers who did not know that there was any distinction & it is only within the last few years that any one was so married. Of course had all the fathers refused, every one woman in the country wd have been no better than those that are represented to their own children as discreditable.[68]

In Red River, Macallum's policy occasioned no public

protest, as the small colonial society was showing signs of becoming obsessed with the question of female virtue. Just the imputation of impropriety could be enough to destroy a young woman's character. In the spring of 1839, for example, James Hargrave was horrified to learn that it was being spread about the colony that he had seduced the serving maid of the Governor's wife. The young woman steadfastly protested her innocence, and the truth was that the cook at Lower Fort Garry, having had his own advances spurned, had concocted the story to get his revenge. Hargrave would have sued for slander but he was cautioned that his desire to uphold a young woman's honour would probably result in more harm than good. Despite her innocence, the publicity "would attach a stain to her character, let it be ever so spotless, that could not easily be washed off."[69]

If Victorian morality taught that virginity was a young woman's greatest possession, it also taught that a wife's greatest sin was adultery. But again, the double standard applied — a wife should forgive a husband such frailty, but a husband could *not* forgive a guilty wife.[70] Simpson, with his racist bias, claimed that mixed-blood women were prone to infidelity; he evidently found that a number of his officers neglected their duties in their jealous attempts to guard against "certain innocent indescretions which these frail brown ones are so apt to indulge in." Other traders, however, were at pains to point out that cases of unfaithfulness were rare.[71] Given the conditions of fur-trade life where husbands and wives might be separated for months on end and where the transport of families was difficult, it was remarkable that so many relationships were as stable as they were. But the wife who was found guilty of committing a "faux pas" was subject to serious condemnation.

Such was the case of Alexander Fisher's wife, Angélique, a step-daughter of the engagé Antoine Savard. During the 1830s, Fisher and his wife had lived happily in New Caledonia. Then in 1841, Fisher received a last minute posting to Fort Good Hope, and owing to the lateness of the season, he had to leave his wife and young children to winter at Fort Chipewyan. For Madame Fisher, the winter was to be a confused and tragic one. Shortly after her husband's departure, her youngest daughter Jane died.

Then during the winter she was subject to the religious zeal of the Wesleyan missionary James Evans, who baptized her on the condition that she would never again sleep with her husband until he promised to marry her according to Christian rite at the first opportunity.[72] Evans's preaching seems to have made little impact on the untutored mind of Fisher's wife, and in her loneliness she succumbed to the attentions of the young postmaster William McMurray. Thus poor Angélique, six months pregnant, arrived to join her husband at Fort Good Hope in the summer of 1842. Fisher was beside himself; he declared that his disgraced wife should have been sent to her mother at Lesser Slave Lake so that he would have been spared the indignity of having to live out the season with her. He vowed vengeance on McMurray, but he could not forgive Angélique whom he summarily left on the beach at Fort Chipewyan the following summer when he took his children out to Montreal. Sympathy was expressed for Fisher's troubles, and his discarding of his wife was considered appropriate. As Hargrave lamented, "If there is hell on this earth to a man it must be the bitter sting of a wife's infidelity."[73]

The few other recorded cases of infidelity further reveal the emphasis placed on the woman's sin and the social pressure which the wronged husbands felt to sever their connection with such worthless women. The man who would tolerate such weakness in a wife could not expect to remain respectable in society.[74] In 1841, Chief Trader Francis Ermatinger, after a notoriously wild youth,[75] settled into commendable domesticity by marrying Catharine Sinclair, a young lady who, it was reputed, would be a credit to her husband even in the civilized world. A daughter named Frances Maria, born at Fort Vancouver in 1843, was her father's pride and joy. In 1846, Ermatinger went on furlough to England, leaving his wife and child with her grandparents, the McLoughlins. To his great dismay he was not allowed to return to the Columbia but was posted to Fort Chipewyan. He sent immediately for his family, but ill health delayed his wife's departure and she had to stay at Fort Edmonton during the winter of 1848. Ermatinger's joy at being re-united with his family at Norway House the following summer soon turned to despair when he discovered that his wife was pregnant. She had been led astray during the winter by young Alexander Christie, Jr, the educated son of the respected chief factor. Shortly after the birth of the child in December, Ermatinger poured out his grief to his friend Hargrave:

> I am, I believe, a doomed man. My last two winters, in this quarter were wretched by solitary but I had hope and employed myself in getting every thing snug about me and succeeded in doing so. Poor reward, I have received for all my care and anxiety. My friend, if ever a woman had a husband in this country, who indulged her every wish and spared no expense to raise her ideas above the common herd, the one with me had but I cannot dwell upon my shame.[76]

Similar sentiments were echoed by Chief Factor John Stuart when he learned that there was reason to question the fidelity of his country wife Mary Taylor during their sojourn at Fort Simpson on the Mackenzie River in the 1830s. The case of Mary Taylor is a complex and sad one. In 1827, after her disappointment over Hargrave, she had agreed to become the country wife of aging Chief Factor Stuart, who had cast up at Norway House, free of any previous connections. Although the disparity in their ages did not augur well, Stuart was initially most happy with his young bride: ". . . she is uncommonly attentive to me . . . as caressing and anxious to please as if I was a young man."[77] About a year after Stuart was posted to Fort Simpson, however, Mary became inextricably involved with a flamboyant young postmaster named François Noel Annance, an Abenaki mixed-blood of good education. In his clandestine correspondence with Stuart's wife, Annance appears as a gallant knight, bent on rescuing his beloved from the clutches of a lecherous and abusive old man,[78] but Mary later charged that Annance had actually raped her and she had then been forced to pretend some attachment for him owing to his threats of violence and blackmail.[79] Old Stuart might have killed Annance had he got the chance, but he also felt that Mary was now not worthy of his esteem. She was a fallen woman, "a disgrace to her sex" — "If she continued to wear the mask of virtue so long it was because no one thought it worth while to tempt her."[80]

Chief Factor John Stuart. His country wife Mary Taylor left him when he "boggled at the Noose Matrimonial".

Both Ermatinger and Stuart were sincerely attached to their mixed-blood wives, but it initially appeared that the dictates of pride and society precluded the possibility of a reconciliation. Ermatinger brought his wife out with him from Fort Chipewyan in 1850, then left her with her parents at Rainy Lake while he proceeded with his daughter to St Thomas where his brother lived. To everyone's surprise the next year he sent for his wife to join him which she eventually did. The couple apparently lived amicably together until Ermatinger's death in 1858, although they were never able to escape the stigma of the scandal.[81] Fur-trade society was scandalized when it was reported that Stuart and Mary Taylor had come out of the Mackenzie District in 1834 "more loving than ever", and Stuart, ever concerned to appear respectable, decided to sever his connection with Mary when he retired to Britain the following year. He made some financial provision for her but acknowledged that she was free to remarry, although he insisted that it be to a white man.[82] Several years later Stuart changed his mind and sent for Mary to come to England, holding out the promise of a church marriage. This time it was Mary's turn for a bitter disappointment. When it became apparent that Mary, in spite of her adoption of English dress and manners, was ill-equipped to shine in the society to which Stuart aspired, the old man decided to go back on his promise. But Mary herself remained adamant; she would not stay with Stuart unless they were properly married. As a result, the couple eventually parted for good in June 1838. In the opinion of some of Stuart's contemporaries, the young mixed-blood woman had been subjected to unjustifiable humiliation. Even the strait-laced Hargrave declared:

> I cannot help admiring the spirit of my old friend Mary in her resolution of separating from Old Aesop [Stuart] when she found he boggled at the Noose Matrimonial. In that he was a fool — for with all her slips aside in this land — she was every way worthy of having this justice done her by him.[83]

Stuart did have the decency to make Mary some financial recompense and paid for her passage back to Rupert's Land, but her prospects for personal happiness were ruined. It pained her friends to see how she had changed, being now given to "fits of depression & despondency."[84]

The fate of Mary Taylor emphasizes the vulnerability of young mixed-blood girls, especially in the upper ranks of fur-trade society. They were being conditioned to become increasingly dependent upon white male protectors, who were supposed to treat ladies with "tender attention". Many fur traders continued to treat mixed-blood women in an honourable fashion, but there was a significant group centering around Governor Simpson who did not. The women who were thus abused were left with no recourse and their situation could be pitiful. The cavalier attitude shown toward native women by some incoming whites in the post-union period was influenced by the growth of racial prejudice which was general throughout the British Empire in the nineteenth-century. In Rupert's Land, racism was aggravated by the Protestant clergy whose attitudes reflected their belief in the superiority of everything British.[85]

In analysing fur-trade society it is important to differentiate racism along sex lines because prejudice affected males in different ways and usually earlier than it did their female counterparts. Indian men were never considered part of fur-trade society, but for a lengthy period, traders were prepared to intermarry freely with their women. The Indian woman eventually lost her place to the mixed-blood woman, although the speed with which this process took place varied according to rank and area. By the post-union period, it was generally considered unsuitable for an officer to have an Indian wife. Those few, who for personal reasons were tempted along these lines, met with criticism and were in danger of hindering their career prospects.[86]

By the nineteenth century, Indian women had lost considerable status, and it was the desire to prevent their daughters from experiencing the same fate which made fur-trade fathers such active promoters of their acculturation. Partly as a result of these efforts, a select group of carefully raised mixed-blood girls continued to be absorbed through marriage into the upper echelons of society, while at the same time their brothers were becoming the victims of racial prejudice which prevented their rising to the ranks of Company officers.[87] Open resentment flared when it was intimated to the sons of Hudson's Bay Company officers that they did not form part of "the first rank of society" and therefore could not expect to be considered desirable husbands for their cultivated female counterparts. In 1834, William Hallett, a son of former officer Henry Hallett, was much aggrieved when the Governor of Assiniboia rejected his suit for a daughter of Chief Factor Allan McDonell in favour of the son of a Selkirk settler. The girl evidently preferred Hallett, who came near to raising the whole of the mixed-blood population of the settlement in an attempt to rescue his sweetheart. The intended foray came to naught and the girl was duly married to the Scottish John Livingstone. The feelings of discrimination, however, were to have long-term repercussions contributing to the dislike which the mixed population of Red River increasingly bore toward Company rule.[88] Governor Simpson himself observed that the fact that the whites chose the best-looking mixed-blood girls produced everlasting jealousies.[89]

As racial prejudice grew and fur-trade society became more

consciously stratified with regard to women, even the position of acculturated mixed-blood females was threatened. Was such a woman, tainted with Indian blood, really the most suitable wife for the gentleman officer of Rupert's Land? The clergy did not think so. Although they felt it necessary to sanctify long-standing country unions, the Church of England missionaries, who were among the first to bring white wives to Rupert's Land, actively discouraged new officers from entering into mixed marriages. In 1835, when the Reverend Cockran heard it rumoured that James Hargrave might succumb to a mixed-blood damsel, he wrote to Hargrave in alarm, urging him to keep in view the noble example of Chief Factor Duncan Finlayson who almost alone among his contemporaries had managed to evade "the snare which has ruined many of our countrymen."[90] The clergy considered that white wives would have a welcome civilizing influence on society, while Company officers such as Simpson and Hargrave expressed the view that a genteel British bride would be an appropriate enhancement to their status. The introduction of white women into Rupert's Land was to have profound implications for fur-trade society: it gave the men a choice of marital partners that could prove detrimental to the position of mixed-blood women, even if they had become "quite English" in their manner.

8

"LOVELY, TENDER EXOTICS"

It was significant to the development of fur-trade society that until the early nineteenth century, virtually no white women had set foot in Rupert's Land. Had it been possible for traders to bring out their wives at an earlier date, it is doubtful whether intermarriage with native women would have been so extensive or marriage *à la façon du pays* so widely accepted. The only exception to this absence of European wives from the fur-trade scene was an ill-starred experiment on the Bay in the 1680s when the wife of Governor Henry Sergeant and her companion Mrs Maurice had been allowed to come out to Albany. The experience of the two British women had been frightful; not only had they to endure the harsh climate and primitive conditions, but they were subject to the French overland attack on the Hudson's Bay Company posts in 1686. Mrs Sergeant was nearly killed in the attack on Albany, and the London Committee conjectured that her husband's concern for her safety had made him reluctant to mount a spirited defence of the fort. Mrs Maurice suffered even greater hazard. In the summer of 1685, her father had anxiously demanded that his daughter be sent home, but the ship on which she sailed was lost in the ice. The survivors, while wintering at Fort Charles, were caught up in de Troyes's attack and Mrs Maurice was wounded. Evidently, the French surgeon was moved enough by the sight of a helpless woman to offer her some medical aid, and she was allowed to return to Albany.[1] In the light of these events the London Committee came to the conclusion that white women at their posts would constitute a burdensome nuisance. Sergeant and his "parcell of women" were recalled and a resolution was passed forbidding any female a passage to Hudson Bay.[2]

In well over a century, there is no evidence that this ruling was ever contravened, with the result that white women were restricted to the periphery of fur-trade life. A substantial number of Hudson's Bay Company employees left wives at home in Britain, and there is evidence that the enforced separation between husbands and wives imposed particular strains upon the women. The London Committee received numerous letters from wives applying for their husbands' wages or requesting that their husbands be sent home before the expiry of their contracts.[3] The anguish which one wife endured during her husband's absence was revealed by the pleas of Mrs John Ballenden to the Committee. This Orkney woman had married her husband, a Company officer of long standing, when he came home to Stromness on furlough in 1796. Two years later, Ballenden returned to York Factory, having contracted to serve for five more years. In April 1801, Mrs Ballenden wrote to the Committee, begging that her husband be allowed to come home by the first ship. She received a firm but courteous refusal; the Company secretary advised her to "wait patiently" with the thought that her husband's improved financial position would compensate for his long absence. Ballenden who was himself aggrieved at being kept from his "tender partner" eventually persuaded the Company to let him retire a year early.[4]

In spite of his British marriage, however, Ballenden also had a native wife and family on the Bay. This phenomenon of the "double family" was not unusual among eighteenth-century Hudson's Bay Company officers; several others such as James Isham and Andrew Graham married British women when they went home on furlough but then returned to the Bay to their native wives.[5] A husband, far away in Rupert's Land, might take another woman to assuage his loneliness, but if the wife left back home succumbed to the temptations of another male, the consequences could be disastrous. In 1681, the Committee was instructed to cut off payments to one Elizabeth Nalridge, as her husband had been informed that "she hath had severall Bastards since her said Husband went away".[6] Given the problems involved in being left behind, it is likely that many women, had they been given the opportunity, would have risked the hardships of life in the Indian Country in order to remain united with their menfolk.

It was not until 1806 that two white women managed to penetrate the fur-trade domain. Both did so on their own initiative, determined to follow their men; their stories are so unusual that they deserve particular mention. The first, a young Orkney lass whose real name was Isabel Gunn, arrived incognito at Moose Factory, in the summer of 1806.[7] She had disguised herself as a boy, signing on with the Company agent at Stromness under the name of John Fubbister. She was apparently intent upon being reunited with her lover, but fate was to keep them apart, for Fubbister was posted to Albany while her man was at Eastmain. During her first season at Albany, this Orkney girl performed the tasks required of a servant so well that she went undetected by her superiors. It seems probable, however, that the Orkney servants knew that a girl was in their midst. The Orkneymen were famous for their closeness and may have agreed to keep her identity a secret; certainly, John Scarth, an old Company hand who had been on the same ship from Stromness, was intimate with her. In the spring, Fubbister took an active part in the freighting operations to supply Albany's inland posts and later was part of the brigade sent to winter at Pembina under Hugh Heney.

Here, Fubbister "worked at anything & well like the rest of the men", until the morning of 29 December. On that day, the Hudson's Bay Company men who had been at the Pembina post of Alexander Henry for the holiday festivities were returning to their own quarters. Young Fubbister, apparently indisposed, asked to remain behind. Henry recorded the dramatic scene that followed:

> I was surprised at the fellow's demand; however, I told him to sit down and warm himself. I returned to my own room, where I had not been long before he sent one of my people, requesting the favor of speaking with me. Accordingly I stepped down to him, and was much surprised to find him extended on the hearth, uttering dreadful lamentations; he stretched out his hands toward me, and in piteous tones begged me to be kind to a poor, helpless, abandoned wretch, who was not of the sex I had supposed, but an unfortunate

*Forts of the Hudson's Bay and North West Companies at Pembina on
the Red River. By Peter Rindisbacher, c. 1822.*

Orkney girl, pregnant, and actually in childbirth. In saying this she opened her jacket, and displayed a pair of beautiful, round, white breasts. . . . In about an hour she was safely delivered of a fine boy, and that same day she was conveyed home in my cariole, where she soon recovered.[8]

Once the true sex of Fubbister became known, there was no question of her continuing in a male role. She was now called Mary and sent back to Albany in the spring. For the next year, she was employed in the traditional female occupation of washerwoman, a task at which she did not excel, and she may also have acted as a "nurse" to the pupils of the school that was established in 1808. Although reluctant to return to Orkney, Isabel Gunn alias John Fubbister was "discharged from your Honours Service" in September 1809 and sent home with her son by the annual ship. According to popular account, she suffered further misfortune and ended her life a vagrant.[9]

The story of the French-Canadian Marie-Anne Gaboury, while equally as full of adventure, had a much happier ending.[10] This young woman from the village of Maskinongé near Three Rivers had worked for several years as an assistant housekeeper for an abbé. Mademoiselle Gaboury found her life completely changed after her marriage to the freeman trapper Jean-Baptiste Lajimonière in April 1806. Lajimonière had come home the previous fall apparently with the intention of settling down, but when spring break-up came the call of the West proved too strong. He told his new bride that he must return to the Indian Country and might be gone for several years. After all efforts to persuade him to change his mind failed, Marie-Anne decided that her only course was to go with her husband no matter what the hardships. In the summer of 1806, the couple made the long trip with the Nor'Wester brigade to Pembina; here Lajimonière joined the freemen, exposing his wife to a nomadic hunting life which taxed her courage and resourcefulness. For the birth of her first child, Marie-Anne sought the shelter of the Hudson's Bay Company post, where a daughter Reine was born on 6 January 1807. In the spring, the Lajimonières left Pembina by canoe for Fort des Prairies (Fort Edmonton), travelling with three other French-Canadian freemen, all of whom had Cree wives. Marie-Anne was grateful for the company of these women and wisely adopted some of their ways, such as carrying her baby in an Indian cradle. As a freeman's wife, Marie-Anne had to endure the discomforts of living on the open prairie for many months; on occasion, she was left alone in camp and was terrified by visits from strange bands of Indians. One of her most hair-raising experiences occurred in August 1808 when she was again pregnant. She was riding her horse, a spirited buffalo runner, with young Reine tucked snugly in one of the saddle bags when she suddenly came upon a herd of buffalo. The horse immediately gave chase and the young mother could only cling desperately to the horse's neck until she was finally rescued by her husband. Later that night, Marie-Anne gave birth to a son, nicknamed La Prairie; within three days she was on her horse again riding back to Fort Edmonton. Marie-Anne and her children were objects of much interest to the Indians; in fact, one Blackfoot woman so coveted her little son that she reputedly tried to kidnap him.

Lajimonière, who was anxious to give his growing family a home, welcomed the news that a permanent settlement was to be established at Red River and returned to the area in 1811. Owing to the rivalry between the fur companies, the colony in its first years was a continual scene of conflict. In the summer of 1815, the settlement was destroyed for the first time by the Nor'Westers and the Métis, but the surviving band of Selkirk settlers managed to re-establish it in the fall under the leadership of Colin Robertson. In October, Lajimonière, at the request of Robertson, undertook the arduous task of carrying dispatches to Lord Selkirk in Montreal to inform him of the state of the colony. It was arranged that Marie-Anne and her four children would be kept at the Hudson's Bay Company post in his absence; in the event of his death, the Company would pay his wife an annuity of seven pounds for the next ten years. The hardy Lajimonière succeeded in getting through to Lord Selkirk, but on his return he was waylaid by the Nor'Westers and held captive at Fort William. There he heard ominous reports of the massacre of Seven Oaks and the capture of the Hudson's Bay Company post by the Nor'Westers. He feared his family might be dead. Marie-Anne had, in fact, fled with her children down the river and found refuge with Chief Peguis and his Ojibwa band who had sided with the settlers in the conflict. She was finally reunited with her husband after he returned to Red River in the fall of 1816. Lajimonière settled his family on the east bank of the Red River on a grant of land which he had received from Lord Selkirk. Madame Lajimonière, a devout Catholic, was of great assistance to the priests when they arrived in the settlement, but there were times in the difficult years of getting established when she wished her husband would take the family back to Lower Canada. The destiny of the Lajimonière family, however, was tied up in the Catholic, Métis community of Red River. Marie-Anne was to live there for over fifty years, and through her daughter, Julie, she became the maternal grandmother of Louis Riel.

Marie-Anne Lajimonière had the distinction of being the first white woman to settle permanently in Western Canada. The founding of the Red River Colony, however, provided for the arrival of an unprecedented number of white women. Eighteen women were among the second party of Selkirk colonists who arrived at York Factory in the summer of 1812, and there were at least twenty in the next group, who were forced to pass a wretched winter at Fort Churchill before undertaking the long trip to Red River. Their coming was significant — as Indian captive and trader John Tanner succinctly observed upon reaching the settlement: "[There] I saw for the first time in many years since I had become a man, a white woman."[11] Understandably, since many of the traders were of Scottish origin themselves, the daughters of the Selkirk settlers were looked upon as a promising source of wives. In 1820, the young clerk Donald Ross wed Mary, a daughter of Alexander McBeath who had come from Kildonan in 1813, and took her to live at Norway House.[12] Another McBeath daughter, Christy, while on a visit to her sister's home in 1824, captivated visiting trader Robert McVicar. There was no minister at Norway House to marry the couple, but on 18 July, they solemnly pledged in front of witnesses to perform "all the relative duties of man and wife" and to incur "all the obligations which the institution of Matrimony enjoins" in accordance with the laws of Scotland. Later at Fort Chipewyan in 1827, the

McVicars had a Church of England ceremony performed by Captain Franklin.[13]

The number of white wives in Rupert's Land was augmented by a group of indigent Swiss townsfolk who arrived in the colony in 1821. Although their young women had primarily been intended as wives for the soldier-settlers of the disbanded de Meuron regiment, they attracted considerable interest from fur traders, young and old.[14] In 1822 after the death of his mixed-blood wife, Chief Factor John Clarke decided to take the Swiss-born Marianne Treutter for a wife. For this old Nor'Wester, the custom of the country was good enough even for a white woman; his refusal to have a church marriage provoked acid comment from the Reverend John West on the need to check the "vicious" habits of the traders: "One of the Chief Factors avowedly a married man takes with him a Swiss girl into the Interior without censure from Council."[15]

To set "a good example" Chief Factor Donald McKenzie took a white wife shortly after he became governor of the colony in 1825. His choice fell on the twenty-year-old daughter of a poor Swiss "gentleman", Miss Adelgonde Droz, who had initially entered McKenzie's household as governess to his three mixed-blood children. McKenzie had "turned off" his native wife several years earlier,[16] and in his new bride, he felt he had won a woman who possessed many more of the qualities esteemed in a wife. In describing Adelgonde to a friend, McKenzie revealed important clues to the qualities that nineteenth-century officers sought in a marital partner. "Strict and exemplary in her conduct", his wife was "the acknowledged model of the sex in this quarter". She was devout, "never missing a sacrament by any chance", and commendably industrious, being "expert with her hands in all that females are accustomed to perform in the continental part of Europe from the bonnet to the slippers". McKenzie did express some reservations about her beauty and intellect. His bride was hardly "a muse for wit", but this, he added, might not be a disadvantage: "for my own part, I esteem her also in consideration of her habit taciturnity for you may rely upon it that nothing can give greater comfort to a husband than the satisfaction of having a wife who is nearly mute."[17]

A Swiss colonist, centre, with his wife and children. From a sketch entitled "Colonists on the Red River in North America" by Peter Rindisbacher, c. 1825.

With the Red River Colony providing the first convenient pool from which to select a white wife, it is suprising that there was not more of a rush on the settlers' daughters. However, several factors operated to check such a development. The Selkirk settlers were reluctant to integrate with the fur traders, whom they probably considered to be tainted with barbarism; they generally kept their daughters for their own kind and remained a close homogeneous group. The Swiss colonists, on the other hand, appear to have been more accommodating, but their mass exodus after the flood of 1826 robbed the traders of further wives from this quarter. By this time Governor Simpson had become sufficiently alarmed by the number of marriages that had taken place to feel it was necessary to stop the trend from spreading among the lesser officers and servants. Native families had cost the Company considerable inconvenience and expense, and the situation would become even worse if the men began to take settlers' daughters into the wilds of the interior. White women would seriously hamper the mobility of their husbands:

> ... it not only frustrates the intentions of the Company and executors, in respect of the Colony, but is a clog on the gentlemen who take them, who cannot do their duty or be disposable, with European women in their train, native women are a serious incumbrance, but with women from the civilized world, it is quite impossible the gentlemen can do their duty.[18]

Simpson began to pressure junior officers to forgo marriage altogether, or at least until the expiry of their first contract.[19]

The Governor felt that, in Red River and perhaps in some of the larger, more accessible posts, the Company's senior officials might enhance their station by taking an English lady for a wife. He had welcomed the arrival of Captain R. P. Pelly and his genteel British wife to the settlement in 1823, anticipating that the governorship of Pelly and his lady would set a higher civilized tone.[20] Although Simpson was concerned that the officers' wives be white, the colour of their skin was only one prerequisite — they must also be *ladies*. Here the daughters of Red River colonists were seen to be regrettably deficient by men with aspirations, such as Simpson and Hargrave. Whatever McKenzie might think of his wife, Simpson considered Adelgonde to be lacking in the accomplishments necessary in a governor's lady; he disapproved of McKenzie's choice, describing her as "a silly, ignorant thing, whose common place wise saws . . . are worse than a blister."[21] And although the daughters of poor Scottish crofters might have the advantage of being white, they were found lamentably lacking in ladylike refinements. Mary Ross was criticized by some officers for being "coarse in mind & natural taste, uneducated & unpolished."[22] Thus, when Governor Simpson and several of his colleagues decided it was time to take a white wife, they did not look to the settlers' daughters of Red River.

In 1829, Governor Simpson and his close friend Chief Factor John George McTavish went on furlough to Great Britain. Although both men had had close attachments with mixed-blood women in Rupert's Land, their intimate private

Kilakotah, a Clatsop woman and country wife of Chief Factor James McMillan until he severed ties with her in 1829. She later married Louis Labonté.

correspondence reveals that for most of this year they were preoccupied with the search for a suitable wife.[23] What they envisaged was a wife who would live up to their middle-class ideal of womanhood — a lady pure and devout, of beauty, genteel accomplishment, and dutiful obedience.[24] In their quest for a "lovely, tender exotic", the two officers were joined by Chief Factor James McMillan who was also on furlough, having come out from the Columbia District where he had severed his ties with his Chinook wife Kilakotah.[25] At first the fur traders, unaccustomed to the society of refined young ladies, were ill at ease in the intricacies of genteel courtship. To McTavish who was surveying the field in Scotland, Simpson wrote encouragingly:

> I see you are something like myself, shy with the fair, we should not be so much so with the Browns . . . muster courage "a faint heart never won a fair Lady".[26]

While the men were apprehensive about their ability to catch the fancy of a pretty "nymph", as Hudson's Bay Company officers they could offer social status and economic security which could be compensation enough. Such was the light in

M. Porritt

Frances Simpson.

which wealthy Nor'Westers, retiring to Canada a few decades earlier, had been viewed:

> The ladies of Montreal and Quebec are immediately on the <u>qui vive</u>; invitations are numerous, the wealthy North-Wester is universally admired; bronzed features, Oxford-grey hairs, and a <u>dégagé tout ensemble</u> impart peculiar interest to his appearance.[27]

In McTavish's case, only the prospect of having to spend some years in Rupert's Land deterred a certain "Miss B." from marrying him, but early in 1830, the old Nor'Wester won the consent of Miss Catherine Turner, a daughter of the late Keith Turner of Turnerhall, Aberdeenshire. The couple was married on 22 February in Edinburgh.[28] Two days later, George Simpson also brought his matrimonial pursuits to a successful conclusion. During the first part of his stay, Simpson had been

Gordon Konantz

Governor George Simpson.

too ill to do much courting; in December he inquired of McTavish "if you have any fair cousin or acquaintance likely to suit an invalid like me". His friend scarcely had time to consider when a few weeks later the Governor wrote ecstatically, "Would you believe it? I am in Love".[29] He had not had to venture outside the family circle but had become infatuated with his beautiful and accomplished eighteen-year-old cousin Frances, who had been a child when he had begun his career as a clerk in her father's London firm. At first, it was decided that the marriage should await Simpson's return from Rupert's Land in the fall of 1830, but the prospect of such a separation prompted him to persuade her parents to give their consent to an immediate wedding. The Simpsons were married on 24 February at St Mary's Church in Middlesex and embarked on a short honeymoon to Tunbridge Wells. The McTavishes hastened to London to join the Simpsons for the sailing to North America. They were to have been joined by James McMillan and his Scottish bride of a few months (the former Miss Eleanor McKinley), but Mrs McMillan's health was not up to the voyage. McMillan proceeded alone to Red River to take charge of the experimental farm; his wife came out via York Factory the following summer, bringing a baby daughter.[30]

Mrs Simpson and Mrs McTavish were the first British women ever to make the long canoe trip from Montreal into the interior. Fur traders expressed astonishment that "ladies" should undertake the journey, but such precautions were taken to minimize the hazards and inconveniences of canoe travel that the expedition took on the air of a genteel camping trip.[31] The two women enjoyed each other's company only as far as Michipicoten, as McTavish was not returning to York Factory but taking charge of Moose Factory, the headquarters of the Southern Department. As the Simpsons proceeded through Rupert's Land, the presence of the Governor's lady made a great stir, especially in the upper echelons of fur-trade society. The officers' behaviour toward Mrs Simpson was representative of the worshipful attitude which was adopted toward "the lady" in nineteenth-century Victorian England.[32] Significantly, as Frances Simpson made her progress from post to post, she was not introduced to a single native wife, while the officers themselves were assiduous in their attempts to appear hospitable and refined.

For some old traders, this was a taxing business. Mrs Simpson was amused by the efforts of Chief Trader Thomas McMurray who undertook to escort her on a tour of the fort and garden when the party reached Lac La Pluie:

> ... old & weather beaten as he was, he surpassed all the Gentlemen I had met with in these Wilds, as a Lady's Man; but altho' our walk did not occupy an hour, it quite exhausted all his fine speeches, and the poor man seemed as much relieved when we returned to the house ... as if he had just been freed from an attack of the Night-Mare.[33]

The visit of the Governor's lady made such an impression that shortly afterward the post was renamed Fort Frances in her honour. Chief Factor John Stuart, in particular, extolled the civilizing influence which the presence of Mrs Simpson would have on the Indian Country; she was a divine creature whose coming heralded improved standards of morality and gentility. He rhapsodized:

> The very first sight of her on landing at Bas de la Riviere strongly reminded me of the Picture Milton has drawn of our first Mother — Grace was in all her steps — heaven in her Eye — In all her gestures Dignity & love, while everything I have seen of her since — seems to denote her such as first Lord Lyttleton represents his first Lady to have been — "Polite as all her life in courts had been — Yet good as she the world had never seen."[34]

In Red River, the "fascinating accomplishments" of Mrs Simpson imparted a whole new air of "high life & gaiety" to society. The Christmas season of 1830 featured select parties given by the Governor, highlights of which were his wife's performances on the recently imported pianoforte.[35]

Regardless of the enthusiasm evinced for the delightful Governor's lady, fur-trade society could not help but be shocked at the callous manner in which Simpson and McTavish had betrayed their mixed-blood consorts. Neither of them had the decency to follow the old custom of "turning off" where at least arrangements were made for a former partner before a new one was taken. Simpson had left Margaret Taylor at Bas de la Rivière under the charge of Chief Factor John Stuart whose country wife was her sister Mary. At the end of August 1829, Margaret had given birth to her second son, later christened John McKenzie Simpson.[36] The glowing reports that the obsequious Stuart wrote to the Governor about Margaret and her little ones emphasized that they were anxious for his return and indicated that there was not an inkling of Simpson's intended course.[37] When Simpson did return with his lovely English bride, Stuart must have been forewarned to have his former partner out of the way.

Stuart and several other officers, notably Donald McKenzie, dared not openly criticize the Governor but they could not restrain themselves from denouncing McTavish for his cruelty to Nancy McKenzie, his country wife of long standing. Stuart, who had taken a paternal interest in Nancy ever since she was a child, wrote bitterly to the former Nor'Wester:

> . . . what could be your aim in discarding her whom you clasped to your bosom in virgin purity and had for 17 Years with you, She was the Wife of your Choice and has born you seven Children, now Stigmatized with ignominy . . . if with a view of domestick happiness you have thus acted, I fear the Aim has been Missed and that remorse will be your portion for life . . . I think it is well . . . our correspondence may cease.[38]

Nancy, or Matooskie to use her Indian name, had had no idea that McTavish would not return; in fact, Hargrave had written to him that all spring Madame and "the little Madrauli-kins" had been paying "a visit to the riverside to see where the road shall open for you."[39] To be "delicately" informed instead of her abandonment caused poor Matooskie such distress that even Hargrave sympathized with her plight. "The first blow was dreadful to witness" he wrote to her uncle Donald McKenzie.[40] McKenzie and Stuart, in trying to insist that Nancy should receive at least a large financial settlement to compensate for the years she had devoted to McTavish, soon found themselves at "hot war" with Governor Simpson who was now manoeuvring to settle the situation by marrying the two mixed-blood women to Company servants. With the promise of a dowry of two hundred pounds, Pierre Leblanc, a respectable carpenter, went courting Nancy McKenzie, who had little choice but to accept him. They were formally married in February 1831. Later in March, Margaret Taylor was married to Amable Hogue.[41]

Simpson, aware of the unpopularity of his action, derived some comfort from the fact that a number of other officers were prepared to follow suit when tempted by the right opportunity. In 1831, Chief Factor William Connolly, who maintained that it was "a most unnatural proceeding" to desert the mother of one's children, had taken his Cree wife Suzanne and family with him when posted to Eastern Canada. Within a year he had repudiated his Indian partner and officially married his attractive cousin Julia Woolrich. While it did little to assuage Suzanne's bitterness, Connolly continued to provide for her and eventually arranged for her to be sent to Red River where she was supported in the Catholic convent until her death in 1862.[42]

The status now attached to having a white wife was considerable. One can speculate that it was indeed the formal bonds of church marriage which protected the position of some of the native wives of the retired chief factors in Red River. Upon the death of their native spouses, most of the colony's retired fur traders took to marrying British schoolmistresses. The first was old James Bird who, in January 1835 shortly after the death of his Indian wife, married the widowed Mary Lowman. The couple's whirlwind marriage was considered in bad taste, especially since Mrs Lowman had left the girls' school without a teacher; but some contemporaries noted approvingly that Bird had become "a reformed man in manner & vigor since his marriage to a white wife."[43] About a year after the death of his Ojibwa wife in 1838, retired Chief Factor Robert Logan married Mrs Bird's former travelling companion Sarah Ingham, who was also a widow.[44] When Miss Anne Armstrong, an aspiring governess, had first arrived in Rupert's Land in 1835, Hargrave had predicted that this "most amiable young lady" might one day "comfort a desolate and longing trader". However, her eventual marriage to recently widowed J. P. Pruden in December 1839 was not destined to be harmonious. Evidently the attempts of this fastidious lady to reform a rough old Indian trader provoked serious discord. It became common knowledge that they were like

> . . . cat & dog, on each side of the hearth, the one spattering & the other snarling . . . certain it is, that their tempers are not suited for each other, & that they will never live happily together.[45]

Chief Factor John Charles grieved over his mixed-blood wife Jane who had died of tuberculosis, but after a few years he continued the trend by marrying Margaret Macallum in February 1844. She had come out from England previously to assist her brother John with the running of the Red River Academy.[46] Of the early British schoolmistresses, only the eccentric Miss Allan failed to marry into Red River society; her

Mrs J. P. Pruden, the former Anne Armstrong, whose attempts to reform her trader husband led to discord.

prospects were apparently terminated with the sudden death of the "old Blue" James Sutherland in 1844.[47]

Throughout the 1830s, the overseas quest for a white wife remained in vogue. As one old trader put it, "the novelty of getting H. Bay stocked with European Ladys" was bound to prompt other officers to avail themselves of their furlough "with no other view than that of getting Spliced to some fair Belinda."[48] This thought was certainly foremost in the mind of newly commissioned Chief Trader John Tod when he departed for Britain in the fall of 1834, having severed his ties with a native wife in New Caledonia. His search was short, for on board ship was Miss Eliza Waugh, who had accompanied Mrs Mary Jones to Red River several years before as a companion and lady's maid. Miss Waugh was reputedly a fine, lively Welsh girl; she had attracted the admiration of several officers in the settlement but apparently did not like life in Red River. Tod, however, managed to win over Miss Eliza, and the couple were married shortly after the ship arrived in England. Permission was granted for Tod to bring his wife back out to Rupert's Land the following year.[49]

It was not until 1837 that those two "paragons of virtue" Chief Factor Duncan Finlayson and Chief Trader James Hargrave were at last free to pursue their intentions of marrying British ladies. Hargrave, while touring in western Scotland, paid a visit to the home of his friends, the young clerks William and Dugald Mactavish, at Campbelton where their father was sheriff. He had not been at Kilchrist House long before he decided that their elder sister Letitia would make an admirable wife: of good family, "her conduct as a daughter and a sister has ever been of the 1st order", and her education had been carefully finished.[50] The call of duty interrupted Hargrave's matrimonial plans, for he was called back to York Factory unexpectedly before he had time to present his official suit. Both proposal and acceptance were conveyed by post, and Hargrave after an impatient season returned to marry Letitia on 8 January 1840.[51] In the meantime, Duncan Finlayson had successfully courted another of the Simpson girls — Isobel, the elder sister of the Governor's wife. On 26 May 1838, this dignified trader recorded in his diary in formal Victorian style:

> I have this day been made the Happiest Man on earth by the declaration from the Sweet lips of the amiable & accomplished Miss Simpson that she would be mine forever.[52]

The couple was married in November, but Isobel was not well enough to accompany her husband to Rupert's Land when he returned to assume the governorship of Assiniboia in 1839. It was arranged that she should come out the following summer with the Hargraves to York Factory where she was met by her husband.[53] The marriages of Hargrave and Finlayson were greeted with approbation throughout the Indian Country; many compliments were bestowed upon "the Scots Bluebell" and "the English Rose".[54]

Indeed, fur-trade society in Rupert's Land during the mid-decades of the nineteenth century presents a fascinating microcosm for the study of "the lady" in society. When set against the background of the Western Canadian frontier, not only are the attitudes of the men thrown into sharp relief, but the limitations which this ideal imposed upon women are starkly revealed. It is evident that many Hudson's Bay Company officers, even those who remained loyal to their native wives, were sincere in their admiration of the attributes of "a lady". As James Hargrave, hearing of the delights of Frances Simpson, enthused:

> There is certainly a charm in an accomplished young lady's society which we rough fur traders can only appreciate . . ., and peculiarly so when beauty, youth & talent are joined, as in this instance, to that sweet affability which makes all around so perfectly at their ease in her company.[55]

While their charms were undoubtedly exaggerated by the deficiencies of native women in this regard, British ladies were also regarded as "the delicate flowers of civilization", a powerful symbol to white men, especially on a frontier where the pull of Indian culture had been strong.[56] The fur traders were full of praise for the British lady who would brave the wilds of Rupert's Land to share her husband's lot. James Douglas wrote to his friend Hargrave upon learning that the fair Letitia had consented to share his life at York Factory: "What a debt of gratitude you incur, through such heroic devotion, which a lifetime of the tenderest attentions can hardly repay."[57] Hargrave was most grateful for the way in which his wife endured life on the bleak shores of Hudson Bay for over ten years. In 1851, he wrote to his wife, who was visiting in Scotland prior to coming out to their new home at Sault Ste Marie, that she was to reward herself with the purchase of "a fine silk velvet gown worthy of being worn by such a wife as you have been to me."[58]

Yet Letitia Hargrave was almost alone among the British wives in making a satisfactory adjustment to fur-trade life.

Douglas and some of the other traders had worried, with justification, that such "tender plants" might not survive being transplanted to so alien a soil. Life in Rupert's Land required considerable physical and psychological adaptation, and the British lady was likely to lack (and would not be encouraged to develop) the bodily strength and mental attitude necessary to make a successful transition. It was ironic that, while the fur traders admired the delicate mould in which a young woman such as Frances Simpson had been fashioned, it was this state which jeopardized her ability to accept life in Red River. As was predicted, the fate of most of the lovely, tender exotics was "to pine and languish in the desert".[59] In fact, the rapid decline in health suffered by some of these ladies was so serious that they soon had to be removed from the Indian Country. The promise of things to come had been seen as early as 1823 when Captain Pelly brought out his British wife to Red River. Every effort was made to ensure the lady's material comfort, but the high hopes that were entertained for Pelly's governorship were dashed by his wife's deteriorating health. She was "a delicate women" who never seemed to be quite at home in the colony, observed Simpson. By 1825, it was apparent that her life was in danger if she did not return to England for medical attention; her husband, feeling that she could never live happily in Red River, felt compelled to resign and they both departed by the fall ship.[60]

In looking at the difficulties suffered by the fur traders' white wives, it is important to emphasize that for them life in Rupert's Land had a very different meaning than it did for their husbands. For the men, it had become a familiar, if somewhat rough world of work where the camaraderie of associates was particularly valued. For white women, however, it meant moving to a strange and physically inferior environment and severing the social and domestic attachments upon which their lives had previously been based.[61] They had not even the prospect of a useful role to play in the fur trade, as did native women. Most of the officers' wives had little desire to leave Britain. They came out to Rupert's Land under the conviction that it was "a wife's most sacred and hallowed duty" to follow and share the fortunes of her husband,[62] but this did little to alleviate the wrench of parting and their loneliness in unfamiliar surroundings.

Frances Simpson's diary reveals that she had had a sheltered upbringing and that she suffered intensely from being separated from the large, affectionate family circle at Grove House in London:

> I can scarcely trust myself to think of the pang which shot thro' my heart, on taking the last "Farewell" of my beloved Father, who was equally overcome at the first parting from any of his children — suffice it to say, that this was to me a moment of bitter sorrow.[63]

Her delicate constitution began to decline immediately. Shortly after the ship sailed from Liverpool in March 1830, the young woman succumbed to such a violent attack of sea-sickness that her husband was prepared to bribe the captain to put her ashore, but stormy weather prevented the landing attempt. She recovered to enjoy being entertained by society in New York and Montreal, and the canoe trip west, but Mrs Simpson found little about her new home in the tiny colony of Red River to cheer her. She was the Governor's lady, provided with the best that the settlement could offer, but her position only accentuated her feelings of isolation and loneliness. She was restricted to seeing the few white wives of the men who were most prominent in society, but even among these, little real companionship could be found. The well-bred Mrs Jones and Mrs McMillan lived too far away for regular visits while Mrs McKenzie and Mrs Cockran were scarcely qualified to become her intimate friends. Simpson was particularly disparaging of Mrs Cockran who had been a scullery maid before marrying a missionary and "shines only when talking of elbow Grease & the scouring of pots & pans."[64]

If Frances Simpson's situation was unenviable, the prospect of being the only white woman at an isolated fur-trade post was even worse. Such fears may have contributed to the unhappy fate of John Tod's wife, Eliza. Tod was to have taken his wife to the Columbia District in 1838, but she began to show signs of mental disorder even before they reached Red River. As a result, the couple was allowed to winter at Bas de la Rivière, where it was hoped a season's quiet rest would restore the nerves

Provincial Archives of British Columbia

Mrs John Tod, née Eliza Waugh.

of the young woman who understandably "felt agitated in being drawn into scenes new to her in almost every point of view."[65] By spring her condition, which had been compounded by motherhood, was so serious that Tod would have taken her to England had he not been unexpectedly required to take charge of Oxford House. During her stay at this post, Mrs Tod became so deranged that it was feared that she would do violence to herself and her child. Tod could get no help to look after her, as the superstitious natives were terrified of the mad woman, but he did manage to take her out to England the following year. Eliza Tod was eventually placed in an asylum, and her husband, who returned to the Columbia, never saw her again.[66] It appears that years of isolation could take their toll even of a strong women such as Mrs Donald Ross who was, for much of her life, the only white wife at Norway House. Shortly after her

Mrs John Tod, fourth wife of Chief Trader John Tod. When Tod returned to the Columbia, he took as his country wife, Sophia Lolo, daughter of a prominent mixed-blood guide at Fort Kamloops.

husband's death, though the family was now living in Red River, she went mad, obsessed with the notion that her children would be massacred by Indians.[67]

Apart from the isolation of fur-trade life, the accommodation for British ladies at the various posts could not help but fall short of the standards to which they were accustomed. Nevertheless the senior officers tried to provide their wives with as much home comfort as possible. Simpson, who had an impressive stone residence built at Lower Fort Garry, began quite a trend for the importation of refinements such as "Piano Forts, Turkey Carpets, and Zenumbra Lamps."[68] Letitia Hargrave's first sight of the uninviting scene at York Factory caused her "to turn my back on the company & cry myself sick", but she eventually became more reconciled when settled in her own separate house, made snug with imported rugs and curtains and "a 1st rate square piano".[69] The wives of chief factors were not, of course, expected to do any menial tasks and were provided with servants. At York Mrs Hargrave had a personal maid, and later an old family servant, Mary Clarke, came out to help her. Several Indian women were hired to do the washing and scrubbing, and the meals were prepared and supervised by the fort's Orkney cook and the old French-Canadian butler.[70]

The wives of the Company's senior officers, however, occupied a position of privilege. The white wives of lesser men could find the lack of comfort and privacy to which they were subject quite taxing. There can be no doubt that Herbert Beaver's unseemly conduct at Fort Vancouver was compounded by his concern for his wife's welfare. Mrs Beaver was constantly complaining: the food was not fit for "civilized beings", their rooms were ill-appointed and too noisy, and the courtyard too muddy for a lady to venture out. Worse still in Beaver's eyes was the fact that his wife was forced to demean herself by doing domestic chores, since they were not provided with suitable servants.[71] In the late 1840s at York Factory, the clerk Robert Clouston was appalled by the poor accommodation provided for himself and his wife Jessy, a daughter of Chief Factor Donald Ross. Although Jessy had been born at Norway House, she had been educated at the schools in Red River to live in a ladylike manner. "Fancy, a woman brought up as Jessy has been", fumed Clouston, having to live in one cold, small room adjoining the general office, which was the center of all the comings and goings of the fort. The Cloustons also lacked the aid of a servant, although after his wife became ill Mrs Hargrave lent them the part-time services of her Indian maid.[72]

Predictably, many of the health problems suffered by white wives related directly to pregnancy and childbirth, the time when they missed most the solace of female relatives and the security of familiar surroundings. The post surgeons did their best to help the women, but the lack of more expert medical attention was frequently lamented. Frances Simpson was much treated by the two doctors of the colony, yet she deteriorated rapidly as her first pregnancy advanced in the spring of 1831. Simpson was distraught at having to leave his wife to attend the annual council meeting at York; he hurried back to Red River in time for the birth of a son which the mother barely survived.[73] Chief Factor McMillan's wife was also subject to constant ill health; after the birth of a daughter in the spring of 1833, her husband actually began to despair of her life.[74] Unfortunately, prejudice prevented white women from utilizing what might have been a source of relief in their confinements. The mixed-blood wives of the officers were unable to convince their white sisters of the effectiveness of the native position for childbirth which involved squatting down beside the bed. Letitia Hargrave recorded that Mrs Gladman was astonished when the doctor complimented her on the delivery of her first child; the mixed-blood woman thought the whole process had been unnecessarily difficult.[75]

If they survived childbirth, the women were constantly worried about the welfare of their children. Infant mortality was something to be expected in the nineteenth century, but it seemed particularly cruel to have to consign a little one to the frozen wastes of Rupert's Land. Letitia Hargrave's greatest sorrow while at York Factory was the death of her second baby in December 1842. One is left to imagine the feelings of Christy McVicar as she suffered through the birth and death of her first child, born in the fall of 1825 at Fort Resolution on the shores of Great Slave Lake.[76] Frances Simpson's delicate state of health was seriously undermined by the death of her infant son in the spring of 1832. Within the next year, Simpson realized that his despondent, ailing wife could not survive in the inhospitable climate of Rupert's Land:

> She has no Society, no Friend, no Relative here but myself, she cannot move about wt. me on my different Journeys and I cannot leave her in the hands of strangers . . . some of them very unfeeling.[77]

He, therefore, took her home to England in the fall of 1833. The Governor's lady never returned to Red River, although she did come out to live at Lachine about a decade later.[78]

All in all, the desire of the Hudson's Bay Company officers to have "a lovely, tender exotic" to grace hearth and home did not prove successful. Only Letitia Hargrave lived for any length of time in Rupert's Land. While her success may be attributed to a hardier Scottish constitution, her access to the best of fur-trade life, and the presence of her brother William at York Factory, she welcomed the prospect of her husband's posting to Sault Ste Marie in 1851.[79] The concern of the officers for their white wives prompted them to retire as soon as possible (as did Robert McVicar and Donald McKenzie in the early 1830s) or at least to seek a more amenable station in Eastern Canada where their families could be nearer civilization. In 1835, John G. McTavish was transferred to the Lake of Two Mountains near Montreal,[80] and neither McMillan nor Finlayson stayed long in Red River. For Isobel Finlayson, life at Lower Fort Garry had unpleasant associations with her sister's unhappy sojourn there, and she too suffered from homesickness and ill health. Finlayson, who considered his wife "too tender a plant to be needlessly exposed to a Siberian climate", was delighted to relinquish the governorship of Assiniboia and remove to the Company depot at Lachine in 1844.[81]

Of all the white women who entered fur-trade society in the first half of the nineteenth century, those who adapted best were not the true "exotics", but women whose background had prepared them for hardship or women for whom life in Rupert's Land promised social and material advancement. Both Mrs Donald Ross, a daughter of a Scottish crofter, and Mrs William Cockran, a former maid-servant, apparently possessed the stamina and resourcefulness necessary to be successful pioneer wives. Through marriage, they also experienced a considerable rise in social status. Mrs Ross was highly conscious of her rank as a chief factor's wife, while Mrs Cockran, as wife of the Hudson's Bay Company chaplain, deemed herself one of the pillars of Red River society. Upon marrying retired chief factors, the British schoolmistresses gained access to the best of Red River society. It was conjectured, probably with some justification, that money and position were the primary reasons why a "fresh morsel" such as Mrs Lowman would put up with such an "old shrivelled bag of dry bones" as James Bird: "A Widow with Two Children & without anything to depend upon, was not likely to let such an opportunity slip of getting £3,000 secured to her."[82] Shortly after her marriage, it was observed that Mrs Bird was a clever woman and "fast rising to the top of the tree."[83] Both she and the new Mrs Pruden were anxious to establish their position as the leaders of Red River society.

White women brought a heightened class-consciousness to Rupert's Land. As the "old Blue" James Sutherland commented:

> We have now here some rich old fellows that have acquired large fortunes in the service, have got married to European females and cut a dash, have introduced a system of extravagance into the place that is followed by all that can afford it.[84]

White women, in intruding upon a society which had previously been limited to native women, were also active agents in the growth of racial prejudice. In a colony which offered the prospect of social mobility, the desire for status and its material trappings was bound to be intense; in Rupert's Land, the increasing social rivalry which can be seen among the women was compounded by the question of race.

9

A QUESTION OF BLOOD

In various parts of the British Empire, a direct relationship can be traced between the growth of racial prejudice and the arrival of white women on the scene. With the appearance of women of their own race, the fur traders began to exhibit prejudices toward native females which had previously been dormant. In the words of James Hargrave, "this influx of white faces has cast a still deeper shade over the faces of our Brunettes in the eyes of many."[1] In fact, the question of colour became an issue for the first time. Traditionally, native wives, apart from the European names often bestowed upon them,[2] had been referred to as "my woman", "the mother of my children", "the old lady" or "the guid wife", terms which reveal no concern for their racial origin. Now the derogatory word "squaw" was increasingly applied to native wives, while Simpson employed a variety of uncomplimentary terms which emphasized colour: "Brown Jug", "swarthy idol" and "bit of brown."[3] Some of the officers also appear to have operated on the premise, seen in other parts of the empire, that care must be taken to keep white ladies from having any contact with native people. Theoretically their delicacy and innocence would be endangered if exposed to the corrupting influence of "savages".[4]

White women showed little inclination to approach their native sisters in terms of equality or friendship. In addition to feeling racially and morally superior to native women, British women expressed an active hostility toward "squaws" because they feared their competition for white husbands. In Rupert's Land, in contrast to other parts of the empire, sexual relations with native women had been sanctioned by a recognized marriage rite which had been upheld and widely practised even by men of the highest rank. Thus, a British woman might find what she regarded as her legitimate place — that of wife and mother — taken by a woman whom she regarded as her inferior in every way. It is significant that perhaps the most overt hostility to native women was voiced by lower-class white women who were highly sensitive to the fact that they might easily be by-passed in favour of a native wife.

An unusual example of the prejudice which lower-class white women showed toward native women was seen in the behaviour of Jane Barnes, a coarse, illiterate barmaid from Portsmouth, England, who in 1813 had accompanied Nor'Wester Donald McTavish on his long ocean voyage to the Columbia. The Englishwoman's position was precarious, because shortly after her arrival, McTavish discarded her in favour of a Chinook woman. Alexander Henry was then moved to offer Jane "protection", but most of the other Nor'Westers found her attempts to play the refined lady ridiculous and resented her disparaging and hypocritical remarks about the native women.[5] Several months after her arrival, the barmaid was again alone when Henry drowned. Her only choices were to become the wife of the son of the Chinook chief, who promised her all the luxury his station would allow,[6] or to return to England. Miss Barnes chose the latter course, deeming herself too good for any Indian, and on the way home via Canton she, at last, secured a husband in the ship's commander.[7]

In fur-trade society, racism compounded the rivalry which has traditionally existed between women when they are trapped by a social structure in which a woman's lot is largely determined by her success in marriage. If women's social status and economic security are only to be derived vicariously through their husbands, this naturally places them in competition with one another for the best mates. In nineteenth-century Canada, a Hudson's Bay Company officer was considered a most respectable catch; some of the chief factors, notably John Charles and John Rowand, had amassed considerable fortunes.[8] In analyzing the women's apparent preoccupation with social position, it also becomes evident that sex roles were an important factor. While a concern for status and its material symbols was certainly not a monopoly of the female sex, such matters gained prominence in the lives of women who could express their worth only within the social realm. In being fashionably attired, furnishing an elegant home, or sporting a fine carriage, a wife was exhibiting her husband's success and enhancing his status. If women tended to become overly zealous in insisting upon the prerogatives which accrued to them because of their husbands, it stemmed from a recognition of their precarious dependency upon their men. Since the failure of the husband would spell the ruin of his womenfolk as well, it is understandable that the women would fight to the best of their ability to preserve their positions. The bitterness of the rivalry which could develop was well illustrated in the fate of the women behind the magnates of the North West Company, who had actively worked to crush their Hudson's Bay Company opponents. In 1836, the young Lord Selkirk, touring in Canada, wrote to his mother that she could at last feel avenged on her foes, the McGillivray women:

> The ladies of the family who you know were the bitterest enemies of all, as they were thwarted by the opposition in the fur trade, in their ambition of being the Queens of Canada, are now living in a very poor way . . . when one remembers how high they used to hold their heads, it is quite a lesson on the instability of human affairs. You know well what vixens there are about Montreal, and you may easily imagine how much these poor women suffer for their former vanity.[9]

Rupert's Land in the post-union period presented an even riper field for rivalry because here not only white women but native women as well became embroiled in the growing social and racial turmoil.[10] While the coming of white women damaged the position of native wives, particularly in the early 1830s, for a number of reasons acculturated mixed-blood women were able to reassert their place within fur-trade society. New white women coming into Rupert's Land in the 1840s found that well-established mixed-blood women would fight to retain their social position. Conflict was fostered by gossip in the small and closely connected community of Red River. The affairs, especially of the notables, were discussed with much relish, and "Dame Rumour" possessed the power to destroy a woman's reputation. This fact was starkly illustrated when the accumulating racial tensions eventually erupted in a scandal in Red River in 1850. The affair threatened to fracture the colony's elite and pitted white women against mixed-blood.

The prospect that the arrival of white women would have serious repercussions for native women in fur-trade society had been seen with the founding of the Red River Settlement. Miles Macdonell, the leader of the colonists, was highly critical of the "squaws" kept by Hudson's Bay Company officers and advised Lord Selkirk that it would be most advantageous if Company servants were allowed to bring white wives out to Rupert's Land and thus end "the iniquitous and scandalous connection formed with Indian women." Macdonell objected to the appointment of any man who had an "Indian family" to a position of importance; in his opinion Peter Fidler, for example, was an unsuitable choice as the permanent surveyor for the settlement because of his native connections.[11] Governor Simpson worked to reinforce the idea that in Red River, at least, only white women could be members of high society. With the arrival of the Pellys in 1823, the Governor of Assiniboia now had a genteel white wife, so that Simpson, during his stay at Fort Garry that season, shunned any visible attachment to a native woman and played the role of exemplary bachelor. He wounded the feelings of Captain Frederick Matthey, a leader of the de Meuron settlers, by refusing to allow him to introduce his mixed-blood wife to Mrs Pelly. Simpson considered Mrs Matthey too disreputable for the society of an English lady, partly because she was a wife *à la façon du pays*.[12]

With the arrival of Frances Simpson, the Governor seemed determined to create an all-white elite in the settlement. Mrs Simpson's female society was restricted to those few white women whose husbands possessed social standing — the chief factors' wives, Mrs McKenzie and Mrs McMillan, and the missionaries' wives, Mrs Jones and Mrs Cockran. Chief Factor Colin Robertson who went so far as to attempt to introduce his native wife to "the Governor's lady" was met with a scathing rebuff. This proud Scotsman had earned Simpson's dislike because his genuine concern for the betterment of his mixed-blood wife Theresa had often resulted in extravagance and a neglect of business.[13] While preparing to take his family to Canada, Robertson brought his wife to Red River in 1831 to visit two of their children who were at school at the parsonage. His hope that Mrs Robertson might also make the acquaintance of the Governor's wife was dashed:

> Robertson brought his bit of Brown wt. him to the Settlement this Spring in hopes that She would pick up a few English manners before visiting the civilized World. . . . I told him distinctly that the thing was impossible which mortified him exceedingly.[14]

The only mixed-blood women who were allowed to come near Mrs Simpson served her in a purely menial capacity. One was the wife of a servant who measured her foot for moccasins; the other, ironically, was McTavish's former wife Nancy who helped to nurse Mrs Simpson while she was recovering from the birth of her first child.[15] As one mixed-blood officer in the Company observed resentfully: ". . . things are not on the same footing as formerly."[16]

At Moose Factory, McTavish had similarly ruffled feelings by refusing to countenance Isabella, the mixed-blood wife of Chief Factor Joseph Beioley. Even Simpson expressed concern lest McTavish go too far in alienating Beioley whose capacities he rated highly. But the Governor fully sympathized with his friend; it was the height of presumption for Beioley to expect that "his bit of circulating copper" should have the society of Mrs McTavish.[17] The mixed-blood families of former Company officers such as that of George Gladman were highly incensed at this treatment, for they considered themselves to be part of the fur-trade elite. Simpson, however, encouraged McTavish to rid them of this illusion:

> I . . . understand that the other Ladies at Moose are violent and indignant at being kept at such a distance, likewise their husbands, the young Gladmans particularly. . . . The greater the distance at which they are kept the better.[18]

Under the regime which Simpson envisaged in the early 1830s, European ladies were expected to treat native females with the polite condescension that a genteel woman would show to her servants or persons of lower rank. Mrs McMillan's behaviour in holding herself aloof from native women was considered most appropriate:

> She . . . has preserved during her whole residence here the same delicacy of feeling a good education gave her in Scotland. — Kind to the native women and children she yet maintains her original rank among them and seeks for society only in her own family.[19]

While their public attitude toward native women might appear tolerant, the private opinions of the white wives indicated a good deal of racial prejudice. Frances Simpson described McTavish's former country wife Nancy McKenzie as "a complete savage, with a coarse blue sort of woollen gown without shape & a blanket fastened round her neck."[20] Her lack of charity toward her may have been aggravated by the fact that she had witnessed the humiliation which her friend Catherine McTavish suffered in dealing with her husband's mixed-blood children. McTavish had made it plain to his new wife that she was expected to act as step-mother to several of his older daughters, but the Scottish woman was scarcely prepared for her first encounter with thirteen-year-old Mary who appeared unannounced one evening while they were still in Montreal:

> [McTavish] rose & took her up to his wife, who got stupid, but shook hands with the Miss who was very pretty & mighty impudent. . . . [Mrs McTavish] got white & red & at last rose & left the room, all the party looking very uncomfortable except [her husband] & the girl. [Mrs Simpson] followed & found her in a violent fit of crying, she said she knew the child was to have been home that night, but thought she wd. have been spared such a public introduction.[21]

Governor Simpson took pains to conceal his mixed-blood progeny from his wife so that she was spared such scenes, but she did confess that "she was always terrified to look about her in case of seeing something disagreeable."

If white women expressed a dislike of native women, the hints which have survived indicate that neither was there any love lost on the part of the native women. It is significant that William Cockran observed that they nursed a strong resentment against European females. Evidently Mrs Cockran had so alienated the women in her husband's congregation by her pretentious airs that when she was taken ill Cockran himself had to look after her; none of the native women would do anything to help her.[22] Considering the grief and loss of status suffered by the native wife who found herself replaced by a white wife, it is not surprising that she might seek revenge on the object which had caused her troubles. According to legend, Jean Baptiste Lajimonière had had an Indian wife, who tried unsuccessfully to poison his new French-Canadian wife Marie Anne.[23] Suzanne, William Connolly's Cree wife, was very angry about losing her place to Julia Woolrich; the Indian woman had the satisfaction of intimating to the white woman that she "had only got her leavings", but it must have been small comfort.[24] Mixed-blood wives such as Margaret Taylor and Nancy McKenzie, who had once been at the top of the fur-trade hierarchy, must have bitterly resented the white ladies who caused them such a loss in status. "What a downfall is here" lamented one sympathizer.[25]

For a number of reasons, however, Simpson was to fail in his desire to exclude mixed-blood women from the upper echelon of fur-trade society. The group of officers who followed the Governor's example in discarding their native wives was small — no more than half a dozen. No doubt others felt momentary pangs of envy and indecision, but for the majority of the Company's officers, feelings of loyalty and devotion prevented them from severing long-established ties. Simpson claimed to have observed Chief Factor Alexander Kennedy "casting a sheep's eye" at Miss Waugh during her stay in Red River, but when Kennedy went on furlough to England in 1829, he wrote to his native wife Aggathas: ". . . be assured that as long as I live I shall never forsake you . . . and if I die I shall not forget you."[26] Kennedy did die unexpectedly while in London, and his will shows his concern to make provision for his "beloved Wife" Aggathas. Many of Simpson's prominent officers, among them John Rowand, John McLoughlin, James Douglas and J. D. Cameron, remained faithful to their native wives, who retained their position as "first ladies" at their husbands' stations. In Red River, the possibility of mixed-blood wives reasserting themselves in prominent society was symbolized in the appointment of Chief Factor Alexander Christie as Governor of Assiniboia in 1835. Simpson had initially discounted Christie, although he was one of the best qualified for the job, because of his native family. The old fur trader, however, could not be shaken in his loyalty to his mixed-blood wife Ann Thomas, whom he formally married shortly after coming to the settlement.[27]

Initially, it does not appear that Mrs Christie played an active role in Red River society even though she was "a Governor's lady". Like most of the Indian and less acculturated mixed-blood wives of prominent men in the colony, her sphere was probably much confined to the sympathetic circle of home and family. The wives of wealthy free trader Andrew McDermot and Alexander Ross were seldom seen in public, except when they went to church.[28] Indeed, many of the older officers seem to have been concerned to protect their "poor homespun country squaws"[29] by keeping them in the background rather than exposing them to the slights and snubs which they might now encounter in the changing social climate of Rupert's Land. Colonel J. H. Lefroy, who travelled through Western Canada in the 1840s, observed that some of the Company officers

> have a curious aversion to allowing their wives to be seen. . . . It seems to indicate a painful consciousness that they are not of their own rank, or an equally painful . . . idea, that a gentleman from the settlements would ridicule their deficiencies.[30]

Although Lefroy was quite flattering in his remarks about native women, traders such as James Douglas knew from bitter experience that many newcomers were less charitable. At Fort Vancouver, his mixed-blood wife Amelia had had to endure the disparging comments of the Beavers; even after her church marriage, they considered Mrs Douglas as "little calculated to improve the manners of society."[31] Later, although now the wife of the Governor of Vancouver Island, she was subject to insult from incoming colonists such as Emma Staines, the wife of the first Church of England minister at Fort Victoria; the two women "did not chum at all — there being too much uppishness about the latter, she being the great woman — the great complaining."[32] As a result, Mrs Douglas concentrated her energies on her family. She was also reluctant to play the role of the Governor's lady because of her hesistant English, but gradually she began to move more in society. In 1861, Lady Franklin and her travelling companion found Amelia Douglas a kind, gentle hostess and thought it was a pity she had kept so much in the background.[33] Several years later, now as Lady Douglas, she was honoured at a testimonial dinner for her husband in New Westminster. She always retained her fondness for the simpler, more Indian ways of her youth, yet Lady Douglas became the gracious chatelaine of her home on James Bay. Her husband was delighted by the way in which "darling, good Mamma" learned to cope with the complex Victorian fashions and "won all hearts with her kindness and geniality."[34]

Many officers were undoubtedly over-protective of their native wives, but a few took determined steps to educate them to be able to cope with the changing social scene. The most notable was Archibald McDonald, whose half-Cree wife Jane came from a humble background, since her father Michel Klyne had never progressed beyond the rank of postmaster. Writing in jest to a friend in 1831, McDonald revealed that his wife was aware of the threat which white women posed for her kind:

> I already feel the benificial effects of the Govr & McTavish's marriages — [Jane] has picked up sense enough to infer from their having changed partners, that the old ones were difficient in learning & that her own case may be the same when tis my turn to visit my Scottish cousins.[35]

Mrs McDonald responded quickly to her husband's attempts to teach her to read and write. He was proud to inform his friends of her excellent academic progress, and he commended her skill in managing her household. She had servants, but she could not bear to be idle: "Her Butter, Cheese, Ham & Bacon would shine in any ordinary market" wrote McDonald from Fort Colvile.[36] His wife, who was also a devout convert to Christianity, welcomed the advice proffered by the wives of the Presbyterian missionaries who came to the Columbia region from the Eastern States in 1839. She was one of the two mixed-blood women who were invited to join the Columbia Maternal Association, a pioneer women's club formed by the missionaries' wives "to seek divine assistance in discharging the responsible duties of mothers and for the early conversion of our children."[37] All in all, Jane Klyne McDonald became the epitome of a respectable Victorian matron. She was not likely to feel at a loss in any society, and when McDonald retired to St Andrews near Montreal in 1849, his wife adapted to her new role with skill and dignity.[38]

If native women who received the support and assistance of their husbands were able to meet the challenge of white women, the younger generation of educated mixed-blood girls in whom the Indian strain was becoming increasingly diluted, were even better equipped to attract the eye of incoming Englishmen. When it became apparent that white women could not adapt to fur-trade life, the prospect of marrying an acculturated mixed-blood girl was again looked upon with favour. A significant number of the young men who became Company officers in the post-union period did not follow the course, urged by Simpson and Hargrave, of steering clear of native attachments. In the late 1830s, Hargrave had cautioned the young clerk Archibald McKinley (a brother of Mrs McMillan) to avoid the foolish temptation of taking "some petticoat or no petticoat as a playmate" to alleviate his loneliness in his station in New Caledonia. In June 1840, however, McKinley married Sarah Julia, a daughter of Peter Skene Ogden who had been his bourgeois. McKinley assured Hargrave:

> the step was not taken without due consideration. I was acquainted with the now Mrs. McK upwards of four years and had sufficient time to judge for myself. . . . so far I have every reason to be thankful for I am as happy as my most sanguine love dreams could lead me to expect.[39]

In Red River in 1836, there were two weddings which helped to re-affirm the status of acculturated mixed-blood women. John Macallum, the master of the Red River Academy, married the accomplished daughter of Chief Factor John Charles. The fact that Betsey's father was one of the wealthiest

Mrs Archibald McKinley, née Sarah Julie Ogden.

men in Rupert's Land was possibly an added inducement.[40] However, the marriage in December 1836 of the promising young clerk John Ballenden and Sarah, the eighteen-year-old daughter of Chief Trader A. R. McLeod, was very much motivated by love. Some misgivings about Ballenden's choice were expressed, but Hargrave, uncharacteristically, declared that Sarah was "a delightful creature" and his friend had "every reason to consider himself a happy man".[41] The Reverend Jones was gratified by such marriages; he felt it was important that the young ladies of his Academy, "being raised from their former condition", should occupy "the station the female ought at all times to occupy in Society".[42] Apart from the ladylike graces which they acquired at the schools in Red River, the

Mrs Schofield, Trail, B.C.

Letitia Hargrave, wife of Chief Factor James Hargrave.

traders' daughters also had the advantage of being acclimatized
to bear some of the hardships that even an officer's wife might
encounter. When Mrs Richard Lane, one of the daughters of
Red River merchant Andrew McDermot, accompanied her
husband to his new posting in the Columbia District in 1846,
she proved to be one of the best snowshoers in the party.[43]

With many mixed-blood women either remaining or
becoming wives of officers, and with the departure of Simpson's
English wife, fur-trade society showed signs of again becoming
more open. By Letitia Hargrave's time, it had become accept-
able for the respectably married mixed-blood wives of officers
to be introduced to European wives. At York Factory in 1840, it
was deemed appropriate for Harriet Gladman, wife of the only

other officer, to call on the Scottish lady. Mrs Hargrave felt that Mrs G. was rather vulgar looking, but she "speaks well & that is a great help. . . . I rather think she is kindly disposed." Letitia came to value the company of the mixed-blood woman, especially when her first child was born. The two wives corresponded after the Gladmans moved to another post in 1841.[44] Mrs Hargrave mixed with other native women of the fort in a way that earlier white ladies would not have countenanced. The Indians were allowed into her house to see her first-born son, and the women, who were delighted to be able to kiss him, exclaimed "Very fat! Very white."[45] On New Year's Day, the chief factor's wife also entertained a select party of ten native women, but she found the ball which was given by the clerks to celebrate the holidays quite beyond the pale:

> I went and sat for a little in a room off that in which they were dancing. It was a humbling affair. 40 squaws old and young with their hair plaited in long tails,

"A Christmas ball in Bachelors' Hall", York Factory, 1843.

nothing on their heads but their everlasting blankets smelling of smoke and everything obnoxious. Babies almost newly born & in their cradles were with their mothers & all nursing them in the face of everyone. I was glad to come home.[46]

As the British wife of one of the senior Company officers, Mrs Hargrave expected to be treated with deference. She could be most cutting to mixed-blood women who gave themselves airs, and even to white women who presumed too much. When Mary Taylor returned from her disappointing trip to Scotland, she met with little kindness from the Scottish lady, who described her as "an awful monster of a black woman" and ridiculed her fondness for jewellery.[47] Mrs Hargrave retained her civility to most of the officers' daughters who passed through the factory, although privately she thought them over-dressed and pretentious. Eventually she confessed to her mother that she could hardly bear the thought of entertaining another mixed-blood woman.[48] Letitia Hargrave was scarcely more charitable to some of the white women who, coming from less genteel backgrounds, were anxious to use the increased social opportunities presented by fur-trade society to make their mark. Former schoolmistresses such as Mrs Bird and Mrs Pruden, who fancied themselves the leaders of Red River society were, in Mrs Hargrave's opinion, mere social upstarts with reputedly shady pasts that hardly made them respectable.[49]

The social rivalry among women was also aggravated by the Protestant missionaries and their wives — particularly after the establishment of Methodist missions at several fur-trade posts in the 1840s. The missionaries, who viewed themselves as pillars of civilization in a barbarous land, felt they were on a social par with, if not superior to, the Hudson's Bay Company chief factors. They and their wives expected to be provided with the best accommodation and provisions that the posts could offer, but their demands were heard with increasing irritation by the Company officers:

We are rather getting tired of Wesleans and quite sick of Episcopalians. . . . The Catholic clergy here let them be what they may elsewhere are exemplary. The Indians see them living perfectly alone & caring for nothing but converting them & often they think more of such men than those who come with families & bully for every luxury & complain of every appearance of neglect getting literally furious on the slightest annoyance felt by them or their accomplished ladies.[50]

At Norway House, the social conflict between Mary Blithe Evans, the Canadian wife of the chief Methodist missionary, and Mary Ross, the chief factor's wife, certainly contributed to the difficulties which James Evans experienced during his ill-starred mission to Rupert's Land.[51] While Mrs Ross might have been criticized by some for her lack of polish, she was highly conscious of her status as a chief factor's wife. She became incensed when the Evanses were installed in the best dwelling in the fort and proceeded to consume rations in excess of those allotted to a senior chief factor's family. By the spring of 1843, the two wives were so much at "open war" that Donald Ross required Evans to move his family from the fort to the Indian village. Mary Evans and her daughter Clarissa were exceedingly wroth at being deprived of the comforts of the post, but evidently they bore a large share of the blame:

> . . . the whole affair has been caused by Mrs. Evans & her daughter's successful rivalry over Mrs. Ross and her children — For they were the derision of the whole passers by for their finery and exhibition of good education and knowledge of astronomy as Mrs. E. used to say — whereas Mrs. Ross & Jane did not know the names of the commonest stars. . .[52]

Mrs Evans also found herself rebuffed by the "best" of fur-trade society. Letitia Hargrave had entertained the missionary's wife at York in the summer of 1841, but, partly because she considered Methodists to be lower class, she was annoyed by the familiarity of the woman's letters and replied with stiff formality. Their correspondence soon ceased. Mrs Finlayson also stopped writing to Mrs Evans because of her penchant for spreading gossip all over the country.[53] Governor Simpson believed that Evans's subsequent attack upon the Company and its policies resulted "from a pique originating in family affairs" and he felt little sympathy for Mrs Evans when sexual scandal removed her husband from office in 1846.[54]

The missionaries' wives, snubbed by the leaders of fur-trade society, in turn believed that there was no question about their superiority over native women. When Mrs George Barnley came out to assist her husband's ministry at Moose Factory in 1845, she soon found that her "tone of superiority" did not sit well with Betsey Miles, the mixed-blood wife of the chief factor. Mrs Miles, who was observed to have "a good deal of the Yankee cut" about her, had adapted rapidly to white ways and was concerned for her social status.[55] Miles and his wife were both anxious to support the advancement of civilization at Moose Factory and had initially welcomed Barnley's mission; Betsey, in fact, had become an "ardent Wesleyan". Relations between the missionary and the Mileses deteriorated rapidly after the arrival of Barnley's "pious European lady", who complained of the accommodation and the food which was provided and expected the chief factor's wife to wait on her hand and foot. In spite of the concerns of her own large family, Mrs Miles would have been happy to give sisterly aid to Mrs Barnley, but the mixed-blood woman grew offended at being treated like a servant. Miles was outraged when his wife was subjected to "a volley of abuse" for supposedly neglecting Mrs Barnley and her child.[56] The situation grew so bad that the Barnleys abandoned Moose Factory in 1847. In the opinion of Chief Factor Miles, Barnley's wife had been in large measure responsible for the failure of her husband's mission; "the studied system of arrogance, insolence and annoyance" which Barnley had pursued had been instigated by his wife who had "no more consideration than the gratification of her own wishes, be that effected at whatever sacrifice and which her hysterics seems always at hand to force him to compliance."[57] By the late 1840s, after being deluged with complaints about the clergymen's wives, Governor Simpson began to seriously doubt the desirability of bringing white ladies out to Rupert's Land:

> European ladies can seldom accommodate themselves to the want of society in Hudson's Bay and affect a supercilious air of superiority over the native wives and daughters of gentlemen in the country.[58]

Simpson had changed his tune; he urged that unmarried missionaries be sent out, but if they must take a wife, a respect-

Chief Factor Robert Miles.

able partner might be found among the acculturated young native ladies of Red River.

Ironically, the diminution in racial prejudice that was evident in fur-trade society at large in the 1840s did not result in a decrease in social and racial rivalry among the women themselves. The fact that native women could still capture white husbands was deeply resented by incoming white women. Letitia Hargrave's maid, Mary Clarke, was loud in her denunciation of "squaws" and lamented the frequency with which Company servants continued to marry them.[59] In some circles, Mrs Donald Ross might be considered of the "same grade as her brown sisters", but this daughter of a Selkirk settler did not think so; she despised the acculturated Mrs Gladman and her pretensions.[60] Mrs Gladman, who had become "very fastidious" as to her company after her association with Mrs Hargrave, found it difficult to break into the "high society" of Red River when she moved there in the early 1840s. Evidently, quite a pecking order had developed in the settlement. Mrs Robert Logan, for example, was not considered within the same league as her former mistress Mrs Bird — although she "endeavours to do the honours of her house as well as she can."[61] Some people had become so sensitive about their position in society that Governor Finlayson complained to Hargrave that it would have required "Beau Nash" to regulate the movements of fashionable Red River couples. It seems that Mrs Finlayson, who was the epitome of good breeding, took refuge behind a pretext of ill health in order to escape from a society which she found objectionable.[62]

Racial tensions were evident between the former British schoolmistresses and their mixed-blood step-daughters. The family of retired Chief Factor Robert Logan had particularly opposed their father's marriage to Mrs Ingham.[63] In the curious Charles-Macallum connection, it was reported that Betsey Macallum did not "pull well" with her step-mother and sister-in-law Mrs Charles, as the latter thought too much of herself.[64] The new Mrs Pruden initially alienated her younger step-daughters by her pretentious airs, but later, owing to the high social standing that several mixed-blood ladies were to achieve, she set about making a fashionable young lady out of the youngest, Caroline, who was reputed to have been the most beautiful girl in Red River.[65] In the late 1840s after the re-appointment of Alexander Christie as the Governor of Assiniboia, it looked as though acculturated mixed-blood women were beginning to shine in the colony. The governor's wife was instrumental in arranging an advantageous match for her daughter Margaret shortly after she returned from schooling in England. In July 1845, Margaret Christie was married to the clerk John Black. Although some of the senior officers, such as Finlayson, expressed surprise at Black's being "caught in that quarter", the young woman thought herself as good as any white woman and "far above the rest of the native Ladies."[66]

Caroline Sinclair (née Pruden), left, reputed to be the most beautiful girl in Red River and Maggie Stewart, née Mowat.

Another mixed-blood woman who was not to be outdone was Sarah Ballenden. In 1848, her husband was given charge of the Company's affairs in Red River, and Mrs Ballenden found herself virtually`at the top of the social pyramid of Rupert's Land. Determined to play an active social role as befitted the wife of a chief factor, she organized dinner parties and balls and regularly presided at the officers' mess at Upper Fort Garry. A highlight of the social season of 1849 was the christening of her infant daughter whom she chose to name Frances Isobel Simpson Ballenden; it was reputedly a "splendid entertainment with abundance of champagne."[67] Such was Sarah Ballenden's social success that it was even predicted that this vivacious young mixed-blood woman was "destined to raise her whole caste above European ladies in their influence on society here."[68] This prospect was not relished by white women coming into the settlement, and when the opportunity of discrediting the chief factor's wife arose, it was eagerly seized upon.

From the moment that Mrs Ballenden returned to Red River after an absence of several years at Sault Ste Marie, she was an object of gossip and speculation. According to one observer, nearly "every act word or deed was marked and commented upon", especially by certain white women who considered themselves the watch-dogs of society.[69] Her popularity with men was considered particularly suspect. After all, had she not, like many mixed-blood girls, been guilty of indiscretion in her youth? And what about the cordiality that had been observed between the chief factor's wife and the gallant Captain Christopher Foss, an officer who had come out with the Chelsea Pensioners in 1848 and now dined at the mess table at the Upper Fort? Mrs Robert Logan was heard to remark that Ballenden's wife was the type who "must always have a sweetheart as well as a husband."[70] Suggestive hints which originated with Mrs Ballenden's German servant girl about the relationship between her mistress and Captain Foss were seized upon and magnified until, by the summer of 1849, it was widely rumoured that the Captain's attentions to Sarah were "of such a character as to entitle Mr. B. to a divorce."[71]

This gossip was to fall on the receptive ears of two white

Margaret Anderson, sister of the first Bishop of Rupert's Land.

women who arrived in Red River in the fall of 1849. The first was Anne Clouston, the daughter of the Company's agent at Stromness, who came out to Rupert's Land to be married to the clerk A. E. Pelly, a relative of the London Governor of the Company, Sir John H. Pelly.[72] The couple was married at York Factory by The Rt Revd David Anderson, the first Church of England Bishop of Rupert's Land, who had come by the same ship as Miss Clouston. The Bishop, a widower with three children, was accompanied by his sister who was to look after his household and help with the running of the academy. Margaret Anderson appears to have been the epitome of the strait-laced, sharp-tongued spinster.[73]

Upon her arrival at the Upper Fort, Mrs Pelly was much disconcerted to find that, in spite of her connections, she was obliged to give precedence to Mrs Ballenden, a woman whom, by race and reputation, she did not consider her social equal. The Scottish woman evidently intended to play the great lady, for even Letitia Hargrave had been aghast at the extravagance of her trousseau:

> Anne brought an immense quantity of finery 5 perfectly new bonnets besides that she wore on board, & scarves, handkerchiefs & shawls as if she had been going to Calcutta.[74]

Instead of the deference she expected, Anne Pelly found that her fastidious and fainting ways were the object of ridicule at the mess table, especially by Captain Foss who was evidently in the habit of casting mocking glances at Mrs Ballenden. Pelly's wife was so incensed by the insulting manner in which she was treated that she actually made herself ill; her husband withdrew from the mess in a huff and shunned the Ballendens.[75]

In her eagerness to discredit Mrs Ballenden, Mrs Pelly viewed the friendly behaviour of Captain Foss and Mrs Ballenden at the mess table as proof of their intimate involvement. She took it upon herself to relay all the current gossip to Major William Caldwell, now Governor of Assiniboia, with the demand that such immorality not be condoned.[76] Ballenden's popularity made Caldwell hesitate to take any open action, but after the chief factor left in June to meet Governor Simpson with the further intention of going on furlough, a concerted effort was made to exclude his wife from respectable society. The Major forbade his family to associate with Mrs Ballenden; Miss Anderson and the Bishop refused to countenance her, and the Cockrans advised some of Sarah's closest friends that she was no longer fit company. Most humiliating of all, Mrs Black, who had always shown a preference for the society of Mrs Pelly, now openly cut her fellow country-woman.[77]

Mrs Ballenden was determined to fight back and she was not without her supporters. She took refuge with the family of her husband's friend, Recorder Adam Thom, whose legal aid she enlisted to clear her name. She obtained a sworn statement from her servant girl who denied any knowledge of an illicit relationship between her mistress and Captain Foss. Thom, as a result of his own investigations, was able to assure the distressed

Annie Ballenden who, it was said, looked much like her mother Sarah.

Ballenden when he returned that the rumours were without foundation.[78] Ballenden did not doubt his wife's innocence and would have been happy to forget the whole unpleasant business, but Mr Black confronted him with a sworn deposition by the mess cook John Davidson and his English wife implicating Sarah with Captain Foss. Significantly, the mess cook's wife was resentful at being required to perform household duties which she considered beneath her dignity and had actively spread rumours about her employer's wife.[79] The issue was further made public when Mr Pelly made similar charges against Foss and Mrs Ballenden in front of Governor Simpson. Pelly had reason to seek revenge against both parties: he himself had previously made advances to Sarah Ballenden and been rebuffed, while Captain Foss had not only ridiculed his wife, but had relieved him of a large sum of money gambling the previous winter.[80]

Foss was so outraged by these accusations that he brought a suit against Pelly, Davidson, and initially Black, and their wives for having instigated a defamatory conspiracy against Mrs Ballenden and himself; his sole purpose, he claimed, was "to clear the reputation of a Lady".[81] The three-day trial which began on 16 July 1850 threw Red River into a turmoil. Although numerous witnesses were called, the evidence proved to be extremely vague and circumstantial; most had to admit that they had just heard and repeated rumours concerning Foss and Mrs Ballenden. The evidence of some of the women, particularly that of Mrs Cockran and Miss Anderson, was full of innuendo and undisguised prejudice.[82] Finally, after several hours of deliberation, the jury declared that Mrs Ballenden had been unjustly slandered, and the defendants were required to pay heavy damages.[83]

From a judicial point of view, the trial was highly irregular, notably because the judge, Adam Thom, had previously acted for the appellants. The real significance of this event, however, lies in the racial animosities which it engendered. Such was the excitement occasioned by the case, lamented Simpson, that "all the inhabitants thought it proper to espouse one side or the other and to regard the verdict as a personal triumph or a personal injury."[84] Sides were drawn along racial lines. Chief

Provincial Archives of Manitoba

Dr John Bunn, prominent mixed-blood doctor of Red River, his wife and child.

among Mrs Ballenden's accusers were those who championed
the supremacy of white women: the Protestant clergy, particularly Bishop Anderson and Reverend Cockran; Governor
Caldwell; and some of the lesser Company officers. On the
other hand, most of Sarah's supporters, including all of the
jurors, were either English mixed-bloods or married to native
women. Two of Mrs Ballenden's most ardent defenders were
Dr John Bunn, a prominent mixed-blood, and the colony's
sheriff Alexander Ross who was married to an Indian woman
and had numerous daughters. The English mixed-bloods who
desired to be assimilated into white society viewed the attack on
Mrs Ballenden as an attempt to discredit mixed-blood women
which would threaten their position in Red River society. In the
words of one cogent observer, the affair seemed to be "a strife
of blood".[85] Adam Thom, whose part in the proceedings had
temporarily lessened his unpopularity among the mixed-bloods,
denounced the intended racial slur. "Altho Mrs. B. might not
have so much starch in her face" he declared, "she had as much
virtue in her heart as any exotic."[86] There can be no doubt that
Anne Pelly's air of superiority occasioned much resentment and
was a root cause of trouble. Her brother, Chief Trader Robert
Clouston, wrote acidly to his father-in-law Donald Ross:

> ... my sister is not a native — therefore must have the
> ill-will of that class. She has self respect and acts in a
> manner entitling her to the respect of others therefore
> she must have the enmity of those who have lost the
> sense of shame.[87]

Thus the colony was seriously split along predominantly
racial lines when the new Associate Governor of the Hudson's
Bay Company, Eden Colvile, arrived in the fall of 1850 with his
English wife Anne. Despite her declared innocence, Mrs
Ballenden had continued to be shunned by "the nobs of
womankind", especially Mrs Caldwell, Miss Anderson and Mrs
Cockran. The animosities resulting from the scandal created an
impossible social situation. Colvile wrote in exasperation to
Simpson:

> Altogether the state of things is most unpleasant,
> though somewhat ludicrous, withal. For instance,
> today, the Bishop & his sister were calling on us, & in

the middle of the visit I heard a knock at the door & suspecting who it was rushed out & found Mr. & Mrs. Ballenden. I had to cram them into another room till the Bishop's visit was over, but as he was then going to see the Pelly's he had to pass through this room, so that I had to bolt out & put them into a third room. It was altogether like a scene in a farce.[88]

Colvile, who took over the governorship of the colony from the unpopular Caldwell, did attempt to heal the breach. Since Ballenden himself was convinced of his wife's innocence, the Governor deemed it only fair that she should be reinstated in society and delighted Ballenden by admitting Sarah to the company of his wife. The wives of the lesser Church of England clergy also re-established relations with Mrs Ballenden.[89] Gradually peace seemed to be returning to the settlement, although it rankled with some that Captain Foss, who was very popular with the English mixed-bloods, had not had the good grace to leave Red River.

During the months immediately following the trial, the Ballendens lived quietly at Lower Fort Garry where they had removed. Governor Colvile found Mrs Ballenden's behaviour so discreet and proper that he began to think that the poor woman "had been more sinned against than sinning." The parsons and their women were "very strait-laced", he declared, and the colony "a dreadful place for scandal". When Ballenden decided that he must go to Britain for medical treatment in the fall of 1850, Colvile favoured his wife by allowing her to remain at the fort; there was no lively mess table at the Lower Fort, but Mrs Ballenden was to take her meals with the clerk W. D. Lane.[90] The winter arrangements began auspiciously enough, but during December the scandal suddenly blew up again, when an unsigned letter, reputedly from Sarah Ballenden to Captain Foss inviting him to visit her at the fort, was intercepted. Although there was never enough evidence to actually prove it, Foss allegedly managed a discreet two-day visit during Colvile's absence. The chagrined Governor, informed of this fact by Thom, now felt obliged to cease all association with Mrs Ballenden. A short time later, the unfortunate woman inextricably incriminated herself by paying a short afternoon visit to the house of retired officer Donald McKenzie, where Foss was living.[91] Soon Mrs Ballenden, finding herself again a social outcast, left the fort and took refuge with a mixed-blood family named Cunninghame.

These events gave Mrs Ballenden's former accusers great satisfaction; in their view, there could be no doubt that she had been guilty from the beginning.[92] Although no further sign of an affair between Sarah and Captain Foss was detected, some of the woman's supporters now also felt obliged to desert her cause. Both Dr Bunn and Adam Thom changed sides, and Thom deemed it necessary to write to Ballenden of his wife's falseness.[93] Far away in Scotland, a grief-stricken and angry Ballenden contemplated divorce, but he changed his mind when he returned to Red River in mid-June 1851 to find his wife ailing. She had just given birth to a son whom he knew to have been his own. While pressured by some that he must divorce his wife if he wished to remain respectable, Ballenden was grateful for the support of others. Alexander Ross pointed out to him that, while Sarah may have appeared indiscreet on one occasion, there was still no concrete proof of her guilt. Ballenden's wife, he felt, had been the victim of unrelenting hatred. "After what I had seen at the trial" declared Ross, "and the unfounded malice got up in certain circles, no earthly power will convince me, that she is guilty, till that guilt be proved."[94] During the summer, after the Ballendens' reconciliation, it was rumoured that Sarah actually "confessed" to her husband, but this fact was contradicted by Ballenden himself. In a pathetic letter written to Simpson later that year, he stoutly defended his wife and begged the Governor to desist from making further uncharitable remarks about her: "I entreat of you, for my sake, if not for hers to cease, and let her rest in peace."[95]

In the fall of 1851 Ballenden was posted to Fort Vancouver, and he would have taken his wife with him if her health had been equal to the journey. Instead, he endeavoured to settle Sarah comfortably in a rented house near The Rapids. Here, Sarah Ballenden, now vilified as "a fallen woman", was to pass a wretched and lonely winter. Her health seriously deteriorated; according to one of her few friends, "if there is such a thing as dying of a broken heart, she cannot live long."[96] In the summer of 1852 Mrs Ballenden, unable to bear the situation in Red River any longer, moved to Norway House where she was generously received by Chief Factor George Barnston and his mixed-blood wife Ellen. Barnston, who had been a friend of Sarah's father and known her since childhood, declared that she might "always find an asylum where I live. Surely utter helplessness merits aid."[97] In 1853, Ballenden's own poor health forced him to retire from the Columbia, and he gave instructions for his family to proceed him to Scotland. There is evidence that a poignant reunion took place between husband and wife in Edinburgh before Sarah died of consumption in December of that year. A short time later Ballenden wrote to his daughter Eliza and told her of the concern which "your own dear mother" had expressed about the welfare of her children as she lay on her deathbed.[98]

The fate of Sarah Ballenden was surely a sad indictment of the operation of the double standard against women. While Mrs Ballenden may well have engaged in a flirtation with Captain Foss, it could not be proved that she had actually committed adultery. Yet gossip and innuendo were enough to convict her. As the Reverend William Cockran cynically observed, ". . . whenever a rumour of this kind is in circulation, I have always found them to turn out correct."[99] In any event, according to the strict code of nineteenth-century morality, the woman must pay the price of any peccadillo. Sarah Ballenden became a social outcast; her reputation was ruined.

The Foss-Pelly scandal, as it came to be called, also provides insights into the way society operated to pit women against one another. Significantly, the mixed-blood woman's strongest condemnation came not from men but from other women. In this situation the women were seen to behave in a petty and vindictive manner; yet they were more deserving of pity than censure. Their actions stemmed in large measure from their being reduced to a precarious dependency on male protectors; they were locked into a system which gave women no autonomous way of establishing their status or worth. The racism evinced by white women, while as inexcusable as that of their male counterparts, was aggravated by what, in their view, was a concrete threat to their own welfare.

The Foss-Pelly scandal had repercussions on fur-trade society because it led to the reinforcement of racial prejudice against native women. Implicit in some of the attitudes expressed at the trial was the notion that a certain moral weakness was inherent in women of even part-Indian extraction. In the words of a contemporary historian, "probably no case ever brought before the Recorder's court . . . had given rise to so much bad feeling, and such deplorable consequences, as did this cause célèbre."[100]

10

"A WORLD WE HAVE LOST"

As a result of the Foss-Pelly scandal, the position of acculturated mixed-blood women was challenged. In the early 1850s, several Company officers again voiced grave reservations about the desirability of taking a native wife. The famous Yukon explorer Chief Trader Robert Campbell summed up the situation:

> It is too well known that few indeed of those joined to the ebony and half ebony damsels of the north are happy or anything like it; and that few or none of them have pleasure, comfort or satisfaction of their Families.[1]

At this time, Campbell was contemplating marriage himself. As a young clerk in the 1830s, he had promised Simpson that he would not encumber himself with a wife and family during active service. Now he had lived the lonely life of a bachelor long enough. Careful to avoid the eligible young ladies of the country, Campbell became engaged to a Scottish woman, Miss Elleonora Sterling, while on furlough in 1853. She came out to Rupert's Land a few years later and was married to Campbell at Fort Chipewyan.[2] A few other Company officers followed Campbell's lead,[3] but there was no marked decline in the 1850s in the pattern of marriage between incoming whites and the acculturated daughters of old Hudson's Bay Company families. In spite of growing racial prejudice, economic and social factors assured mixed-blood women of their place in Red River society at least until 1870, when the transfer of Rupert's Land to Canada signalled the end of the old fur-trade order.[4]

Marriage alliances remained an important avenue to wealth and status in the fur-trade world of the mid-nineteenth

*Chief Trader Richard Hardisty, Sr, and his wife Margaret
(née Sutherland). Their daughter Isabella married Donald
A. Smith, later Lord Strathcona and Mount Royal. c. 1860.*

century. In 1851, for example, the ambitious young Orkneyman
A. G. B. Bannatyne married Annie McDermot, a daughter of
the wealthy free trader Andrew McDermot. Bannatyne's
connection with McDermot laid the basis of his own success as
a merchant and free trader. On the other hand, relations
between the Company and the prominent free traders in the
colony were eased when, in 1864, William Mactavish, the
Governor of Assiniboia, married another of McDermot's
daughters, Mary Sally.[5] There can be no doubt that the beauty
and the accomplishments of the daughters of prominent traders
continued to be powerful drawing cards. Several years after
being posted to the Labrador District of Esquimaux Bay in
1848, Donald A. Smith married Isabella Hardisty, the daughter

Provincial Archives of Manitoba

Mrs William Cowan, née Harriett Sinclair. Undated.

of his chief factor Richard Hardisty and his mixed-blood wife
Margaret Sutherland. Isabella, who had been sent to school in
England, was well equipped to function in her future role as
Lady Strathcona and Mount Royal. In 1852, Dr William
Cowan, who had come to Red River several years before as the
medical officer for a detachment of Chelsea Pensioners, married
Harriett Sinclair, the daughter of the prominent mixed-blood
James Sinclair. In 1848 at the age of sixteen, Harriett had
attracted much favourable comment at a grand ball held at Fort
Garry, and she had then been sent to Knox College in
Galesboro, Illinois, for two years to finish her education.[6]

Provincial Archives of Manitoba

Miss Lizzie Ballenden, one of the two 'perfectly accomplished' daughters of Chief Factor John Ballenden and his wife Sarah. Undated.

In December 1853, the long-awaited Presbyterian minister John Black went against the general wishes of his Scottish congregation and married one of the daughters of Alexander Ross. Certainly the stigma of race cast a shadow over the merits of Henrietta Ross, for it was predicted (albeit wrongly) that Black's unfortunate choice of "a native for a helpmate" would be detrimental to his ministry.[7]

The response of mixed-blood society to the growth of racial prejudice was an ever stronger emphasis on the total emulation of respectable Victorian society. In the 1850s and 1860s,

Provincial Archives of Manitoba

Miss Davis's school for young ladies. c. 1880.

Hudson's Bay Company officers and other aspiring Red River socialites went to great lengths to turn their daughters into "perfectly accomplished" young ladies. The case of Chief Factor John Ballenden's own two daughters, Annie and Lizzie, is illustrative. In 1854, they returned to Red River after nearly a decade of schooling in England. According to one observer:

> . . . they can play elegantly on the Harp, guitar, piano, they sing melodiously and methodically, they can dance and waltz like true English dames . . .[8]

The harp and piano belonging to the Misses Ballenden were carefully transported from York Factory to Red River, while the items listed in their private orders sent to England the next year show that they possessed extensive and fashionable wardrobes.[9] As in most colonial societies, there was undoubtedly a good deal of prestige attached to sending one's children to the mother country for education. In Red River the tradition of providing a fashionable education for girls was furthered in the late 1850s with the establishment of Miss Davis's school for young ladies at St Andrew's.[10] An English governess assisted Miss Davis, whose father had been a Company officer, in providing "a solid English education, with French, Music,

Drawing, Dancing, Plain & Ornamental Needle-Work".
Considerable attention was also paid to the propriety of the
girls' behaviour and their manner of walking and sitting.[11] A
handsome stone dormitory, which could house up to forty
boarders, became a temporary home for many of the daughters
of Company officers posted throughout Rupert's Land. For the
daughters of prominent Roman Catholic families, a similar
ladylike education was provided at the convent established by
the Grey Nuns who had come to Red River in 1844.[12]

Undoubtedly, the acculturation of many mixed-blood
children, particularly of the well-to-do, was successful; however,
it could not be accomplished without paying a price — that
price being the suppression of every vestige of their Indian
heritage. In families where the Indian or mixed-blood mother
had not been educated in the British manner, this process could
cause a heart-rending dilemma. A particularly poignant
example was that of the family of Alexander Ross. In his book
on the history of the settlement, published in 1856, Ross never
alluded to the fact that he had a native family. He may have
fondly hoped that they had integrated into the Scottish
Presbyterian community, but the hostility with which his
daughter's marriage to the Reverend Black was greeted suggests
otherwise. After his father's death in 1856, James Ross, then a
student at the University of Toronto, wrote a letter to his sisters
that revealed the family's difficulty in dealing with racial
prejudice. Within the family circle, their "dear Mama" had
always been cherished, but by the 1850s she was becoming
something of an embarrassment, especially to her more
acculturated daughters. James gently chided his sister Jemima
for attempting to avoid being seen riding to church with her
mother, and he emphasized the need for family loyalty:

> What if mama is an Indian! . . . remember the
> personal qualities that ought to endear mama to us.
> Who more tender-hearted? Who more attached to her
> children & more desirous of their happiness? Who
> more attentive to their wants — anxious about their
> welfare? None. She has all these qualities in a
> wonderful degree and they are the endearing . . . the
> essential qualities of any good mother. What avail

those accomplishments in etiquette & fussy nonsense of which she happens to be destitute? . . . Better far give me my mama with her Christian meekness — her kind affection — her motherly heart — than the cold-hearted so-called lady — who prides herself, it may be, in her fine shape — her clever but foolish jesting — her superficials & secondaries of writing & hairbrushing and gait and posture.[13]

It is significant that in defense of native wives, one hears again and again of their good nature, their generosity and their kindness; it is a measure of the hypocrisy that could be met with in "civilized" society that their families knew that these admirable human qualities would not be enough to overcome the stigma of race. The course taken by most prominent fur-trade families was to attempt to obliterate rather than take pride in their Indian background. James Douglas, who was extremely sensitive to the racial slights which his native family had to endure in the rapidly changing province of British Columbia,[14] took extra precautions to ensure that his youngest daughter Martha was educated to move in the best circles. In letters of affectionate but stern advice written to Martha while she was at school in England, he cautioned her to keep her Indian ancestry a secret from her schoolmates:

I have no objection to your telling the old stories about "Hyass" but pray do not tell the world that they are Mamma's.[15]

Officially Mrs Douglas's part-Cree origin was obscured; as was customary in the census records, she was listed as being Irish like her father.[16] Similarly, in the popular book of reminiscences, *Women of Red River*, published in 1923, many of the pioneer women interviewed were descendants of old Hudson's Bay Company families. They make virtually no mention of their Indian ancestry, but take much pride in their British patrimony.

This fact may indeed be a distinguishing characteristic of the English mixed-blood group which serves to differentiate them from their Métis cousins. Captain Palliser, who led an exploring expedition through Rupert's Land in the late 1850s, observed that there was a sharp difference in attitude between what he called the Scotch and the French half-breeds. The Scottish half-breed was anxious "to profit by the advance of civilization in the old country as well as he can. Should his mother or his wife be Indian women, he is kind to them, but they are not his companions." The French half-breed, on the other hand, felt much more affinity with the hunting and trapping life of the Indians; "his sympathies are all towards his Indian mother, squaw, and especially his (belle mère) mother-in-law".[17] Palliser's comments over-simplify the cultural complexities of the two mixed-blood groups, for there were obviously important class differences within this basic ethnic division. It was the mixed-blood children of the fur-trade elite who particularly aspired to assimilate into their fathers' world, and it was their social and economic status that was most threatened by the advent of white settlement.

The fur-trade society of Rupert's Land was justified in feeling suspicious of the attitudes of the "Canadian" newcomers from Ontario. This small group which began to be a vocal presence in Red River in the 1860s made no secret of the fact that they considered themselves to be the vanguard of civilization in the West. Again there is evidence that the air of racial superiority evinced by the few white women in this group caused social conflict within the colony. In 1868, Charles Mair, an enthusiastic proponent of Ontarian expansion into Rupert's Land, claimed to have witnessed the tension between mixed-blood and white wives at a dinner party given by Alexander Begg, an early Canadian settler. While the affair had been pleasant enough, Mair wrote to his brother in Ontario:

> There are jealousies and heart-burnings, however. Many wealthy people are married to half-breed women, who, having no coat of arms, but a "totem" to look back to, make up for the deficiency by biting at the backs of their "white" sisters. The white sisters fall back upon their whiteness, whilst the husbands meet each other with desparate courtesies and hospitalities, with a view to filthy lucre in the back-ground.[18]

When these unflattering remarks made their way into several Ontario newspapers, including the Toronto *Globe*, the prominent ladies of Red River were outraged by this insult. Mrs

Mr & Mrs A. G. B. Bannatyne with their family: Jimmie, standing beside his mother, Willie, Laura, Lizzie. Rorie is seated in front. c. 1870

Bannatyne, who had been present at the Beggs, was so incensed that, upon encountering Mair in her husband's store, she reputedly slapped his face and "struck him several times with a riding whip."[19] Even though Mair's assessment of the social situation may have contained a germ of truth, his letter is more revealing of his own prejudices and lack of understanding of fur-trade society. This attitude was typical of the settlers from Ontario. Although there were certainly factions within it, the fur trade in Western Canada had, in essence, produced a regional society whose future was threatened by the impending waves of agrarian settlement. It is significant that those Company officials and prominent free-traders who had married into "old" mixed-blood families showed sympathy for the fight waged by Louis Riel and the Métis to secure political and cultural rights for the people of Rupert's Land within the Canadian union.[20]

In the post-1870 Canadian West, the goal, largely of settlers from Ontario, was to establish a modern, agrarian, British society. In this scheme of things, there would be little basis for the continuation of the economic and social exchange between white and native peoples which had been the foundation of the fur trade.[21] Widespread intermarriage between European traders and Indian women and the development of extensive kinship networks had been fundamental to the growth of fur-trade society. In the period of frontier settlement, unions between white men and native women became increasingly rare; they were frowned upon by the dominant white culture, while at the same time the sexual exploitation of native women was allowed to increase.[22] The pattern of western society was now not mixed unions, but the transplanting of *white* wives and the raising of *white* families. Unlike the fur traders, young men of the North West Mounted Police who formed unions with native women were not likely to meet with social approval. In 1882, when William Parker married Mary Calder, a descendant of the old Hudson's Bay Company family of Sinclair, his mother disapproved so much of his choice that she stopped corresponding with him.[23] Incoming settlers' wives, although they might show charitable concern for the welfare of the native people, were appalled by the thought of any intermingling of the races. When the Mooneys (Nellie McClung's parents) moved from Ontario to Manitoba in the early 1880s, Letitia Mooney insisted that the family move on from the Red River area to an all-white settlement because there were "too many jet black eyes and high cheek bones" there.[24]

As the tenets of British culture gained hold in the West, the traditions and practices of fur-trade society were demeaned and forgotten. The nature of the white-native unions which had once characterized fur-trade life was particularly subject to misinterpretation. Marriage *à la façon du pays* came to be regarded as something illegal and immoral. This was not, however, the opinion of Chief Justice Coram Monk who in 1867 ruled on the first case in a Canadian court where the validity of marriage after the fashion of the country was at issue. In this case, a son of Chief Factor William Connolly sued for a share of his father's estate on the grounds that the union between his father and his Cree mother Suzanne Pas-de-Nom had constituted a legal marriage. On the basis of the testimony of numerous witnesses who had lived in Rupert's Land and an extensive examination of the development of marriage law, Monk ruled that Connolly's parents had indeed been lawfully married. Firstly, his mother had been married according to the custom and usages of her own people and secondly, the consent of both parties which was the essential element of civilized marriage had been proved by twenty-eight years of repute, public acknowledgement and cohabitation as man and wife.[25] Connolly had given his name to Suzanne and shown considerable concern for the care and education of his offspring. In a moving summation, the Chief Justice declared:

> It is beyond all question, all controversy, that in the North West among the Crees, among the other Indian tribes or nations, among the Europeans at all stations, posts, and settlements of the Hudson's Bay, this union, contracted under such circumstances, persisted in for such a long period of years, characterized by inviolable fidelity and devotion on both sides, and made more sacred by the birth and education of a numerous family, would have been regarded as a valid marriage in the North West, was legal there; and can this Court, after he brought his wife and family to Canada, after having recognized her here as such, presented her as such to the persons he and she associated with, declare the marriage illegal, null and void? Can I pronounce this connection formed and continued under such circumstances concubinage, and brand his offspring as bastard. . . .I think not. There would be no law, no justice, no sense, no morality in such a judgment.[26]

This ruling, however, did not set a legal precedent. In a subsequent and more influential case, that of *Jones v. Fraser* in 1886, Chief Justice Ramsay ruled that marriage *à la façon du pays* did not constitute a marriage in law. He declared that the court would not accept that "the cohabitation of a civilized man and a savage woman, even for a long period of time, gives rise to the presumption that they consented to be married in our sense of marriage."[27] It has been suggested that Ramsay's ruling was heavily influenced by other legal decisions in the British Empire which reflected a growing antipathy in the nineteenth century toward mixed marriages. The rigidity of subsequent Canadian decisions underscored the inability of the Canadian judicial system to adapt to or make allowances for new social realities which had developed in the Canadian context.[28]

Ramsay's remarks give little credence to the strong bonds of affection and duty which characterized many of the lasting unions between European traders and their native wives. "Many tender ties" did develop in a society which recognized the importance of family and kin and in which native women had a vital contribution to make. The early historical development of Western Canada was based upon a close economic partnership between Indian and white and extensive intermarriage. It is unfortunate that, in terms of its racial ties, the early world of the fur trade became "a world we have lost." Even in fur-trade society, with the increasing impact of white cultural values, prejudice gained hold to such an extent that this potential for racial integration was lost. This is to be regretted, for the blending of European and Indian culture could have been an enriching human experience. Even James Hargrave, in one of his more philosophical moments, was moved to remark of the so-called "savages":

> . . . most of them with no better education than what the light of nature teaches lead more innocent lives and better fulfil the duties of fathers, sons, brothers and *sisters* than many who in the civilized world call themselves Christians.[29]

Abbreviations

Select Bibliography

References

ABBREVIATIONS

A.A.S.B.   Archives de l'archevêché, Saint-Boniface
C.M.S.A.   Church Missionary Society Archives, London
H.B.C.A.   Hudson's Bay Company Archives, Winnipeg
H.B.R.S.   Hudson's Bay Record Society
J.C.C.H.S. *Journal of the Canadian Church Historical Society*
P.A.B.C.   Provincial Archives of British Columbia, Victoria
P.A.M.   Provincial Archives of Manitoba, Winnipeg
P.A.O.   Provincial Archives of Ontario, Toronto
P.A.C.   Public Archives of Canada, Ottawa
P.R.O.   Public Record Office, London
T.R.S.C.   *Transactions of the Royal Society of Canada*
W.C.J.A.   *Western Canadian Journal of Anthropology*

SELECT BIBLIOGRAPHY

I. PRIMARY SOURCES

A. Manuscripts

Archives de l'archevêché, Saint-Boniface
    Henry Fisher Correspondence, 1820-55 (Microfilm copy, Reels Nos.
        1735-1772, courtesy of Father Gaston Carrière, O.M.I. of the
        Séminaire Saint-Paul, Ottawa)
Church Missionary Society Archives, London
    Reverend William Cockran Papers, (CC1/018)
    Reverend David Jones Papers, (CC1/039)
Glenbow Archives, Calgary
    John Sutherland Papers
Hudson's Bay Company Archives, Winnipeg
    Section A: Headquarters Records
    Section B: Post Records
    Section D: Governors' Papers
    Section E: Miscellaneous Records
    Section F: Records of Allied and Subsidiary Companies
    Transcripts of the Selkirk Papers, Red River Correspondence, 1811-1836,
        Copy Nos. 112, 154-161

Transcripts of the Edward Ermatinger Correspondence, Copy Nos. 21-23.
McCord Museum, McGill University
    Robert McVicar Papers
McGill University Library
    Journal of James Mackenzie, 1799-1800
Provincial Archives of British Columbia, Victoria
    Edward Ermatinger Correspondence
    John S. Helmcken. Reminiscences, 1892
    Archibald McDonald Papers
    Charles Ross Papers
    Donald Ross Correspondence
    Canada Official Census Records, Victoria, 1881
Provincial Archives of Manitoba, Winnipeg
    Miss Davis' School Collection
    Alexander Kennedy Papers
    Records of General Quarterly Court of Assiniboia
    Alexander Ross Papers, 1810-1903
Provincial Archives of Ontario, Toronto
    James Keith Estate Papers, 1802-1857 (Microfilm copy)
    John "Le Borgne" McDonald Papers
Public Archives of Canada, Ottawa (Manuscript Group 19)
    Edward Ermatinger Correspondence, 1820-74
    Ermatinger Family Papers, 1766-1966
    Fort Severn Journal, 1768-69
    James Hargrave Correspondence, 1821-1861
    John McLeod Correspondence, 1825-1837
    Charles McKenzie Papers, 1828-1888
    Masson Collection
    Selkirk Papers
    Miles Macdonell Papers
    Andrew Bulger Papers
Public Record Office, London
    Selected Wills of Probate Court
Toronto Public Library, Baldwin Room
    George Nelson Papers, 1802-1839
University of Western Ontario, London, Canada
    James Evans Papers

B. Published Primary Sources

Ballantyne, Robert M. *Hudson Bay; or, Everyday Life in the Wilds of North America.* Edinburgh, 1848.

Burpee, Lawrence J. *Journals and Letters of Pierre Gaultier de Varennes de la Vérendrye and his Sons.* Toronto: Champlain Society, XVI, (1927).

Catholic Church Records of the Pacific Northwest: Vancouver, vols. I and II and Stellamaris Mission. Translated by Mikell de Lores Wormell Warner and annotated by Harriet Duncan Munnick. St. Paul, Oregon, 1972.

"Connolly vs. Woolrich, Superior Court, Montreal, 9 July 1867." *Lower Canada Jurist,* XI: 197-265

Cowie, Isaac. *The Company of Adventurers.* Toronto, 1913.

Curot, Michel. "A Wisconsin Fur Trader's Journal, 1803-1804." *Wisconsin Historical Collections,* 20:396-471.

Coues, Elliot, ed. *New Light on the Early History of the Greater Northwest: The Manuscript Journals of Alexander Henry and of David Thompson, 1799-1814.* Minneapolis, Minn., 1965 [reprint].

Cox, Ross. *The Columbia River.* Edited by Edgar and Jane Stewart. Norman, Okla., 1957.

Davies. K. G., ed. *Letters from Hudson Bay, 1703-40.* London: H.B.R.S., XXV (1965).

———. *Northern Quebec and Labrador Journals and Correspondence, 1819-35.* London: H.B.R.S., XXIV (1963).

Dempsey, Hugh, ed. *William Parker, Mounted Policeman.* Edmonton, 1973.

Doughty, A. G. and Chester Martin, eds., *The Kelsey Papers.* Ottawa, 1929.

Drury, C. M., ed. *First white women over the Rockies . . .* 3 vols. Glendale, Calif., 1963.

Fleming, R. Harvey, ed. *Minutes of Council of the Northern Department of Rupert's Land, 1821-31.* London: H.B.R.S., III (1940).

Franchère, Gabriel. *Narrative of a Voyage to the Northwest Coast of America, 1811-1814.* Edited by Ruben Gold Thwaites. Cleveland, Ohio, 1904.

Franklin, John. *Narrative of a Journey to the Shores of the Polar Sea, 1819-22.* 2 vols. London, 1824 [3rd edition].

———. *Narrative of a Second Expedition to the Shores of the Polar Sea, 1825-27.* London, 1828.

Garry, Nicholas. "Diary of Nicholas Garry". *T.R.S.C.*, Second Series, VI, 11 (1900): 75-204.

Gates, Charles M., ed. *Five Fur Traders of the Northwest.* St. Paul, Minn., 1965 [revised edition].

Glazebrook, G. P. de T., ed. *The Hargrave Correspondence, 1821-1843.* Toronto: Champlain Society, XXIV (1938).

Glover, Richard, ed. *David Thompson's Narrative, 1784-1812.* Toronto: Champlain Society, XL (1962).

Hargrave, J. J. *Red River.* Altona, Man., 1977 [reprint].

Hearne, Samuel. *A Journey to the Northern Ocean.* Edited by Richard Glover. Toronto, 1958.

Henry, Alexander. *Travels and Adventures in Canada and the Indian Territories, 1760-1776.* Edited by James Bain. Boston, 1901.

H.B.C.A., *Report from the Committee, appointed to inquire into the State and Condition of the Countries Adjoining to Hudson's Bay and of the Trade carried on there, 24 April 1749.*

Irving, Washington. *Astoria, or Anecdotes of an Enterprise Beyond the Rocky Mountains.* Norman, Okla., 1964.

Jessett, Thomas E., ed. *Reports and Letters of Herbert Beaver, 1836-38.* Portland, Oregon, 1959.

Jesuits. Letters from Missions. *Black gown and redskins; adventures and travels of the early Jesuit missionaries in North America, 1610-1791.* Edited by Edna Kenton. New York, 1956.

Johnson, Alice M., ed. *Saskatchewan Journals and Correspondence, 1795-1802.* London: H.B.R.S., XXVI (1967).

"Johnstone *et al.* vs. Connolly, Appeal Court, 7 Sept. 1869." *La Revue Légale,* I: 253-400.

Kane, Paul. *Wanderings of an Artist among the Indians of North America.* Edmonton, 1968 [reprint].

Kenney, J. F. *The Founding of Churchill.* Toronto, 1932.

Kenyon, W. A. and J. R. Turnbull, eds. *The Battle for James Bay, 1686.* Toronto, 1971.

Lamb, W. Kaye, ed. *Sixteen Years in the Indian Country: The Journal of Daniel Williams Harmon, 1800-1816.* Toronto, 1957.

———. *The Letters and Journals of Simon Frazer, 1806-1808.* Toronto, 1960.

———. *The Journals and Letters of Sir Alexander Mackenzie.* Cambridge, England, 1970.

Landon, Fred, ed. "Letters of Rev. James Evans." *Ontario Historical Society, Papers and Records,* XXVIII (1932): 47-70.

248

Lefroy, John Henry. *In Search of the Magnetic North: A Soldier-Surveyor's Letters from the North-West 1843-44.* Edited by G. F. G. Stanley. Toronto, 1955.
Lewis, William S. and Murakami, Naojiro, eds. *Ranald McDonald: The Narrative of his early life on the Columbia under the Hudson's Bay Company's regime . . . .* Spokane, Wash., 1923.
"Mackinac Register of Marriages, 1725-1821." *Wisconsin Historical Collections,* XVIII (1908): 469-513.
McClung, Nellie. *Clearing in the West.* Toronto, 1976 [reprint].
McDonald, Archibald. *Peace River: A Canoe Voyage from Hudson's Bay to the Pacific.* Edited by Malcolm McLeod. Edmonton, 1971 [reprint].
MacLeod, Margaret A., ed. *The Letters of Letitia Hargrave.* Toronto: Champlain Society, XXVIII (1947).
Masson, L. R. F. *Les Bourgeois de la Compagnie du Nord-Ouest.* 2 vols. New York, 1960 [reprint].
Merk, Frederick, ed. *Fur Trade and Empire: George Simpson's Journal, 1824-25.* Cambridge, Mass., 1931.
Morton, A. S., ed. *The Journal of Duncan McGillivray . . . at Fort George on the Saskatchewan, 1794-95.* Toronto, 1929.
Morton, W.L., ed. *Alexander Begg's Red River Journal and other papers relative to the Red River Resistance of 1869-70.* Toronto: Champlain Society, XXXIV (1956).
[Mountain, George Jehoshaphat]. *The Journal of the Bishop of Montreal during a Visit to the Church Missionary Society's North-West America Mission.* London, 1849.
Nute, Grace Lee and Richard Bardon, eds. *A Winter in the St. Croix Valley: George Nelson's Reminiscences, 1802-03.* St. Paul, Minn., 1948.
Oliver, E. H., ed. *The Canadian North-West: Its Early Development and Legislative Records.* 2 vols. Ottawa, 1914.
Rich, E. E., ed. *Simpson's Athabasca Journal and Report, 1820-21.* London: H.B.R.S., I (1938).
_____. *Colin Robertson's Letters, 1817-1822.* London: H.B.R.S., II (1939).
_____. *Minutes of the Hudson's Bay Company, 1682-84.* London: H.B.R.S., IX, (1946).
_____. *Simpson's 1828 Journal to the Columbia.* London: H.B.R.S., X, (1947).
_____. *Hudson's Bay Company Letters Outward, 1679-94.* London: H.B.R.S., XI, (1948).
_____. *James Isham's Observations and Notes, 1743-49.* London: H.B.R.S., XII (1949).
_____. *Cumberland House Journals and Inland Journal, 1775-79.* London: H.B.R.S., XIV (1951).
_____. *Cumberland House Journals and Inland Journal, 1779-82.* London: H.B.R.S., XV (1952).
_____. *Moose Fort Journals, 1783-85.* London: H.B.R.S., XVII (1954).
_____. *Eden Colvile's Letters, 1849-52.* London: H.B.R.S., XIX, (1956).
_____. *Hudson's Bay Company Letters Outward, 1688-1696.* London, H.B.R.S., XX (1957).
Robinson, Henry Martyn. *The Great Fur Land; or Sketches of Life in the Hudson's Bay Territory.* New York, 1879.
Robson, Joseph. *An Account of Six Years Residence in Hudson's Bay.* London, 1752.
Ross, Alexander. *Adventures of the First Settlers on the Oregon or Columbia River.* London, 1849.
_____. *The Fur Hunters of the Far West.* 2 vols. London, 1855.
_____. *The Red River Settlement.* Minneapolis, Minn., 1957 [reprint].
"Short Sketch of the Life and Missionary Labours and Happy Death of Sophia Mason." *Church Missionary Gleaner,* XI (1861): 135-40.

Simpson, George. *Narrative of a Journey Round the World, 1841-42*. 2 vols. London, 1847.
Smith, Dorothy B., ed. *Lady Franklin visits the Pacific Northwest*. Victoria: P.A.B.C. Memoir No. XI, 1974.
Spry, Irene, ed. *The Palliser Papers*. Toronto: Champlain Society, XLIV.
Tyrrell, J. B., ed. *Documents relating to the Early History of Hudson's Bay*. Toronto: Champlain Society, XVIII (1931).
_____. *Journals of Samuel Hearne and Philip Turnor, 1774-1792*. Toronto: Champlain Society, XXI (1934).
Umfreville, Edward. *The Present State of Hudson's Bay*. Edited by W. S. Wallace. Toronto, 1954 [reprint].
Wallace, W. Stewart, ed. *Documents relating to the North West Company*. Toronto: Champlain Society, XXII (1934).
_____. "Lefroy's Journey to the North-West". *T.R.S.C.*, Third Series, XXXII, 11 (1938): 67-96.
West, John. *The Substance of a Journal during a residence at the Red River Colony, 1820-23*. London, 1827.
Wilkes, Charles. *Narrative of the United States Exploring Expedition, 1838-1842*. 5 vols. Philadelphia, 1845.
Williams, Glyndwr, ed. *Andrew Graham's Observations on Hudson's Bay, 1767-91*. London: H.B.R.S., XXVII (1969).
_____. *Peter Skene Odgen's Snake Country Journals, 1827-29*. London: H.B.R.S., XXVIII (1971).
Zaremba, Eve, ed. *Privilege of Sex: A Century of Canadian Women*. Toronto, 1974.

II. SECONDARY SOURCES

Arthur, Elizabeth. "Charles McKenzie, l'homme seul." *Ontario History*, LXX (March 1978): 39-62.
Avery, M. W. "An additional chapter on Jane Barnes." *Pacific Northwest Quarterly*, 42 (1951): 330-332.
Bailey, Alfred G. *The Conflict of European and Eastern Algonkian Cultures 1504-1700: A Study in Canadian Civilization*. Toronto, 1969 [2nd edition].
Barker, Burt Brown. *The McLoughlin Empire and Its Rulers*. Glendale, Calif., 1959.
Bartholomew, G. W. "Recognition of polygamous marriages in Canada." *International and Comparative Law Quarterly*, 10 (1961): 305-27.
Bayley, Dennis. *A Londoner in Rupert's Land: Thomas Bunn of the Hudson's Bay Company*. Winnipeg, 1969.
Binns, Archie. *Peter Skene Ogden: Fur Trader*. Portland, Oregon, 1967.
Bishop, Charles. "Henley House Massacres." *The Beaver*, Autumn 1976, 36-41.
Bolt, Christine. *Victorian Attitudes to Race*. Toronto, 1971.
Bolus, Malvina. "The Son of I. Gunn." *The Beaver*, Winter 1971, 23-26.
Bredin, T. F. "The Red River Academy." *The Beaver*, Winter 1974, 10-17.
Brown, Jennifer. "Company Men and Native Families: Fur Trade Social and Domestic Relations in Canada's Old Northwest." Ph. D., University of Chicago, 1976.
_____. "Changing Views of Fur Trade Marriage and Domesticity: James Hargrave, His Colleagues, and 'The Sex' ", *Western Canadian Journal of Anthropology*, 6, 3 (1976): 92-105.
_____. "A Colony of Very Useful Hands." *The Beaver*, Spring 1977, 39-45.
_____. "Ultimate Respectability: Fur Trade Children in the 'Civilized World' ", *The Beaver*, Winter 1977, 4-10 and Spring 1978, 48-55.

_____. "Linguistic Solitudes in the Fur Trade: Some Changing Social Categories and their Implications" in Carol Judd and Arthur Ray, eds. *Old Trails and New Directions: Papers of the Third North American Fur Trade Conference*, Toronto, 1980.

Burwash, Nathaniel. "The gift to a nation of a written language." *T.R.S.C.*, Third Series, V, 11 (1911): 3-21.

Campbell, Maria. *Halfbreed*. Toronto, 1973.

Campbell, Marjorie Wilkins. *The North West Company*. Toronto, 1957.

_____. *The Saskatchewan*. Toronto, 1965.

_____. *William McGillivray, Lord of the North West*. Toronto, 1962.

_____. "Her Ladyship, My Squaw." *The Beaver*, Autumn 1954, 14-17.

Chalmers, John W. "Social Stratification of the Fur Trade." *Alberta Historical Review*, Winter 1969, 10-20.

Chaput, Donald. "The 'Misses Nolin' of Red River", *The Beaver*, Winter 1975, 14-17.

Clark, Alice. *Working Life of Women in the Seventeenth Century*. London, 1919.

Cline, Gloria G. *Peter Skene Ogden and the Hudson's Bay Company*. Norman, Okla., 1974.

Clouston, J. Storer. "Orkney and the Hudson's Bay Company." *The Beaver*, December 1936, 4-8; March 1937, 39-43; September 1937, 37-39.

Cole, Jean Murray. "Exile in the Wilderness." *The Beaver*, Summer 1972, 7-14.

Colman, Mary Elizabeth. "Schoolboy at Fort Victoria." *The Beaver*, December 1951, 18-22.

Cunnington, C. Willett. *English women's clothing in the 19th Century*. London, 1937.

Curtis, E. S. *The North American Indian*. 20 vols. New York, 1907.

Davidson, Gordon Charles. *The North West Company*. Berkeley, 1918.

Driver, H. E. *Indians of North America*. Chicago, 1961.

Drury, C. M. "The Columbia Maternal Association." *Oregon Historical Quarterly*, 39 (1938): 99-122.

Dugas, Georges. *La Première Canadienne au Nord-Ouest*. Winnipeg, 1907.

Eccles, W. J. *The Canadian Frontier, 1534-1760*. Albuquerque, 1969.

Elliott, T. C. "Marguerite Wadin McKay McLoughlin." *Oregon Historical Quarterly*, 36 (1935): 338-47.

Fisher, Robin. *Contact and Conflict: Indian-European Relations in British Columbia, 1774-1890*. Vancouver, 1977.

Foster, John E. "The Country-born in the Red River Settlement: 1820-1850." Ph.D., University of Alberta, 1972.

_____. "Missionaries, Mixed-Bloods and the Fur Trade: Four Letters of the Rev. William Cockran, Red River Settlement, 1830-33", *Western Canadian Journal of Anthropology*, 3, 1 (1972): 94-125.

_____. "Rupert's Land and the Red River Settlement, 1820-70", in L. G. Thomas, ed. *The Prairie West to 1905: A Canadian Sourcebook*. Toronto, 1975.

Fox, Claire. "Pregnancy, Childbirth and Infancy in Anglo-American Culture, 1675-1830." Ph.D., University of Pennsylvania, 1966.

Galbraith, John S. *The Little Emperor; Governor Simpson of the Hudson's Bay Company*. Toronto, 1976.

Gibbon, J. M. "The Coureur de Bois and his birthright." *T.R.S.C.*, Third Series, XXX, 11 (1936): 61-78.

Giraud, Marcel. *Le Métis Canadien*. Paris, 1945.

Gray, John M. *Lord Selkirk of Red River*. London, 1963.

Griffiths, N. E. S. *Penelope's Web: Some Perceptions of Women in European and Canadian Society*. Toronto, 1976.

Harris, R. Cole and John Warkentin. *Canada Before Confederation*. Toronto, 1974.

Healy, W. J. *Women of Red River*, Winnipeg, 1923.

Henriques, Fernando. *Children of Caliban: Miscegenation*. London, 1974.

Houghton, W. E. *The Victorian Frame of Mind, 1830-70*. London, 1957.

Innis, Harold A. *The Fur Trade in Canada*. Toronto, 1962 [revised edition].

Jacobs, Wilbur. "The Fatal Confrontation: Early Native-White Relations on the Frontiers of Australia, New Guinea and America — a Comparative Study." *Pacific Historical Review*, 40 (1971): 283-309.

Jaenen, C. *Friend and Foe; Aspects of French-Amerindian Contact in the 16th and 17th Centuries*. Toronto, 1976.

Jenness, Diamond. *The Indians of Canada*. Ottawa, 1955.

Johansson, Sheila. " 'Herstory' as History: A New Field or Another Fad?" in Berenice Carroll, ed. *Liberating Women's History*, Chicago, 1976.

Johnson, Alice M. "Ambassadress of Peace." *The Beaver*, December 1952, 42-45.

———. "York Boat Journal." *The Beaver*, September 1951, 32-35 and December 1951, 32-37.

Johnston, Jean. *Wilderness Women*. Toronto, 1976.

Josephy Jr., Alvin M. *The Artist was a Young Man: The Life Story of Peter Rindisbacher*. Fort Worth, Texas, 1970.

Kelly-Gadol, Joan. "The Social Relation of the Sexes: Methodological Implications of Women's History." *Signs*, I, 4 (1976): 809-824.

Knafla, Louis. "Marriage Customs, Law and Litigation in the Northwest, 1800-1914." Paper presented to the Annual Meeting of the Canadian Historical Association, 1978.

Landes, Ruth. *The Ojibwa Woman*. New York, 1971.

Lent, D. Geneva. *West of the Mountains: James Sinclair and the Hudson's Bay Company*. Seattle, 1963.

Lewis, Oscar. *The Effects of White Contact Upon Blackfoot Culture with Special Reference to the Role of the Fur Trade*. New York, 1942.

Lugrin, N. deB. *The pioneer women of Vancouver Island, 1843-1866*. Victoria, 1928.

Lurie, Nancy O. "Indian Women: A Legacy of Freedom." *The American Way*, April 1972, 28-35.

McDonald, Angus. "A Few Items of the West." *Washington Historical Quarterly*, 8, 3 (1917): 188-229.

McElroy, Ann. "The Negotiation of Sex-Role Identity In Eastern Arctic Culture Change." *Western Canadian Journal of Anthropology*, 6, 3 (1976): 184-197.

MacGregor, J. G. *Peter Fidler: Canada's Forgotten Surveyor, 1769-1822*. Toronto, 1966.

———. *John Rowand, Czar of the Prairies*. Saskatoon, 1978.

MacKay, Douglas. *The Honourable Company*. Toronto, 1966 [revised edition].

McKelvie, B.A. "Successor to Simpson." *The Beaver*, September 1951, 41-45.

Mackenzie, Cecil W. *Donald Mackenzie: "King of the Northwest"*. Los Angeles, 1937.

MacLeod, M. A. and Morton, W. L. *Cuthbert Grant of Grantown*. Toronto, 1963.

———. "Red River New Year." *The Beaver*, December 1953, 43-47.

MacLeod, William Christie. *The American Indian Frontier*. New York, 1928.

Mitchell, Elaine. "A Red River Gossip." *The Beaver*, Spring 1961, 4-11.

Morice, A. G. *Dictionnaire historique des Canadiens et des métis français de l'Ouest*. Quebec City, 1908.

———. *The History of the Northern Interior of British Columbia*. Fairfield, Wash., 1971 [reprint].

Morton, A. S. *A History of the Canadian West to 1870-71*. London, 1939.
_____. *Sir George Simpson, Overseas Governor of the Hudson's Bay Company*. Toronto, 1944.
_____. "The Place of the Red River Settlement in the Plans of the Hudson's Bay Company, 1812-1825." C.H.A. *Annual Report, 1929*, 103-109.
Morton, W. L. *Manitoba: A History*. Toronto, 1967.
_____. "The Canadian Métis." *The Beaver*, September 1950, 3-7.
_____. "Donald A. Smith and Governor George Simpson." *The Beaver*, Autumn 1978, 4-9.
"Mr. Beaver Objects." *The Beaver*, September 1941, 10-13.
Murphy, Yoland and R. F. Murphy, *Women of the Forest*, New York, 1974.
Neill, E. D. "History of the Ojibways and their connection with Fur Traders . . . ." *Minnesota Historical Collections*, 5 (1885): 395-511.
Nute, Grace Lee. *The Voyageur*. New York, 1931.
_____. "Journey for Frances." *The Beaver*, December 1953, 50-54; March 1954, 12-17; June 1954, 12-18.
O'Meara, Walter. *Daughters of the Country: The Women of the Fur Traders and Mountain Men*. New York, 1968.
_____. "Adventures in Local History." *Minnesota History*, 31, 1 (1950): 1-10.
Packard, Pearl. *The Reluctant Pioneer*. Montreal, 1968.
Pannekoek, Frits. "The Churches and the Social Structure in the Red River Area, 1818-1870." Ph.D., Queen's University, 1973.
_____. "Protestant Agricultural Zions of the Western Indian." *Journal of the Canadian Church Historical Society*, XIV, 3 (1972): 55-66.
_____. "The Rev. James Evans and the Social Antagonisms of Fur Trade Society, 1840-1846." in R. Allen, ed. *Religion and Society in the Prairie West*. Regina, 1974.
_____. "The Rev. Griffiths Owen Corbett and the Red River Civil War of 1869-70." *Canadian Historical Review*, LVII, 2 (1976): 133-149.
Pearsall, Ronald. *The Worm in the Bud: The World of Victorian Sexuality*. London, 1971.
Pescatello, Ann. *Power and Pawn: The Female in Iberian Families, Societies and Cultures*. London, 1976.
Porter, K. W. "Jane Barnes, first white woman in Oregon." *Oregon Historical Quarterly*, 31 (1930): 125-135.
Pritchett, John Perry. *The Red River Valley, 1811-1849*. New Haven, 1942.
Ray, Arthur J. *Indians in the Fur Trade, 1660-1870*. Toronto, 1974.
Rich, E. E. *The History of the Hudson's Bay Company, 1670-1870*. 2 vols. London, H.B.R.S., XXI and XXII.
Ross, Eric. *Beyond the River and the Bay*. Toronto, 1973.
Sanders, Douglas. "Indian Women: A Brief History of Their Roles and Rights." *McGill Law Journal*, 21, 4 (1975): 656-672.
Saum, Lewis O. *The Fur Trader and the Indian*. Seattle, 1965.
Saunders, R. M. "The emergence of the coureur des bois as a social type." C.H.A. *Annual Report*, 1939, 22-33.
Séguin, R. L. "La Canadienne au XVIIe et XVIIIe siècles." *Revue de l'histoire de l'amérique française*, XIII (1960): 492-508.
Skelton, Isabel. *The backwoodswoman, a chronicle of pioneer homelife in Upper and Lower Canada*. Toronto, 1924.
Slater, Hollis and Muriel Cree. "Cathedral of the Pioneers." *The Beaver*, December 1940, 10-13.
Smith, Marion B. "The Lady Nobody Knows." *British Columbia: a centennial anthology*. Vancouver, 1958.
Spear, Percival. *The Nabobs: A Study of the Social Life of the English in 18th Century India*. London, 1963.
Spindler, L. S. and G. D. "Male and female adaptations in culture change." *American Anthropologist*, 60 (1958): 217-233.

Spry, Irene. "The Transition from a Nomadic to a Settled Economy in Western Canada, 1856-96." *T.R.S.C.*, Fourth Series, VI, 11 (1968): 187-201.

Stevenson, J. A. "Disaster in the Dalles." *The Beaver*, September 1942, 19-21.

Stubbs, Roy St. George. *Four Recorders of Rupert's Land*. Winnipeg, 1967.

Terrell, John U. and Donna M. *Indian Women of the Western Morning: Their Early Life in Early America*. New York, 1976.

Thomas, Keith. "The Double Standard." *Journal of the History of Ideas*, 20 (1959): 195-216.

Thompson, A.N. "John West: A Study of the Conflict between Civilization and the Fur Trade." *Journal of Canadian Church Historical Society*, XII, 3 (1970): 44-57.

_____. "The Wife of the Missionary." *Journal of Canadian Church Historical Society*, XV, 2: 35-44.

Van Kirk, Sylvia. "The Role of Women in the Fur Trade Society of the Canadian West, 1700-1850". Ph.D., University of London, 1975.

_____. "Women and the Fur Trade." *The Beaver*, Winter 1972, 4-21.

_____. "Thanadelthur." *The Beaver*, Spring 1974, 40-45.

_____. "'The Custom of the Country': An Examination of Fur Trade Marriage Practices" in L. H. Thomas, ed. *Essays on Western History*. Edmonton, 1976.

_____. "Women in Between: Indian Women in Fur Trade Society." *Historical Papers, 1977*, 31-46.

Wallace, W. S. *The Pedlars from Quebec and other Papers on the Nor'Westers*. Toronto, 1954.

Walton, F. P. *Scotch Marriages, regular and irregular*. Edinburgh, 1893.

Welter, Barbara. "The Cult of True Womanhood: 1820-1860." *American Quarterly*, 18, 2 (1966): 151-174.

Williams, Glyndwr. "Highlights of the First 200 Years of the Hudson's Bay Company." *The Beaver*, Autumn 1970.

Wilson, Clifford. *Campbell of the Yukon*. Toronto, 1970.

254

REFERENCES

Introduction

1 G. P. deT. Glazebrook, ed., *The Hargrave Correspondence 1821-1843* (Toronto: Champlain Society, XXIV), 310-311.
2 See Harold A. Innis, *The Fur Trade in Canada* (Toronto, 1962); A. S. Morton, *A History of the Canadian West to 1870-71* (London, 1939); and E. E. Rich, *The History of the Hudson's Bay Company, 1670-1870*, 2 vols. (London: H.B.R.S., XXI and XXII).
3 John Foster, "Rupert's Land and the Red River Settlement, 1820-1870" in L. G. Thomas, ed., *The Prairie West to 1905* (Toronto, 1975), p. 21.
4 For a good general discussion of the Indian tribes of Canada, see Diamond Jenness, *The Indians of Canada* (Ottawa, 1955).
5 The only published work on this subject is a popular work by Walter O'Meara, *Daughters of the Country: The Women of the Fur Traders and Mountain Men* (New York, 1968). In Lewis Saum's *The Fur Trader and the Indian* (Seattle, 1965), there is only a brief, superficial mention of this important aspect of Indian-white relations. Marcel Giraud, however, lays useful groundwork in his massive study *Le Métis Canadien* (Paris, 1945).
6 For a useful overview of the process of miscegenation in India, Africa and the Americas, see Fernando Henriques, *Children of Caliban: Miscegenation* (London, 1974).
7 For a discussion of women's role in pre-industrial society, see Alice Clark, *Working Life of Women in the Seventeenth Century* (London, 1919).
8 In this study, the term "mixed-blood" will be used to describe people of Indian-European origin. Like the French word "Métis", it accommodates all gradations of racial mixture and does not carry the pejorative connotation of the word "half-breed". For a discussion of both contemporary and modern terms and the problems connected with their usage, see Jennifer Brown, "Linguistic Solitudes in the Fur Trade: Some Changing Social Categories and their Implications" in C. M. Judd and A. J. Ray, eds., *Old Trails and New Directions: Papers of the Third North American Fur Trade Conference* (Toronto, 1980).
9 Joan Kelly-Gadol, "The Social Relation of the Sexes: Methodological Implications of Women's History", *Signs*, I, 4 (1976): 809-824.
10 See particularly Yolanda and R. F. Murphy, *Women of the Forest* (New York, 1974).
11 See Henriques, *Children of Caliban*.
12 This view is again articulated in a recent important text by R. C. Harris and John Warkentin, *Canada Before Confederation* (Toronto, 1974), 245.
13 See Arthur J. Ray, *Indians in the Fur Trade. 1660-1870* (Toronto, 1974) and Robin Fisher, *Contact and Conflict, Indian-European Relations in British Columbia, 1774-1890* (Vancouver, 1977).
14 Sheila Johansson, "'Herstory' as History: A New Field or Another Fad" in Berenice Carroll, ed., *Liberating Women's History*, 400-430.

Chapter One: Enter the White Man

1   The influence of the concepts of hierarchy and class is an important theme in the historical development of Canadian society as can be seen in the French experience on the frontier. See W. J. Eccles, *The Canadian Frontier, 1534-1760* (Albuquerque, 1969).

2   "The Company's Political Relations with the Indians", in L. G. Thomas, ed., *The Prairie West to 1905* (Toronto, 1975), 29-30.

3   E. E. Rich, ed., *Minutes of the Hudson's Bay Company, 1679-82* (Toronto: Champlain Society, VIII), 250.

4   Eric Ross, *Beyond the River and the Bay* (Toronto, 1973), 19-22.

5   Jennifer Brown, " 'Company Men and Native Families': Fur Trade Social and Domestic Relations in Canada's Old Northwest" (Ph.D., University of Chicago, 1976), 92.

6   *Ibid.,* 53.

7   E. E. Rich, ed. *Copy-Book of Letters Outward, 1679-1694* (Toronto: Champlain Society, XI), 81, 126.

8   Richard Glover, ed., *David Thompson's Narrative, 1784-1812* (Toronto: Champlain Society, XL), 108-09.

9   Ross, *Beyond the River and the Bay,* 160.

10   W. Kaye Lamb, ed., *Sixteen Years in the Indian Country: The Journal of Daniel Williams Harmon, 1800-1816* (Toronto, 1957), 197-98; Ross Cox, *The Columbia River,* edited by Edgar and Jane Stewart (Norman, Okla., 1957), 354-58.

11   For a detailed discussion of the kinship networks which characterized the personnel structure of the North West Company, see Brown, " 'Company Men and Native Families' ", 104-116.

12   Lawrence Burpee, ed., *Journals and Letters of Pierre Gaultier de Varennes de la Vérendrye and his Sons* (Toronto: Champlain Society, XVI), 149; A. S. Morton, *A History of the Canadian West to 1870-71* (London, 1939), 180-82, 86.

13   H.B.C.A., A.11/4, fo. 29.

14   Morton, *History of the Canadian West,* 349.

15   Eccles, *The Canadian Frontier,* 149; H.B.C.A., B.239/a/72, fo. 36.

16   Edward Umfreville, *The Present State of Hudson's Bay,* ed. by W. S. Wallace (Toronto, 1954), 109.

17   Rich, *Letters Outward, 1679-1694,* 79.

18   Glyndwr Williams, ed., *Andrew Graham's Observations on Hudson's Bay, 1767-91* (London: H.B.R.S., XXVII), 248; Umfreville, *Present State of Hudson's Bay,* 154.

19   Rich, *Letters Outward, 1679-1694,* 40-41.

20   *Ibid.*

21   H.B.C.A., A.6/3, fo. 53-53d; Samuel Hearne, *A Journey to the Northern Ocean,* edited by Richard Glover (Toronto, 1958), lxv.

22   K. G. Davies, ed., *Letters from Hudson Bay, 1703-40* (London: H.B.R.S., XXV), 270-71.

23   H.B.C.A., B.135/a/17, fo. 16d.

24   H.B.C.A., Company Annals, No. 8 (1749), 6.

25   The choicest parts of the meat were always reserved for the men, and in times of scarcity the women were reduced to a diet of berries and roots. Samuel Hearne observed that several Chipewyan women died of starvation on the journey back from the Coppermine River in 1772 (Hearne, *Journey to Northern Ocean,* 190).

26   H.B.C.A., B.3/a/1, fo. 28.

27   H.B.C.A., B.3/a/63, fo. 14.

28   More comparison between the work done by Indian and white women might have been forthcoming if any of the writers had been French-Canadian. In New France, visitors observed that the girls lost their beauty prematurely because of their laborious life, having to undertake masculine occupations such as working in the fields, see R. L. Séguin, *La Canadienne au XVIIe et XVIIIe siècles"*, *Revue de l'histoire de l'amérique français*, XIII (1960): 492-508.

29   A. G. Doughty and C. Martin, eds., *The Kelsey Papers* (Ottawa, 1929), 21-22.

30   W. Kaye Lamb, ed., *The Journals and Letters of Sir Alexander Mackenzie*, (Cambridge, England, 1970), 135; see also Williams, *Graham's Observations*, 177-78.

31   Lamb, *Journals of Mackenzie*, 135; Glover, *Thompson's Narrative*, 106.

32   Hearne, *Journey to Northern Ocean*, 56: ". . . custom makes it sit light on those whose lot it is to bear it." See also Isaac Cowie, *The Company of Adventurers* (Toronto, 1913), 318-19.

33   Glover, *Thompson's Narrative*, 125.

34   Hearne, *Journey to Northern Ocean*, 35.

35   *Ibid.*, 56, 35. A stone was equal to fourteen pounds.

36   Claire Fox, "Pregnancy, Childbirth and Infancy in Anglo-American Culture: 1675-1830" (Ph.D., University of Pennsylvania, 1966), 118.

37   Williams, *Graham's Observations*, 177; also Lamb, *Journals of Mackenzie*, 250; Lamb, *Sixteen Years in Indian Country*, 79-80; L. R. F. Masson, *Les Bourgeois de la Compagnie du Nord-Ouest* (New York, 1960), I: 286-87.

38   Lamb, *Sixteen Years in Indian Country*, 218; Margaret A. MacLeod, ed., *The Letters of Letitia Hargrave* (Toronto: Champlain Society, XXVIII), 97.

39   Hearne, *Journey to Northern Ocean*, 59.

40   E. E. Rich, ed., *James Isham's Observations and Notes, 1743-49.* (London, H.B.R.S., XII), 104.

41   *Ibid.* The example of Indian women nursing their own children was used in the campaign in the eighteenth century against the widespread employment of wet nurses in Europe, see Fox, "Pregnancy, Childbirth and Infancy", 196, and Cornelius Jaenen, *Friend and Foe: Aspects of French-Amerindian Cultural Contact in the 16th and 17th Centuries* (Toronto, 1976), 32-33.

42   P.A.C., MG 19 D2, Fort Severn Journal, 1768-69, I, Pt. 11: 57; MacLeod, *Letitia's Letters*, 94-95; Alexander Ross, *The Red River Settlement* (Minneapolis, 1957), 95, 192.

43   MacLeod, *Letitia's Letters*, 87.

44   Rich, *Isham's Observations*, 105-06.

45   John Henry Lefroy, *In Search of the Magnetic North: A Soldier-Surveyor's Letters from the North-West 1843-44*, edited by G. F. G. Stanley (Toronto, 1955), 130.

46   Lamb, *Journals of Mackenzie*, 133-34.

47   Alexander Henry, *Travels and Adventures in Canada and the Indian Territories, 1760-1776*, edited by James Bain (Boston, 1901), 247; Williams, *Graham's Observations*, 150.

48   Henry, *Travels and Adventures*, 293, 302, 312; Glover, *Thompson's Narrative*, 177, 255; Cox, *Columbia River*, 71; Gabriel Franchère, *Narrative of a Voyage to the Northwest Coast of America, 1811-1814*, edited by R. G. Thwaites (Cleveland, Ohio, 1904), 325-26.

49   Hearne, *Journey to Northern Ocean*, 56.

50   Rich, *Isham's Observations*, 79; Masson, *Les Bourgeois*, II: 247-48.

51   Hearne, *Journey to Northern Ocean*, 81.

52   Glover, *Thompson's Narrative*, 348, 362, 376; Elliot Coues, ed., *New Light on the Early History of the Greater Northwest: The Manuscript Journals of Alexander Henry and David Thompson, 1799-1814*. (Minneapolis, Minn., 1965), 749, 849.
53   Rich, *Isham's Observations*, 80; Williams, *Graham's Observations*, 153.
54   H. E. Driver, *Indians of North America* (Chicago, 1961), 265.
55   Rich, *Isham's Observations*, 101.
56   Williams, *Graham's Observations*, 175; Masson, *Les Bourgeois*, II: 251-52.
57   Glover, *Thompson's Narrative*, 82; Lamb, *Sixteen Years in Indian Country*, 53.
58   Williams, *Graham's Observations*, 158; Glover, *Thompson's Narrative*, 251; Alexander Ross, *Adventures of the First Settlers on the Oregon or Columbia River* (London, 1849), 280-81.
59   Hearne, *Journey to Northern Ocean*, 67-69.
60   Glover, *Thompson's Narrative*, 126-27.
61   Rich, *Isham's Observations*, 95; Hearne, *Journey to Northern Ocean*, 83-84; Williams, *Graham's Observations*, 157-58.
62   Charles Bishop, "The Henley House Massacres", *The Beaver* (Autumn 1976), 40.
63   Hearne, *Journey to Northern Ocean*, 82; Lamb, *Journals of Mackenzie*, 134; Coues, *New Light on Greater Northwest*, 515, 517; Cox, *The Columbia River*, 166-67.
64   Lamb, *Journals of Mackenzie*, 324; Coues, *New Light on Greater Northwest*, 324; Glover, *Thompson's Narrative*, 177.
65   H.B.C.A., *Report from the Committee, appointed to inquire into the State and Condition of the Countries Adjoining to Hudson's Bay and of the Trade carried on there, 24 April 1749*, 219.
66   Henry, *Travels and Adventures*, 248, 333.
67   A.S. Morton, ed., *The Journal of Duncan McGillivray . . . at Fort George on the Saskatchewan, 1794-95* (Toronto, 1929), 46; Coues, *New Light on Greater Northwest*, 735.
68   Cox, *The Columbia River*, 166-67.
69   Rich, *Isham's Observations*, 103-06; see also Hearne, *Journey to Northern Ocean*, 81.
70   H.B.C.A., E. 2/4, fo. 16; Joseph Robson, *An Account of Six Years Residence in Hudson's Bay* (London, 1752), 52.
71.   H.B.C.A., A.5/1, fo. 54d; B.239/a/66, fo. 37.

Chapter Two: The Custom of the Country

1   Jesuits, Letters from Missions, *Black gown and redskins; adventures and travels of the early Jesuit missionaries in North America (1610-1791)*, edited by Edna Kenton (New York, 1956), 397-405.
2   Charles Bishop, "Henley House Massacres". *The Beaver* (Autumn 1976), 39.
3   Toronto Public Library, Baldwin Room, George Nelson Papers, Journal 1810-11, 41-42; Frederick Merk, ed., *Fur Trade and Empire: George Simpson's Journal, 1824-25* (Cambridge, Mass., 1931), 99.
4   "Connolly vs. Woolrich, Superior Court, Montreal, 9 July 1867", *Lower Canada Jurist*, XI: 197, 234, (hereafter referred to as "Connolly Case, 1867". See also W. Kaye Lamb, ed., *Sixteen Years in the Indian Country: The Journal of Daniel Williams Harmon, 1800-1816* (Toronto, 1957), 62-63.
5   H.B.C.A., E.2/4, fo. 22d; B.239/a/40, fo. 80.
6   H.B.C.A., B.135/a/14, fo. 32; B.3/a/63, fo. 18d.

7   *Catholic Church Records of the Pacific Northwest: Vancouver, vols. I and II and Stellamaris Mission,* translated by Mikell de Lores Wormell Warner and annotated by Harriet Duncan Munnick, (St. Paul, Oregon, 1972), Vanc. I, B-34, 3rd p.

8   Gloria G. Cline, *Peter Skene Ogden and the Hudson's Bay Company* (Norman, Okla., 1974), 29.

9   Coues, Elliot, ed. *New Light on the Early History of the Greater Northwest: The Manuscript Journals of Alexander Henry and of David Thompson, 1799-1814* (Minneapolis, Minn., 1965), 901. For an account of this marriage reputedly derived from McDougall's Astoria journal, see Washington Irving, *Astoria, or Anecdotes of an Enterprise Beyond the Rocky Mountains* (Norman, Okla., 1964), 461-63.

10.   Frederick Merk, ed., *Fur Trade and Empire: George Simpson's Journal, 1824-25* (Cambridge, Mass., 1931), 86-87, 104-05.

11   Ross Cox, *The Columbia River*, edited by Edgar and Jane Stewart, (Norman, Okla., 1957).

12   Lamb, *Sixteen Years in Indian Country*, 137. For details of Boucher's career, see A. G. Morice, *The History of the Northern Interior of British Columbia* (Fairfield, Wash., 1971), 253-57.

13   A. S. Morton, ed. *The Journal of Duncan McGillivray . . . at Fort George on the Sasskatchewan, 1794-95* (Toronto, 1929), 41.

14   E. E. Rich, ed., *Simpson's Athabasca Journal and Report, 1820-21* (London: H.B.R.S., I), 392.

15   George Simpson, *Narrative of a Journey Round the World, 1841-42* (London, 1847), I, 231.

16   H.B.C.A., B.3/a/63, fo. 18-18d.

17   J. G. MacGregor, *Peter Fidler: Canada's Forgotten Surveyor* (Toronto, 1966), 252.

18   Alexander Ross, *Adventures of the First Settlers on the Oregon or Columbia River* (London, 1849), 280; H.B.C.A., A.36/11, Will of Alexander Ross, 5 June 1856.

19   H.B.C.A., D.5/30, fo. 364.

20   E. E. Rich, ed., *Hudson's Bay Company Letters Outward, 1679-94* (London, H.B.R.S., XI), 235; H.B.C.A., A.6/4, fo. 48. For a discussion of the experience of the first white women on Hudson Bay, see Chapter 8.

21   Ann M. Pescatello, *Power and Pawn: The Female in Iberian Families, Societies and Cultures* (London, 1976), 137, 141, 154; Percival Spear, *The Nabobs: A Study of the Social Life of the English in 18th Century India* (London, 1963), 82, 140.

22   G. P. deT. Glazebrook, ed., *The Hargrave Correspondence, 1821-1843* (Toronto: Champlain Society, XXIV), 381. Author's emphasis.

23   Alexander Ross, *The Fur Hunters of the Far West* (London, 1855), I: 296.

24   Coues, *New Light on Greater Northwest*, 228.

25   Lamb, *Sixteen Years in Indian Country*, 53.

26   Cox, *Columbia River*, 209.

27   Coues, *New Light on Greater Northwest*, 901.

28   Cox, *Columbia River*, 142-43.

29   *Ibid.*, 209-11; Lamb, *Sixteen Years in Indian Country*, 28-29.

30   H.B.C.A., B.3/b/2, fo. 12; B.135/a/11, fo. 64.

31   Coues, *New Light on Greater Northwest*, 211.

32   E. E. Rich, ed. *James Isham's Observations and Notes, 1743-49* (London, H.B.R.S., XII), 322, 325; H.B.C.A., A.11/2, fos. 173-74; A.6/7, fo. 110d.

33   Samuel Hearne, *A Journey to the Northern Ocean*, edited by Richard Glover (Toronto, 1958), 39-40.

34 P.R.O., Prob. 11/1322, fo. 256, Will of Matthew Cocking, 27 Jan. 1797.

35 H.B.C.A., Selkirk Papers, Copy No. 154, pp. 62-63, 74. Lady Selkirk wrote to her husband in 1818: ". . . it is only a Scotch Clergyman that will bring more decent proceedings among Hudson's Bay traders. According to Graffenreid, the offence to Bird and Thomas was, that you disapproved of more than one Indian wife . . . Bird has three Indian ladies it seems. . . ." (Selkirk Papers, Copy No. 159, pp. 886-87.

36 J. B. Tyrrell, ed., *Journals of Samuel Hearne and Philip Turnor, 1774-1792* (Toronto: Champlain Society, XXI), 275.

37 "Connolly Case, 1867", 239.

38 Tyrrell, *Journals of Hearne and Turnor*, 252-53.

39 H.B.C.A., B.42/a/136a, fo. 18d.

40 H.B.C.A., A.6/6, fo. 100.

41 H.B.C.A., B.239/b/78, fo. 12; A.6/16, fo. 246.

42 W. Stewart Wallace, ed. *Documents relating to the North West Company* (Toronto: Champlain Society, XXII), 211.

43 Lamb, *Sixteen Years in Indian Country*, 62-63; Coues, *New Light on Greater Northwest*, 58, 162; Nelson Papers, Journal 1803-04, 3, 6-8.

44 Nelson Papers, Reminiscences, Pt. 5, 206-07.

45 Lamb, *Sixteen Years in Indian Country*, 98.

46 "Johnstone *et al.* vs. Connolly, Appeal Court, 7 Sept. 1869", *La Revue Légale*, I: 280 (hereafter cited as "Connolly Appeal Case, 1869").

47 Rich, *Isham's Observations*, 95.

48 H.B.C.A., E.2/7, fo. 24d.

49 Glyndwr Williams, ed., *Andrew Graham's Observations on Hudson's Bay, 1767-91* (London: H.B.R.S., XXVII), 248.

50 H.B.C.A., B.239/a/50, fo. 5-5d.

51 H.B.C.A., B.3/a/46, fos. 5, 17.

52 H.B.C.A., A.11/43, fo. 114d.

53 H.B.C.A., B.42/a/36, fos. 19d-20, 23; B.42/a/38, fos. 26d-28.

54 H.B.C.A., B.42/a/38, fos. 13-15.

55 H.B.C.A., B.135/a/11, fos. 46-47, 64-66.

56 This and the following quotations are taken from George Rushworth's account of the "real cause" of the attack on Henley House, H.B.C.A., A.11/2, fos. 173-74. For a discussion of the two Indian attacks on Henley House in the 1750s, see Bishop, "Henley House Massacres", *The Beaver* (Autumn 1976), 36-41.

57 H.B.C.A., A.6/9, fos. 29d-30.

58 When forbidden open contact with Indian women, some Company servants took to sneaking over the walls at night to the Indian tents and debauching the women with presents of liquor (H.B.C.A., B.42/a/38, fos. 13-15). While attacks upon HBC men were rare, in 1788 William Appleby was murdered by an irate Indian husband for taking unsanctioned liberties with his wife (H.B.C.A., B.239/b/50, fo. 18d).

59 H.B.C.A., B.22/a/6, fo. 8d.

60 P.R.O., Will of Matthew Cocking.

61 H.B.C.A., A.36/3, Will of William Bolland, 12 July 1804; P.R.O., Prob. 11/1785, fo. 551, Will of John Favell, 19 Feb. 1784; Prob. 11/1141, fo. 229, Will of Robert Goodwin, Codicil, 22 April 1803.

62 H.B.C.A., A.36/6, Will of William Flett, 9 Nov. 1823.

63 H.B.C.A., E.2/7, fo. 5d; Alexander Henry, *Travels and Adventures in Canada and the Indian Territories*, edited by James Bain (Boston, 1901), 248.

64 Chief Factor John Dugald Cameron eventually took his Cree wife Mary to settle in Upper Canada. Captain Roderick McKenzie was so devoted to his native family that he never left the Indian Country. His marriage to Angélique, the daughter of an Ojibwa chief, lasted through his early

days as a Nor'Wester, his long service in the Hudson's Bay Company and his retirement to Red River.

65   P.A.C., Masson Collection, No. 15, Journal of a Nor'Wester, 1978, 18; H.B.C.A., B.89/a/2, fo. 2.
66   Marcel Giraud, *Le Métis Canadien* (Paris, 1945), 361-62.
67   Coues, *New Light on Greater Northwest*, 206.
68   H.B.C.A., B.39/a/22, fo. 42; Nelson Papers, Journal 1808-1810, 19 March 1810; W. Kaye Lamb, ed. *The Journals and Letters of Sir Alexander Mackenzie* (Cambridge, England, 1970), 423.
69   Rich, *Simpson's Athabasca Journal*, 88.
70   Tyrrell, *Journals of Hearne and Turnor*, 514.
71   "Connolly Case, 1867", 229.
72   Gabriel Franchère, *Narrative of a Voyage to the Northwest Coast of America, 1811-1814*, edited by Ruben Gold Thwaites (Cleveland, Ohio, 1904), 366-67, 388.
73   This woman is also referred to in the journals as Rico higgin, Rue hegan and Ruwehegan.
74   P.R.O., Prob. 11/784, Will of Robert Pilgrim, 23 Nov. 1750, fo. 396.
75   H.B.C.A., A.6/8, fo. 54d.
76   H.B.C.A., B.135/a/14, fo. 32; B.239/a/79, fo. 45.
77   Cox, *Columbia River*, 224, 359-61; P.A.C., James Hargrave Correspondence, Hargrave to parents, Fort Garry, 29 Jan. 1827.
78   Wallace, *Documents of N.W.C.*, 478-79.
79   Jennifer Brown, "Company Men and Native Families: Fur Trade Social and Domestic Relations in Canada's Old Northwest." (Ph.D, University of Chicago, 1976), 222.
80   Marjorie Wilkins Campbell, *Lord of the Northwest* (Toronto, 1962), 277.
81   It should be noted that quite a few of the bourgeois did send their mixed-blood children down to Eastern Canada to be educated, see Jennifer Brown, "Ultimate Respectability: Fur Trade Children in the 'Civilized World' ", *The Beaver* (Winter 1977), 4-10.
82   Cox, *Columbia River*, 361; see also "Connolly Appeal Case, 1869", 289.
83   Lamb, *Sixteen Years in Indian Country*, 98.
84   P.A.C., Hargrave Correspondence, Hargrave to parents, 29 Jan. 1827.
85   H.B.C.A., B.3/b/49a, fo. 10d.
86   Lamb, *Sixteen Years in Indian Country*, 5-6.
87   "Connolly Appeal Case, 1869", 284.
88   "Connolly Case, 1867", 231; see also "Connolly Appeal Case, 1869", 280-82.
89   P.A.C., Ermatinger Family Papers, Series 4, Will of Charles Oakes Ermatinger, 4 July 1831; "Connolly Case, 1867", 237.
90   Archie Binns, *Peter Skene Ogden: Fur Trader* (Portland, Oregon, 1967), 355.
91   "Connolly Case, 1867", 237.
92   H.B.C.A., B.223/b/20, fo. 62-62d. See also F. P. Walton, *Scottish Marriages, regular and irregular* (Edinburgh, 1893).

Chapter Three: Your Honors Servants

1   Jesuits. Letters from Missions. *Black gown and redskins; adventures and travels of the early Jesuit missionaries in North America, 1610-1791*, edited by Edna Kenton (New York, 1956), 401-02.
2   H.B.C.A., B.239/b/79, fos. 40d-41; see also J. B. Tyrrell, ed., *Journals of Samuel Hearne and Philip Turnor, 1774-1792* (Toronto: Champlain Society, XXI), 327, n.6; H.B.C.A., A.11/116, fo. 77d.

3   P.A.C., Masson Collection, No. 3, "An Account of the Chipwean Indians", 22.
4   H.B.C.A., B.239/a/105, fo. 11; B.42/a/36, fo. 23; B.42/a/5, fo. 7.
5   W. Kaye Lamb, ed., *The Journals and Letters of Sir Alexander Mackenzie* (Cambridge, England, 1970), 220.
6   Tyrrell, *Journals of Hearne and Turnor*, 125.
7   Lamb, *Journals of Mackenzie*, 424.
8   H.B.C.A., B.239/b/79, fo. 41.
9   P.A.C., Masson Collection, No. 6, John Porter's Journal, 29; H.B.C.A., B.121/a/4, fo. 48d.
10   Elliott Coues, ed., *New Light on the Early History of the Greater Northwest: The Manuscript Journals of Alexander Henry and of David Thompson, 1799-1814* (Minneapolis, Minn., 1965), 582-83; Charles M. Gates, ed., *Five Fur Traders of the Northwest* (St. Paul, Minn., 1965), 161; L. R. F. Masson, *Les Bourgeois de la Compagnie du Nord-Ouest* (New York, 1960), I: 288.
11   H.B.C.A., B.39/a/16, fo. 21.
12   Gabriel Franchère, *Narrative of a Voyage to the Northwest Coast of America, 1811-1814*, edited by R. G. Thwaites (Cleveland, Ohio, 1904), 5.
13   H.B.C.A., B.239/a/131-33 *passim*.
14   Michel Curot, "A Wisconsin Fur-Trader's Journal, 1803-04", *Wisconsin Historical Collections*, XX: 442-43.
15   Gates, *Five Fur Traders*, 237; Curot, "Journal, 1803-04", 441.
16   H.B.C.A., B.27/a/14, fo. 98.
17   Coues, *New Light on Greater Northwest*, 485.
18   Richard Glover, ed., *David Thompson's Narrative, 1784-1812* (Toronto: Champlain Society, XL), 55.
19   Coues, *New Light on Greater Northwest*, 859; Ross Cox, *The Columbia River*, edited by Edgar and Jane Stewart (Norman, Okla., 1957), 266.
20   H.B.C.A., B.39/a/16, fos. 4d-13 *passim*.
21   H.B.C.A., B.89/a/2, fos. 7, 10d.
22   Margaret A. MacLeod, ed. *The Letters of Letitia Hargrave* (Toronto: Champlain Society, XXVIII), lii.
23   The following account is taken from the George Nelson Papers, Journal, 29 Jan.-23 June 1815.
24   H.B.C.A., B.239/a/126, fo. 14.
25   MacLeod, *Letitia's Letters*, 85.
26   H.B.C.A., B.239/b/79, fo. 40d; see also Tyrrell, *Journals of Hearne and Turnor*, 237, n.6.
27   Coues, *New Light on Greater Northwest*, 615; Gates, *Five Fur Traders*, 217; E. E. Rich, ed., *Simpson's Athabasca Journal and Report, 1820-21* (London: H.B.R.S., I), 342.
28   Coues, *New Light on Greater Northwest*, 622; Gates, *Five Fur Traders*, 250-52; Curot, "Journal, 1803-04", 460.
29   H.B.C.A., B.239/a/130, fos. 22d-28 *passim*.
30   Lamb, *Journals of Mackenzie*, 165.
31   H.B.C.A., A.11/44, fo. 95.
32   H.B.C.A., B.239/a/99, fo. 18d: Colen further adds that "this occasions much murmuring among the Men and forces many to leave the Service sooner than they wished to". Unfortunately, no further information has been found to explain either the cause or ultimate outcome of this action.
33   The services of Indian women are mentioned in all four versions of Anthony Henday's journal in the Company archives, see H.B.C.A., B.239/a/40; E.2/4, fos. 35-60; E.2/6, fos. 10d-38d and E.2/11, fos. 1-40d). The most complete references are to be found in E.2/6 and E.2/11.

34   Samuel Hearne, *A Journey to the Northern Ocean*, edited by Richard Glover, (Toronto, 1958), 35.

35   The services rendered by Indian women were recognized to such an extent that Sir Alexander Mackenzie recommended to Captain John Franklin, the British explorer, that Indian women should accompany his overland expedition in 1819 (Masson, *Les Bourgeois*, I: 136).

36   A. G. Doughty and Chester Martin, eds., *The Kelsey Papers* (Ottawa, 1929), xv.

37   H.B.C.A., E.2/4, fo. 52-52d. This version gives the most complete account of the warnings Henday received from his Cree helpmate, but see also E.2/6, fos. 17, 27, 29d.

38   H.B.C.A., B.239/a/48, fo. 47; B.239/a/53, fo. 40d; A.11/115, fo. 85.

39   Tyrrell, *Journals of Hearne and Turnor*, 252-3, 274.

40   Alexander Henry, *Travels and Adventures in Canada and the Indian Territories, 1760-1776*, edited by James Bain (Boston, 1901), 326.

41   H.B.C.A., B.89/a/2, fo.10.

42   H.B.C.A., B.182/a/6, fo. 3. Eskimo women also served as interpreters, see B. 182/a/9, fo. 37. On the West Main, an Eskimo woman called Doll was sent from York to Churchill to accompany the sloop as interpreter on a northward journey in 1764 to acquaint the natives of "our Friendly Intentions", B.42/b/9, fos. 2, 4; A. 11/4, fos. 1-2.

43   H.B.C.A.,B.22/e/1, fo. 9d.

44   Rich, *Simpson's Athabasca Journal*, 231.

45   *Ibid.*, 264.

46   Coues, *New Light*, 793; Frederick Merk, ed. *Fur Trade and Empire: George Simpson's Journal, 1824-25* (Cambridge, Mass., 1931), 104-05; H.B.C.A., D.5/8, fo. 147.

47   The story of Thanadelthur is told in remarkable detail in Governor Knight's journals, H.B.C.A., B.239/a/1-3. See Sylvia Van Kirk, "Thanadelthur", *The Beaver* (Spring 1974), 40-45 for a fuller interpretation.

48   Lamb, *Journals of Mackenzie*, 152.

49   H.B.C.A., B.239/a/40, fos. 41d, 80.

50   Tyrrell, *Journals of Hearne and Turnor*, 273.

51   H.B.C.A., B.135/a/11, fo. 62d.

52   H.B.C.A., B.239/b/78, fo. 55.

53   Glover; *Thompson's Narrative*, 67. Thompson also states that it was the women's prerogative to trade dried provisions, 235.

54   Gates, *Five Fur Traders*, 129.

55   P.A.C., Masson Collection, No. 1, Journal of Charles Chaboillez, 1797-98, 30-43 *passim*.

56   Alexander Ross, *Adventures of the first Settlers on the Oregon or Columbia River* (London, 1849), 106-07.

57   Henry, *Travels and Adventures*, 61; Walter O'Meara, *Daughters of the Country* (New York, 1968), 276-77.

58   H.B.C.A., B.135/a/14, fo. 32.

59   H.B.C.A., B.135/e/3, fo. 9. While the hunt of individual women was generally not large enough to be detailed, that of one Watichusksqwow at York was probably not unusual. On 27 November 1814, she traded 1 silver fox, 2 white foxes, 3 martens, 2 musquash, and 41 rabbits plus the flesh of 10; she was back a fortnight later with 18 more skins, half of them foxes (H.B.C.A., B.239/a/121, fos. 8d-10).

60   H.B.C.A., A.11/19, fo. 1d; B.135/c/1, fo. 269.

Chapter Four: Women in Between

1   Several other anthropological studies support this view of native women

being active agents of economic change. Ann McElroy in her article "The Negotiation of Sex-Role Identity in Arctic Culture Change", *Western Canadian Journal of Anthropology*, 6, 3: 184-197, discusses the important role of Eskimo women in helping Arctic explorers. Inter-racial contact, she argues, was of more benefit to Eskimo women than men. Similarly in Yolanda and Robert Murphy's *Women of the forest* (New York, 1974), a study of the Mundurucu tribe of Amazonian Brazil, the women actively championed the erosion of traditional village life and the concomitant blurring of economic sex roles which came with the introduction of the rubber trade in order to alleviate their onerous domestic duties.

2   N.E.S. Griffiths, *Penelope's Web: Some Perceptions of Women in European and Canadian Society* (Toronto, 1976), 8.

3   Charles Bishop, "Henley House Massacres", *The Beaver* (Autumn 1976), 38.

4   P.A.C., Masson Collection, No. 1, Journal of Charles Chaboillez, 1797-98. 24; Toronto Public Library, Baldwin Room, George Nelson Papers, Journal and Reminiscences 1825-26, 66.

5   Frederick Merk, ed. *Fur Trade and Empire: George Simpson's Journal, 1824-25* (Cambridge, Mass., 1931), 104; Elliot Coues, ed. *New Light on the Early History of the Greater Northwest: The Manuscript Journals of Alexander Henry and of David Thompson, 1799-1814* (Minneapolis, Minn., 1965), 793.

6   Nelson Papers, Journals and Reminiscences 1825-26, 60.

7   Richard Glover, ed. *David Thompson's Narrative, 1784-1812* (Toronto: Champlain Society, XL), 45.

8   Ross Cox, *The Columbia River*, edited by Edgar and Jane Stewart (Norman, Okla., 1957), 377. The phenomenon of Indian women looking to the whites for succor and thus being favourably disposed toward their presence appears to be widespread. Similar instances can even be found in the American frontier experience, see W. C. MacLeod, *The American Indian Frontier* (New York, 1928), 260, 359, n.1.

9   Sylvia Van Kirk, "Thanadelthur", *The Beaver* (Spring 1974), 44-45.

10   Merk, *Fur Trade and Empire*, 104-05; H.B.C.A., D.5/8, fo. 147.

11   Alexander Ross, *The Fur Hunters of the Far West*, I: 297.

12   The story of "Ko-come-ne-pe-ca" has been pieced together from the following sources: H.B.C.A., E.24/1; John Franklin, *Narrative of a Second Expedition to the Shores of the Polar Sea 1825-27* (London, 1828), 305-06; Glover, *Thompson's Narrative*, 366-67; Gabriel Franchère, *Narrative of a Voyage to the Northwest Coast of America, 1811-1814*, edited by Ruben Gold Thwaites (Cleveland, Ohio, 1904), 251; Alexander Ross, *Adventures of the First Settlers on the Oregon or Columbia River* (London, 1849), 101, 153-54.

13   Ross, *Adventures on the Columbia*, 154. Ko-come-ne-pe-ca reputedly became a distinguished warrior and ultimately died of battle wounds.

14   P.A.C., Masson Collection, No. 3, "An Account of the Chipwean Indians", 23-24.

15   *Ibid.*

16   Owing to the lack of statistics, it is impossible to state with any accuracy the total number of Indian women who became wives of the fur traders. According to Alexander Henry's estimate of the population in the North West in 1805, there were 368 native wives attached to the Nor'Westers. In terms of the total number of women within the tribes, it appears that those who actually became traders' wives constituted a very small percentage, although this would vary with the tribes. See Coues, *New Light on Greater Northwest*, 282.

17   L. R. F. Masson, *Les Bourgeois de la Compagnie du Nord-Ouest* (New

York, 1960), I: 293; J. B. Tyrrell, ed. *Journals of Samuel Hearne and Philip Turnor, 1774-1792* (Toronto: Champlain Society, XXI), 275.

18   Alexander Henry, *Travels and Adventures in Canada and the Indian Territories, 1760-1776*, edited by James Bain (Boston, 1901), 248.

19   Ross, *Fur Hunters*, I: 296-97.

20   W. Kaye Lamb, ed., *Sixteen Years in the Indian Country: The Journal of Daniel Williams Harmon, 1800-1816* (Toronto, 1957), 29; Nelson Papers, Journal 1810-11, 42.

21   Coues, *New Light on Greater Northwest*, 71-73, 163, 169, 274.

22   Franchère, *Narrative of a Voyage*, 327.

23   P.A.C., Masson Collection, No. 7, John Thomson's Journal, 1798, 10.

24   "Johnstone *et al.* vs. Connolly, Appeal Court, 7 Sept. 1869," *La Revue Légale*, I: 280-82; Tyrrell, *Journals of Hearne and Turnor*, 252.

25   Michel Curot, "A Wisconsin Fur Trader's Journal, 1803-1804", *Wisconsin Historical Collections*, 20: 449, 453. "Mr. Grant's Girl" also received the same treatment, see Charles M Gates, ed., *Five Fur Traders of the Northwest* (St. Paul, Minn., 1965), 234.

26   Masson, *Les Bourgeois*, II: 373.

27   Toronto Public Library, Nelson Papers, Journal 1810-11, 41; Reminiscences, Pt. 5, 225.

28   Cox, *Columbia River*, 148.

29   Coues, *New Light on Greater Northwest*, 914; Ross, *Fur Hunters*, II: 236.

30   See H.B.C.A., A. 16/111 *passim.*

31   Masson, *Les Bourgeois*, II: 263.

32   P.A.C., Selkirk Papers, vol. 49, John McNab's Journal, 1816, 180.

33   Tyrrell, *Journals of Hearne and Turnor*, 275.

34   A. S. Morton, ed., *The Journal of Duncan McGillivray . . . at Fort George on the Saskatchewan, 1794-95* (Toronto, 1929), 34; Masson, *Les Bourgeois*, I: 256.

35   Nancy O. Lurie, "Indian Women: A Legacy of Freedom", *The American Way* (April 1972), 28-35. This theme was also developed by the British feminist Anna Jameson when she visited the Indians in Upper Canada in the 1830's, see Eve Zaremba, ed., *Privilege of Sex: A Century of Canadian Women* (Toronto, 1974), 45-50.

36   Nelson Papers, Journal 1810-11, 41-42.

37   Nelson Papers, Journal 1803-04, 10-28 *passim.*

38   E. E. Rich, ed., *Simpson's Athabasca Journal and Report, 1820-21* (London: H.B.R.S., I), 271-72.

39   H.B.C.A., B.39/a/16, fos. 6-49d *passim.*

40   Merk, *Fur Trade and Empire,* 99.

41   H.B.C.A., D.4/1, fo. 29.

42   H.B.C.A., D.3/3, fo. 51.

43   Merk, *Fur Trade and Empire*, 99.

44   John Franklin, *Narrative of a Journey to the Shores of the Polar Sea, 1819-22* (London, 1824, 3rd ed.), 101, 106.

45   John West, *The Substance of a Journal during a residence at the Red River Colony, 1820-23* (London, 1827), 16.

46   Masson, *Les Bourgeois*, II: 384-85.

47   Cox, *Columbia River*, 354.

48   West, *Red River Journal*, 54.

49   Franklin, *Narrative of a Journey*, 60, 86.

50   J. S. Galbraith, *The Little Emperor: Governor Simpson of the Hudson's Bay Company* (Toronto, 1976), 68; for a further discussion of this phenomenon, see Jennifer Brown, "A Demographic Transition in the Fur Trade Country", *Western Canadian Journal of Anthropology*, 6, 1: 68.

51   Brown, "A Demographic Transition", 67.
52   C.M.S.A., CC1/018, vol. 1, Cockran to the Secretaries, 11 August 1828.
53   W. J. Healy, *Women of Red River* (Winnipeg, 1923), 163-66.
54   Lamb, *Sixteen Years in Indian Country*, 138, 186.
55   Merk, *Fur Trade and Empire*, 101; for a description of head-flattening, see Paul Kane, *Wanderings of an Artist* (Edmonton, 1968), 123-24.
56   H.B.C.A., B.239/a/103, fo. 14d.
57   West, *Red River Journal*, 16; John Foster, "Missionaries, Mixed-Bloods and the Fur Trade"; *Western Canadian Journal of Anthropology*, 3, 1 (1972): 111.
58   P.A.C., Thomson's Journal, 1798, 20.
59   McCord Museum, Montreal, Robert McVicar Correspondence, 19 July 1825.
60   Margaret A. MacLeod, ed. *The Letters of Letitia Hargrave* (Toronto, Champlain Society, XXVIII), 72, 127.
61   McGill University Library, Masson Collection, Journal of James Mackenzie, 9 April 1800; Masson, *Les Bourgeois*, II: 384-85. For further examples of Indian women being sold by the traders, see Gates, 179, 240 and Masson, I: 288, 294.
62   The following account of this incident is derived from the Île à la Crosse journal, H.B.C.A., B.89/a/2, fos. 5-36d *passim*. For another example of native women being used as pawns in the fur trade rivalry, see H.B.C.A., B.158/a/1, fo. 7d.
63   Tyrrell, *Journals of Hearne and Turnor*, 449-50; Masson, *Les Bourgeois*, II: 387-88.
64   W. Kaye Lamb, *The Journals and Letters of Sir Alexander Mackenzie* (Cambridge, England, 1970), 255; Rich, *Simpson's Athabasca Journal*, 388.
65   P.A.C., Masson Collection, No. 8, Ferdinand Wentzel's Journal, 1805, 41.
66   H.B.C.A., B.59/b/24, fo. 27.
67   Toronto Public Library, Nelson Papers, Reminiscences, Pt. 5, 225.
68   Nelson Papers, Journal 1810-11, 41-42.
69   W. Stewart Wallace, ed., *Documents relating to the North West Company* (Toronto: Champlain Society, XXII), 211.
70   To give teeth to the resolution, every bourgeois or wintering partner was to be liable to a fine of one hundred pounds if he or any person in his department was found guilty of taking an Indian wife. There are only two recorded instances of fines actually having been levied, however; one in the district of Sault Ste. Marie and one in Red River, both long established areas.
71   While in charge of Fort George, the clerk James Murray Yale formed a liaison with a daughter of Talphe, although she had previously been purchased by a Carrier man Tzee-aze. Tzee-aze continued to carry on a clandestine relationship with this woman while she was living with Yale, a fact which was discovered by the interpreter Joseph Beignoit during Yale's absence from the fort. Beignoit's threat to inform Yale of this affair apparently provoked Tzee-aze and an accomplice to murder the interpreter and another servant to ensure their silence, see H.B.C.A., B.119/a/1, fos. 59, 67 and B.119/b/1, 77.
72   Merk, *Fur Trade and Empire*, 127.
73   Lamb, *Sixteen Years in Indian Country*, 5; Coues, *New Light on Greater Northwest*, 555.
74   Ross Cox stated that the daily ration at the fur trade posts was eight pounds of meat for a man, four pounds for a woman and two for a child, *Columbia River*, 354.
75   In 1803 when the young XY clerk George Nelson succumbed to the

urging of his Indian guide and took his daughter for a wife, he was roundly censured by his superiors for doing so, Nelson Papers, Journal 1803-04, 3-34 *passim.* Just before it was absorbed into the North West Company, the XY Company had a total of 520 men, only 37 of whom had wives, Coues, *New Light on Greater Northwest*, 282.

76 H.B.C.A., B.239/b/78, fo. 39d.
77 H.B.C.A., B.42/a/136a, fo. 2d.
78 H.B.C.A., B.239/b/82, fos. 9d-10; B.135/k/1, fos. 16d-17; Franklin, *Narrative of a Journey*, 162.
79 Wallace, *Documents of N.W.C.*, 211.

Chapter Five: Daughters of the Country

1 E. E. Rich, ed. *James Isham's Observations and Notes, 1743-49* (London: H.B.R.S., XII), 79.
2 H.B.C.A., E.8/5, fo. 126.
3 Glyndwr Williams, ed. *Andrew Graham's Observations on Hudson's Bay, 1767-91* (London: H.B.R.S., XXVII), 145. It would appear that many of the Home Guard Indians around the H.B.C. posts were actually first or second generation mixed-bloods (H.B.C.A., B.239/a/105, fo. 28; B.3/a/104, fo. 8).
4 H.B.C.A., A.5/1, fo. 152d.
5 Samuel Hearne, *A Journey to the Northern Ocean*, edited by Richard Glover (Toronto, 1958), 82n; H.B.C.A., A.11/117, fo. 60d.
6 H.B.C.A., A.36/12, Will of James Spence, 6 November 1795; P.R.O., Prob.11/1322, fo. 256, Will of Matthew Cocking, 27 Jan. 1797.
7 John Henry Lefroy, *In Search of the Magnetic North: A Soldier-Surveyor's Letters from the North-West 1843-44*, edited by G. F. G. Stanley (Toronto, 1955), 113, 119. See also Paul Kane, *Wanderings of an Artist among the Indians of North America* (Edmonton, 1968), 221. Mrs Lewes's father was not the John Ballenden who was governor of York Factory at the turn of the century.
8 The romantic story of Rowand's rescue was first recorded by J. H. Lefroy, see W. S. Wallace, "Lefroy's Journey to the North-West", *T.R.S.C.*, Third Series, XXXII, 11 (1938): 93. Various versions of her name appear in the records such as Lisette Humphraville, Louise Ompherville or Umfrieville.
9 Williams, *Graham's Observations*, 145.
10 H.B.C.A., A.6/12, fo. 77d; B.239/b/78, fo. 34; P.R.O., Prob. 11/1110, fo. 569, Will of Ferdinand Jacobs, 30 October 1782. Thucautch's account for 1792 (B.239/d/93, fo. 48d) was:

Blankets .... No. 6	£2- 8-0
Cloth Blue .... Yds. 9	2-18-6
[Cloth] Green .... " 5	1-12-6
[Cloth] Red .... " 8	2-12-0
Needles .... Doz. 4	0- 2-0
Knives Common Clasp .... No. 3	0- 1-6
[Knives] Yew Handle .... " 3	0- 1-0
Twine .... Ski 3	0- 4-6

11 H.B.C.A., B.239/b/79, fo. 28d.
12 L. R. F. Masson, *Les Bourgeois de la Compagnie du Nord-Ouest*, II:41.
13 H.B.C.A., A.11/115, fo. 144d. The first known child to have been taken to England was the three-year-old daughter of Albany governor Joseph Adams in 1737.
14 H.B.C.A., A.6/12, fo. 88. See also A.11/114, fo. 192 and A.6/12, fo. 60d.

15 H.B.C.A., A.6/16, fos. 159d-160.
16 Hearne, *Journey to Northern Ocean*, 82n.
17 H.B.C.A., A.16/111, fos. 65d; A.16/112, fo. 12.
18 H.B.C.A., A.16/112, fos. 12d-13, 30-31d.
19 *Ibid.*, fo. 63.
20 Margaret A. MacLeod, *The Letters of Letitia Hargrave* (Toronto: Champlain Society, XXVIII), 73.
21 Charles Wilkes, *Narrative of the United States Exploring Expedition, 1838-1842* (Philadelphia, 1845), 4: 396. See also MacLeod, *Letitia's Letters*, 126 and Alvin M. Josephy, jr., *The Artist was a Young Man: The Life Story of Peter Rindisbacher* (Fort Worth, Texas, 1970).
22 Alexander Ross, *The Red River Settlement* (Minneapolis, Minn., 1957), 191.
23 Ross Cox, *The Columbia River*, edited by Edgar and Jane Stewart (Norman, Okla., 1957), 360.
24 *Catholic Church Records of the Pacific Northwest: Vancouver, vols. I and II and Stellamaris Mission*, translated by Mikell de Lores Wormell Warner and annotated by Harriet Duncan Munnick, (St. Paul, Oregon, 1972), A-37. Pambrun's wife Catherine was a granddaughter of former HBC officer Edward Umfreville, being the daughter of Thomas Humperville and his native wife Anne. She was born in 1805.
25 H.B.C.A., A.6/15, fo. 102d.
26 Charles M. Gates, ed., *Five Fur Traders of the Northwest* (St. Paul, Minn., 1965), 133. McLeod's emphasis. See also W. Kaye Lamb, ed., *Sixteen Years in the Indian Country: The Journal of Daniel Williams Harmon, 1800-1816* (Toronto, 1957), 40.
27 H.B.C.A., A.6/17, fos. 108d-109; B.239/b/78, fos. 57d-58. For more detail on this educational program, see Jennifer Brown, "'A Colony of Very Useful Hands'", *The Beaver* (Spring 1977), 39-45.
28 H.B.C.A., B.239/b/79, fo. 53d. For other expressions of concern about the free way in which Indian women discussed sexual matters, see Cox, *Columbia River*, 359; John Franklin, *Narrative of a Journey to the Shores of the Polar Sea, 1819-22*, 85-86; and C.M.S.A., CC1/018, vol. 1, Cockran to the Secretaries, 3 Aug. 1831.
29 H.B.C.A., A.1/49, fo. 70; A.6/17, fos. 119-120.
30 Dennis Bayley, *A Londoner in Rupert's Land: Thomas Bunn of the Hudson's Bay Company* (Winnipeg, 1969), 31.
31 H.B.C.A., B.59/z/2, Eastmain School Register, 29 Aug. 1811.
32 H.B.C.A., B.3/a/112, fos. 1-4. Letitia Hargrave states that Harriet Vincent's mother was a daughter of John McNab, Chief Factor at York Factory. But according to Thomas Vincent's own will (H.B.C.A., A.36/14), her mother was Jane Renton, and no connection with the McNabs has been discovered.
33 H.B.C.A., A.16/111, fo. 51; A.36/13, Will of William Thomas, 10 January 1817.
34 H.B.C.A., B.4/b/1, fos. 2d-3.
35 John West, *The Substance of a Journal during a residence at the Red River Colony, 1820-23* (London, 1827), 136. Sally's mother was a mixed-blood woman, Jane Flett.
36 Franklin, *Narrative of a Journey, 1819-1822*, 85-86.
37 Lamb, *Sixteen Years in Indian Country*, 50.
38 H.B.C.A., A.11/4, fo. 210.
39 P.R.O., Prob. 11/1002, fo. 374, Will of Moses Norton, 27 May 1769 and Codicil, 8 Dec. 1773.
40 Hearne, *Journey to Northern Ocean*, 81.
41 *Ibid.*, 228.
42 H.B.C.A., B.4/b/1, fos. 15d-16. Stuart also acted as guardian for the

children of Alexander Roderick McLeod, see D.5/14, fo. 275.

43 H.B.C.A., A.36/13, Will of Thomas Thomas, 10 November 1827. See also B.135/c/2, fo. 139. Under British law at this time, a wife's property became that of her husband.

44 For example, Mary, a daughter of Albany officer John Favell, became the wife of inland officer John R. McKay of Brandon House (P.R.O., Prob.11/1785, fo. 551, Will of John Favell, 19 Feb. 1784). Of Matthew Cocking's daughters, the eldest, Ke-che-cow-e-com-coot, became the country wife of Thomas Stayner, governor of Churchill in the 1790s while the other two became wives of William Hemmings Cook who was in charge of York Factory in the early 1800s (H.B.C.A., B.239/c/1, fo. 201).

45 P.A.C., Charles McKenzie Papers, McKenzie to Hector Aeneas, 12 Sept. 1851.

46 Lamb, *Sixteen Years in Indian Country*, 98. Other examples include the daughters of the engagé André Poitras and his Cree wife who married prominent bourgeois. Magdelaine became the wife of John "Le Prêtre" Macdonnell while Marie married John "Le Borgne" McDonald.

47 Franklin, *Narrative of a Journey, 1819-1822*, 86.

48 Cox, *Columbia River*, 356.

49 The wife of Peter Warren Dease, Elizabeth Chouinard, was probably a daughter of the engagé Charles Chouinard alias Quebec. Thomas McMurray married a daughter of Joachim Cardinalle, while William McIntosh married Sarah Gladue, the daughter of a freeman and his Indian wife.

50 Lefroy, *In Search of Magnetic North*, 26.

51 R. H. Fleming, ed., *Minutes of Council of the Northern Department of Rupert's Land*, 1821-31 (London: H.B.R.S., III), 378; Cox, *Columbia River*, 360.

52 H.B.C.A., D.5/9, fo. 338; P.A.C., Charles McKenzie Papers, Letters to Hector Aeneas, 12 Sept. 1851, 28 Nov. 1853, 1 May 1854.

53 Elizabeth Arthur, "Charles McKenzie, l'homme seul", *Ontario History*, LXX (March 1978), 45.

54 P.A.C., James Hargrave Correspondence, vol. 21, Hargrave to Christie, 13 June 1832; see also Isaac Cowie, *The Company of Adventurers* (Toronto, 1913), 213-14.

55 H.B.C.A., B.135/a/136, fo. 7d; B.27/a/14, fos. 10, 105, 108.

56 H.B.C.A., D.5/18, fos. 535d-536; see also Kane, *Wanderings of an Artist*, 93, 261.

57 J. G. McGregor, *John Rowand, Czar of the Prairies* (Saskatoon, 1978), 172.

58 E. E. Rich, ed., *Simpson's Athabasca Journal and Report, 1820-21* (London: H.B.R.S., I), 245.

59 Cowie, *Company of Adventurers*, 204; see also Wilkes, *Narrative of U.S. Expedition*, 4: 396-97.

60 H.B.C.A., D.5/20, fo. 308.

61 Nancy Boucher was the mixed-blood daughter of Nor'Wester James McDougall, who lived in New Caledonia for many years. She likely became Boucher's country wife in the early 1820s after his Carrier wife had apparently died.

62 The best account of this incident is that of Father Morice in his *History of the Northern Interior of British Columbia* (Fairfield, Wash., 1971), 139-152. He corrects errors made by previous authors such as John McLean and H. H. Bancroft. Morice's account had been followed by Marion B. Smith in her article "The Lady Nobody Knows", *British Columbia, A Centennial Anthology* (Vancouver, 1958), 473-74, but the

account in N. de B. Lugrin, *The Pioneer Women of Vancouver Island, 1843-66* (Victoria, 1928), 12-14, is inaccurate and exaggerated.

63   George Simpson, *Narrative of a Journey Round the World, 1841-42* (London, 1847), 204.

64   Alexander Ross, *The Fur Hunters of the Far West* (London, 1855), I: 289.

65   P.A.C., Selkirk Papers, vol. 49, John McNab's Journal, 1816, 183.

66   Lugrin, *Women of Vancouver Island*, 16.

67   Cox, *Columbia River*, 235; Toronto Public Library, Baldwin Room, George Nelson Papers, Journal 1819, 1-5 *passim*.

68   Ross, *Fur Hunters*, I: 289.

69   Jennifer Brown, "Company Men and Native Families: Fur Trade Social and Domestic Relations in Canada's Old Northwest" (Ph.D., University of Chicago, 1976), 169-173.

70   "Johnstone *et al.* vs. Connolly, Appeal Court, 7 Sept. 1869", *La Revue Légale*, I: 286.

71   Quoted in Brown, "Company Men and Native Wives", 172.

72   Nelson Papers, Journal 1808-1810, 3 Sept. 1808.

73   H.B.C.A., B. 235/c/1, fos. 3d-4.

74   MacLeod, *Letitia's Letters*, 82; H.B.C.A., A.36/14, Will of Thomas Vincent, 13 January 1826 and revised Will, 24 March 1832; A.6/19, fo. 32.

75   "Connolly Appeal Case, 1869", 286-87.

76   *Ibid.*, 284-85, 282.

77   For details of the Ogden case, see Archie Binns, *Peter Skene Ogden, Fur Trader* (Portland, Oregon, 1967), 355-58; see H.B.C.A., A.38/23-26 for voluminous correspondence on the Black case.

78   H.B.C.A., A.36/9, fos. 127, 132.

79   H.B.C.A., A.36/10, Will of Alexander Roderick McLeod, 16 June 1828 and fos. 17-19. The identity of McLeod's half-breed wife is unknown.

80   H.B.C.A., B.156/z/1, fo. 96. Quite a number of these marriage contracts are to be found in the miscellaneous (z) file under the headings of the various posts.

81   H.B.C.A., B.47/z/1; B.89/z/1, fo. 1; B.231/z/1, fos. 54-55.

82   Wilkes, *Narrative of U.S. Expedition*, 4: 419.

83   H.B.C.A., B.223/b/20, fos. 62-62d.

84   H.B.C.A., B.239/k/2, fo. 183d.

85   MacLeod, *Letitia's Letters*, 83. H.B.C.A., E.24/4, J. Stuart to J. G. McTavish, 16 August 1830. It should be remembered that infanticide was not unknown in Indian society in times of famine or distress.

86   P.A.C., Hargrave Correspondence, vol. 23, Hargrave to Nichol Finlayson, 10 Dec. 1838; H.B.C.A., D.5/11, fo. 85. In 1826, Chief Trader Cuthbert Cumming left his family in Red River when posted to the Southern Department. He provided for his family, but when after more than a decade, he still had not received a northern posting, his native wife gave up hope of a reunion and married someone else (Hargrave Corres., vol. 22, Hargrave to Cumming, 6 August 1835).

87   H.B.C.A., D.5/20, fo. 308; B. 135/a/136, fo. 28d.

88   H.B.C.A., B.239/c/1, fo. 181; T. C. Elliott, "Marguerite Wadin McKay McLoughlin", *Oregon Historical Quarterly*, XXXVI: 340-43.

89   The story of Françoise Boucher is told in Cox, *Columbia River*, 363-64; H.B.C.A., A.36/9, Will of Joseph McGillivray, 1 June 1830.

90   MacLeod, *Letitia's Letters*, 82-83.

91   H.B.C.A., E.4/1b, fo. 209; B.239/c/1, fo. 134.

92   H.B.C.A., B.4/b/1, fo. 18; B.239/a/136, fo. 173.

93   H.B.C.A., B.4/b/1, fo. 18-18d.

Chapter Six: My Only Consolation

1   Frederick Merk, ed., *Fur Trade and Empire: George Simpson's Journal, 1824-25* (Cambridge, Mass., 1931), 11-12, 58. Simpson's emphasis.

2   Elliot Coues, ed., *New Light on the Early History of the Greater Northwest: The Manuscript Journals of Alexander Henry and of David Thompson, 1799-1814* (Minneapolis, Minn., 1965), 553-555.

3   Ross Cox, *The Columbia River*, edited by Edgar and Jane Stewart (Norman, Okla., 1957), 360.

4   H.B.C.A., A.16/112, fos. 12d-13.

5   Charles Wilkes, *Narrative of the United States Exploring Expedition, 1838-1842* (Philadelphia, 1845), 4: 350; 5: 129.

6   Jean Cole, "Exile in the Wilderness", *The Beaver*, Summer 1972, 10.

7   Margaret A. MacLeod, ed., *The Letters of Letitia Hargrave* (Toronto: Champlain Society, XXVIII), 87.

8   H.B.C.A., B.27/a/14, fos. 58-59.

9   Charles M. Gates, ed., *Five Fur Traders of the Northwest* (St. Paul, Minn., 1965), 162.

10   John Franklin, *Narrative of a Journey to the Shores of the Polar Sea, 1819-1822* (London, 1824), 54; see also Paul Kane, *Wanderings of an Artist among the Indians of North America* (Edmonton, 1968), 264.

11   John Henry Lefroy, *In Search of the Magnetic North: A Soldier-Surveyor's Letters from the North-West, 1843-44*, edited by G. F. G. Stanley (Toronto, 1955), 92.

12   Gates, *Five Fur Traders*, 94.

13   W. S. Wallace, "Lefroy's Journey to the North-West", *T.R.S.C.*, Third Series, XXXII, 11 (1938): 71; see also H.B.C.A., B.135/c/2, fo. 71d.

14   R. Harvey Fleming, ed., *Minutes of Council of the Northern Department of Rupert's Land, 1821-31* (London: H.B.R.S., III), 358-59; H.B.C.A., D.4/85, fos. 69-70.

15   H.B.C.A., B.39/a/22, fos. 27d-28.

16   Fleming, *Minutes of Council*, 94-95.

17   E. E. Rich, ed., *Simpson's Athabasca Journal and Report, 1820-21* (London: H.B.R.S., I), 23-24.

18   P.A.C., John McLeod Correspondence, p. 166; H.B.C.A., D.5/1, fo. 236.

19   Merk, *Fur Trade and Empire*, 131.

20   Fleming, *Minutes of Council*, 153; for a similar ruling for the Southern Department, see H.B.C.A., D.5/2, fo. 7.

21   Fleming, *Minutes of Council*, 60-61.

22   W. Kaye Lamb, ed., *Sixteen Years in the Indian Country: The Journal of Daniel Williams Harmon, 1800-1816* (Toronto, 1957), 194.

23   P.A.B.C., Edward Ermatinger Correspondence, John Work to Ermatinger, 10 Jan. 1846.

24   Lamb, *Sixteen Years in Indian Country*, 186.

25   Dorothy B. Smith, ed., *Lady Franklin visits the Pacific Northwest* (Victoria: P.A.B.C., Memoir No. XI, 1974), 22-23.

26   H.B.C.A., B.198/e/6, fos. 5d-6.

27   Quoted in J. G. MacGregor, *John Rowand, Czar of the Prairies* (Saskatoon, 1978), 67.

28   P.A.B.C., Charles Ross Papers, "Isabella Ross".

29   N. de B. Lugrin, *The pioneer women of Vancouver Island, 1843-1866* (Victoria, 1928), 62-63.

30   P.A.B.C., Ermatinger Correspondence, Work to Ermatinger, 15 February 1841.

272

31   P.A.C., Charles McKenzie Papers, McKenzie to Hector Aeneas, 1 May 1854.
32   P.A.C., James Hargrave Correspondence, vol. 8, 2189; G. P. de T. Glazebrook, ed., *The Hargrave Correspondence, 1821-1843* (Toronto: Champlain Society, XXIV), 400. Betsey Finlayson was a daughter of Chief Factor Alexander Kennedy and his Cree wife. She evidently spoke excellent English and was "quite the lady".
33   MacLeod, *Letitia's Letters*, xxiv.
34   P.A.C., Hargrave Corres., vol. 6, 1341-42; Walter E. Houghton, *The Victorian Frame of Mind* (London, 1957), 343-44.
35   P.A.C., Hargrave Corres., vol. 5, 1009; vol. 6, 1158.
36   H.B.C.A., D.5/6, fo. 33d.
37   P.A.B.C., Ed. Ermatinger Corres., Arch. McDonald to Edward Ermatinger, 30 March 1842.
38   H.B.C.A., D.5/14, fos. 216-216d.
39   P.A.C., Hargrave Corres., vol. 13, 3744; see also vol. 12, 3227.
40   Walter O'Meara, *Daughters of the Country: The Women of the Fur Traders and Mountain Men* (New York, 1968), 274-75. Thompson had married Charlotte *à la façon du pays* in 1798; she was a daughter of the bourgeois Patrick Small.
41   P.A.C., Miles Macdonell Papers, 149. Macdonell died in 1850, but his wife Magdeleine survived him by twenty years, dying in 1870 at the age of 87.
42   Lamb, *Sixteen Years in Indian Country*, 194-195.
43   Cox, *Columbia River*, 361.
44   Glazebrook, *Hargrave Correspondence*, 195, see also 12, 113.
45   H.B.C.A., D.5/26, fo. 258.
46   H.B.C.A., D.5/7, fo. 274; P.A.C., Hargrave Corres., vol. 9: 2230.
47   H.B.C.A., D.5/12, fo. 64d.
48   P.A.C., Hargrave Corres., vol. 12: 3516; Glazebrook, *Hargrave Correspondence*, 313, 437.
49   H.B.C.A., A.6/20, fo. 77d.
50   H.B.C.A., D.5/10, fos. 549-549d; D.5/12, fos. 64-64d, 400d, 544; D.5/14, fos. 381-381d.
51   H.B.C.A., D.5/20, fo. 69; see also D.5/23, fos. 88-88d, P.A.C., Hargrave Corres., vol. 27, 28 March 1852.
52   H.B.C.A., D.5/10, fo. 218.
53   P.A.C., Hargrave Corres., vol. 15: 4401.
54   P.A.C., Hargrave Corres., vol. 27, 18 and 28 March 1852. After her husband's death in 1859, Nanette Keith returned to Canada to live with the Swanston family.
55   P.A.C., Hargrave Corres., vol. 21, Hargrave to Donald McKenzie, 5 Dec. 1826.
56   H.B.C.A., E.8/5, fo. 126.
57   Alexander Ross, *The Fur Hunters of the Far West*, 160, 198, 233.
58   Fleming, *Minutes of Council*, 3, 33-35.
59   H.B.C.A., Edward Ermatinger Correspondence, Copy No 22, 160.
60   Lugrin, *Women of Vancouver Island*, 64.
61   H.B.C.A., B.239/b/82, fos. 9d-10.

Chapter Seven: Quite English in her Manner

1   For an analysis of the attitudes of the Protestant missionaries, see Frits Pannekoek, "Protestant Agricultural Zions for the Western Indian", *Journal of the Canadian Church Historical Society*, XIV, 3(1972), 55-66.

2   R. Harvey Fleming, ed., *Minutes of Council of the Northern Depart-ment of Rupert's Land, 1821-31* (London: H.B.R.S., III), 95; H.B.C.A., B.239/c/1, fo. 132; E.4/1b, fo. 211. Mary Allez married Grant Forest in September 1824.

3   No complete list of the girls who attended Mrs. Cockran's school has been discovered, but they included Maria, Governor Simpson's daughter by Betsey Sinclair, and Flora McTavish, a daughter of Chief Factor J. G. McTavish.

4   Donald Chaput, "The 'Misses Nolin' of Red River", *The Beaver* (Winter 1975), 17. This school only lasted a few years as the Nolin sisters went to teach at the Catholic mission founded by Father Belcourt at Baie St. Paul in 1834.

5   C.M.S.A., CC1/039, D. Jones to Rev. Bickersteth, 31 Jan. 1827; CC1/018, vol. 1, W. Cockran to Secretaries, 30 July 1827.

6   J. Hargrave to Wm. Cockran, 4 Aug. 1833 as quoted in Jennifer Brown, "Company Men and Native Familes: Fur Trade Domestic and Social Relations in Canada's Old Northwest" (Ph.D, University of Chicago, 1976), 299; C.M.S.A., CC1/039, D. Jones to Secretaries, 25 July 1833.

7   Keith Thomas, "The Double Standard", *Journal of the History of Ideas*, 20(1959): 214.

8   John Henry Lefroy, *In Search of the Magnetic North: A Soldier-Surveyor's Letters from the North-West, 1843-44*, edited by G. F. G. Stanley (Toronto, 1955), 76: "It is curious that in this country while the distinction between the Bourgeois and the voyageurs and servants is properly maintained, there is very little difference between their wives and daughters."

9   C.M.S.A., CC1/018, vol. 1, Wm. Cockran to Secretaries, 20 July 1831 and Cockran to Rev. T. Woodroofe, 3 August 1831.

10 C.M.S.A., CC1/039, G. Simpson to D. Jones, 14 July 1832 and Jones to Secretaries, 14 August 1832; H.B.C.A., B.235/z/3, fo. 547.

11 P.A.C., James Hargrave Correspondence, vol. 4: 475; P.A.B.C., Donald Ross Correspondence, G. Simpson to D. Ross, 20 Dec. 1832. Annabella McKenzie married John Clarke Spence in Red River on 11 Sept. 1832 (H.B.C.A., E.4/1b, fo. 235).

12 P.A.B.C., D. Ross Corres., Ross to Rev. Jones, 4 Jan. 1833.

13 Elaine Mitchell, "A Red River Gossip", *The Beaver* (Spring 1961), 9.

14 H.B.C.A., B.135/c/2, fo. 139; P.A.C., Hargrave Corres., vol. 4: 731.

15 H.B.C.A., D.4/22, fo. 47; Selkirk Papers, Copy No. 161, 1254.

16 Jones's Journal, 6 November 1836 as quoted in A. N. Thompson, "The Wife of a Missionary", *J.C.C.H.S.*, XV, 2 (1973): 40.

17 G. P. de T. Glazebrook, ed., *The Hargrave Correspondence, 1821-1843* (Toronto: Champlain Society, XXIV), 241; H.B.C.A., E.4/1b, fo. 262.

18 Margaret A. MacLeod, ed., *The Letters of Letitia Hargrave* (Toronto: Champlain Society, XXVIII), 206.

19 Glazebrook, *Hargrave Correspondence*, 229; Mitchell, "A Red River Gossip", 9.

20 J. Hargrave to A. McDermot. 26 July 1839 as quoted in Brown, "Company Men and Native Families", 299.

21 P.A.B.C., D. Ross Corres., R. Clouston to D. Ross, 20 Nov. 1847.

22 University of Western Ontario Archives, James Evans Papers, Evans to Ephriam Evans, 3 July 1843.

23 "A Short Sketch of the Life and Missionary Labours and Happy Death of Sophia Mason", *Church Missionary Gleaner*, 1861, 138-140. See also H.B.C.A., D.4/70, fos. 215, 219-21 for Simpson's favourable comments on Sophia Mason.

24 H.B.C.A., E.8/5, fos. 126-129.

274

25   John West, *The Substance of a Journal during a residence at the Red River Colony, 1820-23* (London, 1827), 26, 51-52; A.N. Thompson, "John West: A Study of the Conflict between Civilization and the Fur Trade", *J.C.C.H.S., XII, 3(1970): 52.*

26   These gentlemen and their Indian wives were married early in 1821, see H.B.C.A., E.4/1b, fos. 192d, 195d.

27   H.B.C.A., E.4/1b, fo. 191. The first couple which West had married were HBC officer Thomas Bunn and his half-breed wife Phoebe Sinclair at the Rock Depot on 9 September 1820.

28   C.M.S.A., CC1/039, D. Jones to Rev. Pratt, 24 July 1824.

29   Frederick Merk, ed., *Fur Trade and Empire: George Simpson's Journal, 1824-25* (Cambridge, Mass., 1931), 108.

30   Thomas E. Jessett, ed., *Reports and Letters of Herbert Beaver, 1836-38* (Portland, Oregon, 1959), 2, 86.

31   Marguerite Wadin was the daughter of the early Canadian trader Jean-Etienne Wadin and an unknown Indian woman.

32   Jessett, *Beaver's Letters*, 141; C. M. Drury, ed., *First white women over the Rockies . . .,* (Glendale, Cal., 1963) I: 111.

33   Jessett, *Beaver's Letters*, 119.

34   *Ibid.*, 77, 93.

35   Marion B. Smith, "The Lady Nobody Knows", *British Columbia: a centennial anthology* (Vancouver, 1958), 473-75.

36   Jessett, *Beaver's Letters*, 147-48, 120, 143-45.

37   *Catholic Church Records of the Pacific Northwest: Vancouver, vols. I and II and Stellamaris Mission*, translated by Mikell de Lores Wormell Warner and annotated by Harriet Duncan Munnick (St. Paul, Oregon, 1972), Vanc. 11: 5, 6 & 7.

38   *Ibid.*, 4 & 5; 8 & 9; 41 & 42.

39   C.M.S.A., CC1/018, vol. 3, Cockran's Journal, 3 March 1829.

40   C.M.S.A., CC1/039, Jones's Journal, 9 June 1835: "This laudable practice is now becoming General, in fact the revolution in these respects during the past 10 years has been immense."

41   P.A.B.C., Edward Ermatinger Correspondence, Archibald McDonald to Ed. Ermatinger, 1 April 1836. Author's emphasis. Other notable church marriages in 1835 were Chief Factor John Charles and Jane Auld, 2 February and Chief Trader Francis Heron and Isabella Chalifoux, 16 July (H.B.C.A., E.4/1b, fos. 243, 244).

42   P.A.B.C., D. Ross Corres., Thomas Simpson to D. Ross, 20 Feb. 1836.

43   H.B.C.A., D.5/25, fo. 82d.

44   *Catholic Church Records*, Vanc. 1: 8 & 9.

45   For a more detailed discussion of these views as they apply in the fur trade context, see Jennifer Brown, "Changing Views of Fur Trade Marriage and Domesticity: James Hargrave, His Colleagues and 'The Sex' ", *Western Canadian Journal of Anthropology*, 6, 3(1976), 92-105.

46   P.A.C., Hargrave Corres., vol. 7: 1574.

47   *Ibid.*, vol. 8: 1925-26; vol. 22, Hargrave to John Rendall, 20 April 1837.

48   *Ibid.*, vol. 22, Hargrave to Letitia Mactavish, 24 July 1838.

49   *Ibid.*, vol. 23, Hargrave to George Barnston, 1 Dec. 1842. Grant's Oxford House "wife" was married off to a servant called Stater. A few years after he moved to the Columbia, Grant wed Helen McDonald, the widow of William Kittson.

50   H.B.C.A., B.135/a/125, fo. 15.

51   E. E. Rich, ed., *Simpson's Athabasca Journal and Report, 1820-21* (London: H.B.R.S., I), 23-24.

52   "Johnstone *et al.* vs. Connolly, Appeal Court, 7 Sept. 1869", *La Revue Légale*, I: 288.

53   H.B.C.A., B.239/a/130, fo. 38d. This entry was crossed out by someone at a later date.
54   H.B.C.A., B.239/c/1, fo. 92. Betsey Sinclair soon found a real husband in the clerk Robert Miles. She proved herself an admirable and adaptable wife, and I have found no evidence to support the speculations of Geneva Lent and Dennis Bayley that she was a woman of loose character.
55   H.B.C.A., B.239/c/1, fo. 283.
56   According to the York Factory Journal, B.239/a/136, fo. llld. "G.S." was born 11 Feb. 1827. He was christened George Stewart Simpson by the Rev. Jones at York Factory on 19 August 1828.
57   This woman may have been Mary Keith, a daughter of Chief Factor James Keith. In 1830, Simpson helped to arrange the betrothal of Mary Keith to his ex-servant Thomas Taylor.
58   H.B.C.A.., D.5/3, fos. 168-69.
59   H.B.C.A., B.239/c/1, fos. 360, 366.
60   P.A.C., Hargrave Corres., vol. 21, Hargrave to John McLeod, 12 July 1827 and 5 Dec. 1826.
61   Glazebrook, *Hargrave Correspondence*, 274. Wallace was on his way to the Columbia; tragically the young couple enjoyed only a brief honeymoon for both were drowned in a serious brigade accident at the Dalles rapids in the fall of 1838, see J. A. Stevenson, "Disaster at the Dalles", *The Beaver* (Fall 1942), 19-21.
62   MacLeod. *Letitia's Letters*, 219. Margaret, a daughter of William Sinclair, Jr, married Major Darling at Norway House in 1848 and went to live in England.
63   While the idea of a "double standard" in the sexual behaviour of men and women has existed for centuries, it seems to have become most sharply developed in the nineteenth century, see Thomas, "Double Standard", 195-216.
64   Hargrave to Geo. Simpson, 20 Feb. 1833 as quoted in Brown, "Changing Views of Fur Trade Marriage", 96.
65   Jessett, *Beaver's Letters*, 57.
66   H.B.C.A., E.4/1a, fos. 57, 93, 104d. In a few instances, the term "reputed wife" is used but this was likely at the insistence of the traders themselves who demanded some acknowledgement of their existing marital relationship.
67   Jessett, *Beaver's Letters*, 141.
68   MacLeod, *Letitia's Letters*, 177-78.
69   P.A.C., Hargrave Corres., vol. 23, Hargrave to John Rowand, 2 July 1839; vol. 7: 1716.
70   Thomas, "Double Standard", 201-02, see also Duncan Crow, *The Victorian Woman* (London, 1971), 53-55.
71   Merk, *Fur Trade and Empire*, 58, 131-32; Ross Cox, *The Columbia River*, 360-61. Chief Factor John Stuart also defended the morals of native women against the unflattering observations of Captain Franklin, see H.B.C.A., E.24/4, J. Stuart to Franklin, 12 Dec. 1826 and 10 August 1827.
72   H.B.C.A., D.5/7, fos. 261-261d, 263.
73   P.A.C., Hargrave Corres., vol. 23, Hargrave to J. L. Lewes, 1 April 1843; Glazebrook, *Hargrave Correspondence*, 453.
74   H.B.C.A., Ermatinger Corres., Copy No. 21, 9; D.5/31, fo. 143d.
75   In the late 1820s when a clerk in the Kamloops district, Ermatinger was involved in a tempestuous affair with a Shuswap woman, whom he called "Cleopatra". When this woman took an Indian lover, Ermatinger, in a jealous rage, created a scandal by instructing one of the Company's

servants to cut off the offending paramour's ears (H.B.C.A., D.4/125, fo. 78; A.34/2, fos. 25d-26).

76 P.A.C., Hargrave Corres., vol. 14; 4288. The baby was apparently left with a nurse at Fort Chipewyan and died in infancy.

77 H.B.C.A., B.4/b/1, fo. 3; E.24/5, Fort Simpson Journal, 19 Feb. 1834. During his posting at Carlton House from 1824-26, Stuart had a country wife called Catherine La Vallé by whom he had two sons. It is possible she may have died.

78 H.B.C.A., B.200/a/15, fos. 51-51d, 52d. Annance's final note to Mary casts him in the role of a tragic lover:
"My dearest love, now the fatal die is cast and we part forever . . . If my heart bleeds I only blame myself for having loved an object which is not for me . . . farewell — may you enjoy the happiness which you have refused me."

79 H.B.C.A., E.24/5.

80 P.A.C., John McLeod Correspondence, 356-57.

81 In his will, Francis Ermatinger left all his property to his daughter and his "beloved wife" Catharine. Apparently, life in Upper Canada became so unbearable for Mrs. Ermatinger after her husband's death that she returned to Rupert's Land. She died in Red River in 1876.

82 P.A.C., Hargrave Corres., vol. 6: 1216.

83 Ibid., vol. 23, Hargrave to Nichol Finlayson, 10 Dec. 1838.

84 Ibid., vol. 23, Hargrave to Simpson, 5 Sept. 1839. Mary Taylor appears to have spent the rest of her life with her relatives. In 1843, she went to live with her brother Thomas and his family at Lac Seul. By the terms of Stuart's will of 1832, Mary was to inherit 500 pounds upon his death in 1847. In his papers, however, was found a draft will which made no mention of Mary and gave more generous legacies to his two Scottish sisters. Although the sisters were unsuccessful in their suit to totally disinherit Mary, they did somehow manage to have her legacy reduced to 350 pounds (H.B.C.A., D.5/20, fo. 448; D.5/29, fo. 110; D.5/30, fo. 105; D.5/31, fo. 482).

85 For a discussion of the racist attitudes of the Protestant clergy, see Frits Pannekoek, "The Churches and the Social Structure in the Red River Area, 1818-1870" (Ph.D., Queen's University, 1973).

86 P.A.B.C., Ermatinger Correspondence, Arch. McDonald to Ermatinger, 20 Feb. 1831.

87 For a full discussion of the growing racial prejudice against young mixed-blood males which hampered their advancement in the Company's service, see Brown, "Company Men and Native Families".

88 Alexander Ross, The Red River Settlement (Minneapolis, Minn., 1957), 238-39; P.A.B.C., D. Ross Correspondence., T. Simpson to Ross, 7 Dec. 1834.

89 H.B.C.A., Selkirk Papers, Copy No. 160a, 139.

90 P.A.C., Hargrave Corres., vol. 5: 1078.

Chapter Eight: Lovely, Tender Exotics

1   E. E. Rich, ed., Hudson's Bay Company Letters Outward, 1679-94 (London, H.B.R.S., XI), 144; W.A. Kenyon and J. R. Turnbull, The Battle for James Bay 1686 (Toronto, 1971), 75-76, 97.

2   Rich, Letters Outward, 1679-94, 235.

3   H.B.C.A., A.1/49, fos. 28d, 15, 36, 37d.

4   H.B.C.A., A.5/4, fo. 77-77d; B.239/b/79, fo. 37d.

5   In 1769, Andrew Graham married Patricia Sherer, the daughter of an

Edinburgh merchant, upon his return to Britain after an absence of twenty years. His mixed-blood children were born after his return to the Bay (Glyndwr Williams, ed., *Andrew Graham's Observations on Hudson's Bay, 1767-91* (London: H.B.R.S., XXVII), 333-349). James Isham stayed in England for two years after marrying his English wife Catherine in 1748, but he then returned to his native family at York Factory. Although Isham provided support for his English wife and daughter, the marriage did not survive his long absence (E. E. Rich, ed., *James Isham's Observations and Notes, 1743-49* (London: H.B.R.S., XII), 322-25). Governor Richard Norton and his son Moses both had a white and an Indian wife.

6   E. E. Rich, ed., *Minutes of the Hudson's Bay Company, 1682-84* (London: H.B.R.S., VIII), 151.

7   The story of Isabel Gunn has been well told by Malvina Bolus in "The Son of I. Gunn", *The Beaver* (Winter 1971), 23-26.

8   Elliot Coues, ed. *New Light on the Early History of the Greater Northwest: The Manuscript Journals of Alexander Henry and of David Thompson, 1799-1814* (Minneapolis, Minn., 1965), 426.

9   *Ibid.*, 427n.

10   When an old lady, Marie-Anne Lajimonière told her story to Father Georges Dugas. All subsequent accounts are based on his book, *La Première Canadienne au Nord-Ouest* (Winnipeg, 1907). The most recent and fullest secondary account is Jean Johnston, *Wilderness Women* (Toronto, 1973), 121-152, but see also "Marie-Anne Gaboury", *Dictionary of Canadian Biography*, X: 296-97.

11   W. J. Healy, *Women of Red River* (Winnipeg, 1923), 2-6.

12   No actual record of this marriage exists, but it is possible that the Rosses were married by James Sutherland, an elder of the Scottish Presbyterian Church, who initially acted as minister for the settlers.

13   P.A.B.C., Donald Ross Corres., Marriage certificate of Robert McVicar and Christy McBeath.

14   P.A.C., James Hargrave Correspondence, vol. 21, Hargrave to Richard Grant, 5 Dec. 1826.

15   A. N. Thompson, "John West: A Study of the Conflict between Civilization and the Fur Trade", *J.C.C.H.S.*, XII, 3(1970): 53. Clarke did not receive church sanction for his marriage until he took Marianne and their family out to Montreal in 1830.

16   H.B.C.A., E.4/1b, fo. 214; P.A.C., Hargrave Corres., vol. I: 62. Although absolute proof is lacking, all evidence points to McKenzie's country wife being Mary McKay, a daughter of Alexander McKay and Marguerite Wadin McKay McLoughlin. She was married off to William Sinclair, Jr.

17   Missouri Historical Society, W. P. Hunt Papers, D. McKenzie to W. P. Hunt, 25 June 1827 (courtesy of Jennifer Brown).

18   H.B.C.A., Selkirk Papers, Copy No. 160a, 1157C.

19   H.B.C.A., D.5/4, fo. 57.

20   H.B.C.A., Selkirk Papers, Copy No. 160a, 1108-11.

21   H.B.C.A., B.135/c/2, fo. 6d.

22   P.A.C., Hargrave Corres., vol. 22, Hargrave to D. Mactavish, 18 May 1838.

23   Simpson had been intent on going home to find a white wife as early as 1824. Later, for a brief period he may have contemplated marrying Margaret Taylor, but was easily persuaded against taking such a step (H.B.C.A., D.5/3, fo. 168).

24   For a discussion of the Victorian ideal of womanhood, see Barbara Welter, "The Cult of True Womanhood: 1820-1860", *American Quarterly*, 18(1966): 151-174. The phrase "lovely tender exotic" was first used

278

by James Douglas, see G. P. de T. Glazebrook, *The Hargrave Correspondence, 1821-1843* (Toronto: Champlain Society, XXIV), 310-11.

25   P.A.C., John McLeod Correspondence, 213.

26   H.B.C.A., B.135/c/2, fos. 33d-34.

27   Ross Cox, *The Columbia River*, edited by Edgar and Jane Stewart (Norman, Okla., 1957), 361-62.

28   A. S. Morton, *Sir George Simpson, Overseas Governor of the Hudson's Bay Company* (Toronto, 1944), 164; P.A.C., Hargrave Corres., vol. 1: 214-15.

29   H.B.C.A., B.135/c/2, fos. 33d-34, 35d.

30   Glazebrook, *Hargrave Correspondence*, 85.

31   See G. L. Nute, "Journey for Frances", *The Beaver*, December 1953, 50-54; March 1954, 12-17; Summer 1954, 12-18.

32   W. E. Houghton, *The Victorian Frame of Mind, 1830-70* (London, 1957), 350.

33   Nute, "Journey for Frances", March 1954, 17.

34   H.B.C.A., B.4/b/1, fos. 8d-9; see also Glazebrook, *Hargrave Correspondence*, 57.

35   P.A.C., Hargrave Corres., vol. 1: 275-6; Glazebrook, *Hargrave Correspondence*, 61.

36   H.B.C.A., B.4/b/1, fos. 2d-3; E.4/1a, fo. 80.

37   H.B.C.A., B.4/b/1, fos. 2d-3, 7.

38   H.B.C.A., E.24/4, fo. 12.

39   P.A.C., Hargrave Corres., vol. 21, Hargrave to J. G. McTavish, 26 May 1830.

40   *Ibid.*, Hargrave to D. McKenzie, 1 July 1830.

41   H.B.C.A., B.135/c/2, fos. 56-57, 63d; B.235/z/3, fo. 547a; E.4/1b, fo. 230d.

42   H.B.C.A., B.135/c/2, fo. 96. For full particulars of Connolly's action, see "Connolly vs. Woolrich, Superior Court, Montreal 9 July 1867", *Lower Canada Jurist*, XI: 197-265.

43   Glazebrook, *Hargrave Correspondence*, 181, 187, 189; P.A.C., Hargrave Corres., vol. 23, Hargrave to D. McKenzie, 9 July 1839.

44   P.A.C., Hargrave Corres., vol. 7: 1746; E.4/1b, fo. 262.

45   *Ibid.*, vol. 22, Hargrave to Allan Mcdonell, 10 Dec. 1835; Glazebrook, *Hargrave Correspondence*, 330-31; Margaret A. MacLeod, ed., *The Letters of Letitia Hargrave* (Toronto: Champlain Society, XXVIII) 28, 218.

46   P.A.C., Hargrave Corres., vol. 8: 2172-73; E.4/2, fo. 90.

47   Glazebrook, *Hargrave Correspondence*, 330; MacLeod, *Letitia's Letters*, 218.

48   Glazebrook, *Hargrave Correspondence*, 66.

49   H.B.C.A., Edward Ermatinger Corres., Copy No. 21, 27; B.4/b/1, fo. 5; B.135/c/2, fos. 64-64d, 73d; A.6/23, fo. 109.

50   J. Hargrave to Wm. Lockie, 8 Sept. 1838 as quoted in Jennifer Brown, "Changing Views of Fur Trade Marriage and Domesticity: James Hargrave, His Colleagues, and 'The Sex' ", *Western Canadian Journal of Anthropology*, 6, 3 (1976): 92-105.

51   MacLeod, *Letitia's Letters*, xxv-xxvi, 3-5, 271-76.

52   H.B.C.A., E.12/4, fo. 31.

53   H.B.C.A., E.12/1, fo. 51.

54   Glazebrook, *Hargrave Correspondence*, 309, 318, 332, 358-59, 361, 370-71.

55   P.A.C., Hargrave Corres., vol. 21, Hargrave to John Stuart, 10 Feb. 1831.

56   This ideal of womanhood was also upheld in Upper Canada. Anna

Jameson on her visit to the colony in the 1830s recorded that a backwoods farmer told her that he could not marry a woman who did not accord with his Old Country ideal of feminine elegance and refinement. He had a vision of "a beautiful creature, with the figure of a sylph and the head of a sibyl, bending over her harp. . . ." Eve Zaremba, ed., *Privilege of Sex* (Toronto, 1974), 40-41.

57   Glazebrook, *Hargrave Correspondence*, 311.

58   MacLeod, *Letitia's Letters*, cxlii.

59   Glazebrook, *Hargrave Correspondence*, 311.

60   H.B.C.A., Selkirk Papers, Copy No. 160a, fos. 1108-12; B.239/c/1, fo. 132; Frederick Merk, ed., *Fur Trade and Empire: George Simpson's Journal, 1824-25* (Cambridge, Mass., 1931), 164.

61   See Anna Jameson's comments on this problem among pioneer women in Upper Canada, in Zaremba, *Privilege of Sex*, 42-44.

62   H.B.C.A., E.12/5, fos. 1-2.

63   H.B.C.A., D.6/4, fo. 2.

64   H.B.C.A., B.135/c/2, fos. 54, 64d-65.

65   P.A.C., Hargrave Corres., vol. 22, Hargrave to John Tod, 10 Dec. 1835.

66   H.B.C.A., Ermatinger Corres., Copy No. 21: 30, 35; A.6/24, fo. 85; D.4/62, fo. 64; D.5/10, fo. 384. After this tragic experience, Tod took another country wife, Sophia Lolo, who was the daughter of a prominent mixed-blood guide at Fort Kamloops. Eliza Tod died in 1857, leaving Tod free to marry Sophia after his retirement to Victoria.

67   H.B.C.A., D.5/38, fo. 227d.

68   Donald Ross to Robert Miles, 6 January 1831 as quoted in Jennifer Brown, "Company Men and Native Families: Fur Trade Social and Domestic Relations in Canada's Old Northwest" (Ph.D., University of Chicago, 1976), 10; see also P.A.B.C., D. Ross Corres., T. Simpson to Ross, 12 March 1831 and Glazebrook, *Hargrave Correspondence*, 59.

69   MacLeod, *Letitia's Letters*, 58, 60-61.

70   *Ibid.*, 99-100, 112-113, 127.

71   "Mr. Beaver Objects", *The Beaver* (September 1941), 13; Thomas E. Jessett, ed., *Reports and Letters of Herbert Beaver, 1836-38* (Portland, Oregon, 1959), 81.

72   P.A.B.C., D. Ross Corres., R. Clouston to D. Ross, 28 Sept. 1848, 25 Feb. 1849, 27 March 1849.

73   H.B.C.A., B.135/c/2, fo. 70.

74   P.A.C., Hargrave Corres., vol. 3: 575.

75   MacLeod, *Letitia's Letters*, 96-97, 168.

76   McCord Museum, McGill University, Robert McVicar Papers, John Richardson to R. McVicar, 7 Sept. 1825 and 27 June 1826.

77   H.B.C.A., B.135/c/2, fos. 76d-77, 83, 100.

78   Frances Simpson seems to have conformed to the stereotype of the delicate, ailing Victorian wife. She remained a semi-invalid for the rest of her life and barely survived three more pregnancies.

79   It was a tragic irony that after surviving so many years at York Factory, Letitia Hargrave was to die of cholera shortly after settling in Sault Ste Marie.

80   H.B.C.A., B.135/c/2, fo. 115.

81   P.A.C., Hargrave Corres., vol. 8: 1959, 2195.

82   Glazebrook, *Hargrave Correspondence*, 189.

83   *Ibid.*, 241; MacLeod, *Letitia's Letters*, 217-218.

84   Glenbow Archives, Calgary, James Sutherland Papers, James Sutherland to John Sutherland, 7 August 1838.

Chapter Nine: A Question of Blood

1   P.A.C., Hargrave Correspondence, vol. 21, Hargrave to Charles Ross, 1 Dec. 1830.

2   The European names given to native wives are an interesting indices of the popularity of various names for women in the nineteenth century. The most common was Mary, but also popular were Margaret, Harriett, Jane, Susan, Sarah and Elizabeth.

3   P.A.C., Hargrave Corres., vol. 1: 214-15.

4   See Fernando Henriques, *Children of Caliban: Miscegenation* (London, 1974), xi, 97, 119, 120, 168.

5   Elliot Coues, ed., *New Light on the Early History of the Greater Northwest: The Manuscript Journals of Alexander Henry and of David Thompson, 1799-1814* (Minneapolis, Minn., 1965), 898, 908; Ross Cox, *The Columbia River*, edited by Edgar and Jane Stewart (Norman, Okla., 1957), 158n.

6   Cox, *Columbia River*, 157.

7   Mary Avery, "An Additional Chapter on Jane Barnes", *Pacific Northwest Quarterly*, 42(1951): 331. In 1819, Mistress Robson with her husband and two children made a brief return visit to the Columbia. According to the clerk Alexander McKenzie, the former barmaid had not improved for all her worldly travel. "I should offend your modesty were I to mention specimens of what she intended as wit and humour during her stay with us," he wrote to a friend (H.B.C.A., F.3/2, fo. 194).

8   Chief Factor John Charles was rumoured to be one of the wealthiest men in Rupert's Land, worth about 40,000 pounds; Chief Factor John Rowand left each of his three daughters a legacy of 7,500 pounds.

9   H.B.C.A., Selkirk Papers, Copy No. 161, 1260-61.

10 For an examination of the social and economic stresses that plagued Red River in the first half of the nineteenth century, see Frits Pannekoek, "The Churches and the Social Structure in the Red River Area, 1818-1870" (Ph.D., Queen's University, 1973).

11 H.B.C.A., Selkirk Papers, Copy No. 154, fos. 62-65.

12 H.B.C.A., B.239/c/1, fo. 127. Matthey's country wife seems to have been a mixed-blood woman whom he wed in 1819. He eventually attempted to betray this woman in a most cruel manner. Having decided to return to Europe in 1824, he led his wife to believe that she was to accompany him. Then, upon embarkation at York Factory, he tried to wrest their children from her and leave her behind. None of the onlookers, who were outraged by this unfeeling and deceptive action, would assist him so Matthey finally had to take his wife along (P.A.C., Hargrave Corres., vol. 1: 41).

13 E. E. Rich, ed., *Colin Robertson's Letters, 1817-1822* (London: H.B.R.S., II), cxxii. The Robertsons had been married by David Jones at Oxford House in 1828.

14 H.B.C.A., B.135/c/2, fos. 73, 79.

15 *Ibid.*, fo. 74d.

16 H.B.C.A., Edward Ermatinger Correspondence, Copy No. 23, 271; B.135/c/2, fo. 64d.

17 H.B.C.A., B.135/c/2, fo. 78. Isabella was a daughter of former Company officer John McKay and a native woman, Mary Favell.

18 *Ibid.*, fo. 74.

19 P.A.C., Hargrave Corres., vol. 22, Hargrave to Letitia Mactavish, 27 May 1838.

20 Margaret A. MacLeod, ed., *The Letters of Letitia Hargrave* (Toronto: Champlain Society, XXVIII), 34-36.

21 *Ibid.*
22 C.M.S.A., CC1/018, Cockran's Journal, 13 April 1838; Cockran to the Lay Secretary, 17 June 1840.
23 Jean Johnston, *Wilderness Women* (Toronto, 1976), 129-130.
24 "Connolly vs. Woolrich, Superior Court, Montreal, 9 July 1867", *Lower Canada Jurist*, XI: 237-38; "Johnstone *et al.* vs. Connolly, Appeal Court, 7 Sept. 1869", *La Revue Légale*, I:310.
25 H.B.C.A., Ermatinger Corres., Copy No. 23, 271. Margaret Taylor Hogue appears to have lived out her life in Red River in increasing poverty. Nancy McKenzie Leblanc was also to experience further tragedy. In 1838, her husband and three of her children were drowned while on the way to the Columbia. She eventually went to live at Fort Victoria with her daughter Grace who married Captain Charles Dodd of the *S.S. Beaver.*
26 P.A.M., Alexander Kennedy Papers, Alex. Kennedy to his wife, 14 August 1829.
27 H.B.C.A., B.135/c/2, fo. 106.
28 Elaine Mitchell, "A Red River Gossip", *The Beaver* (Spring 1961), 8.
29 P.A.C., Hargrave Corres., vol. 1: 214-15.
30 John Henry Lefroy, *In Search of the Magnetic North: A Soldier-Surveyor's Letters from the North-West, 1843-44*, edited by G. F. G. Stanley (Toronto, 1955), 26.
31 Thomas E. Jessett, ed., *Reports and Letters of Herbert Beaver, 1836-38* (Portland, Oregon, 1959), 35.
32 P.A.B.C., John S. Helmcken Reminiscences, 1892, 42.
33 Dorothy B. Smith, ed., *Lady Franklin visits the Pacific Northwest* (Victoria: P.A.B.C., Memoir No. XI, 1974), 22-23.
34 Marion B. Smith, "The Lady Nobody Knows", *British Columbia: a centennial anthology* (Vancouver, 1958), 479; Angus McDonald, "A Few Items of the West", *Washington Historical Quarterly*, 8, 3(1917): 225.
35 P.A.B.C., Edward Ermatinger Correspondence, Arch. McDonald to Ermatinger, 20 Feb. 1831.
36 *Ibid.*, 20 Feb. 1833; Jean Cole, "Exile in the Wilderness", *The Beaver* (Summer 1972), 10.
37 C. M. Drury, "The Columbia Maternal Association", *Oregon Historical Quarterly*, 39(1938): 101.
38 P.A.B.C., Ermatinger Corres., Arch. McDonald to Ermatinger, 12 April 1849; William S. Lewis and Naojiro Murakami, eds., *Ranald McDonald: The Narrative of his early life on the Columbia under the Hudson's Bay Company's regime. . . .* (Spokane, Wash., 1923), 83-84n.
39 P.A.C., Hargrave Corres., vol. 23, Hargrave to A. McKinley, 10 Dec. 1838; vol. 8: 1964-65. When officer John Bell married Nancy, a daughter of Chief Factor Peter Warren Dease, in 1830, Hargrave had conceded that the daughter of a well-established officer could be considered "a judicious and respectable choice."
40 P.A.C., Hargrave Corres., vol. 22, Hargrave to Letitia Mactavish, 24 July 1838.
41 *Ibid.*, vol. 23, Hargrave to Mrs. T. Isbister, 23 May 1839 and Hargrave to John Ballenden, 7 Sept. 1839; P.A.B.C., Donald Ross Correspondence, T. Simpson to Ross, 31 May 1837.
42 T. F. Bredin, "The Red River Academy", *The Beaver* (Winter 1974), 14.
43 Paul Kane, *Wanderings of an Artist among the Indians of North America* (Edmonton, 1968), 108.
44 MacLeod, *Letitia's Letters*, 73-74, 97, 106.

45   *Ibid.*, 96.
46   *Ibid.*, 94-95, 111.
47   *Ibid.*, 87.
48   P.A.C., Hargrave Corres., vol. 27, Letitia to Mrs. Mactavish, 27 Feb. 1854.
49   MacLeod, *Letitia's Letters*, 217-18. It was rumoured that Mrs. Lowman was not really a widow and that her first husband was alive in England; Miss Armstrong was reputed to have been in the habit of sleeping with the ship's captain on her voyage out to the colony.
50   MacLeod, *Letitia's Letters*, 164.
51   For a detailed discussion of the James Evans scandal, see Frits Pannekoek, "The Rev. James Evans and the Social Antagonisms of Fur Trade Society, 1840-1846" in R. Allen, ed., *Religion and Society in the Prairie West* (Regina, 1974), 1-18.
52   MacLeod, *Letitia's Letters*, 113, 142, 150-51, 157-58.
53   *Ibid.*, 107, 182; P.A.B.C., D. Ross Corres., Simpson to D. Ross, 29 Dec. 1845.
54   H.B.C.A., D.4/65, fo. 51; D.4/70, fo. 221.
55   H.B.C.A., Ermatinger Corres., Copy No. 23, 298.
56   The conflict between Miles and Barnley is documented in detail in H.B.C.A., A.11/46, fos. 46-69.
57   H.B.C.A., D.5/19, fo. 159d.
58   H.B.C.A., D.4/70, fo. 118.
59   MacLeod, *Letitia's Letters*, 259-60.
60   *Ibid.*, 106, 109.
61   Mitchell, "Red River Gossip", 9.
62   H.B.C.A., D.5/7, fos. 96d, 192; P.A.C., Hargrave Corres., vol. 8: 2193; MacLeod, *Letitia's Letters*, 52-53.
63   H.B.C.A., D.5/7, fo. 185d.
64   MacLeod, *Letitia's Letters*, 261.
65   H.B.C.A., D.5/7, fo. 185d; W. J. Healy, *Women of Red River* (Winnipeg, 1923), 26, 42.
66   H.B.C.A., D.5/13, fo. 395d-96; P.A.B.C., D. Ross Corres., John McBeath to Ross, 6 Aug. 1850.
67   P.A.C., Hargrave Corres., vol. 27, Letitia Hargrave to Flora Mactavish, 1 June 1850. Mrs. Ballenden had named her first daughter Anne Christie after the Governor's wife.
68   H.B.C.A., D.5/31, fo. 247.
69   P.A.B.C., D. Ross Corres., Wm. Todd to Ross, 20 July 1850.
70   P.A.M., Records of the General Quarterly Court of Assiniboia, "Foss vs. Pelly, 16-18 July 1850", 185-86, 203.
71   MacLeod, *Letitia's Letters*, 247.
72   P.A.B.C., D. Ross Corres., R. Clouston to D. Ross, 29 June 1849.
73   H.B.C.A., D.5/30, fo. 206.
74   MacLeod, *Letitia's Letters*, 247; see also P.A.C., Hargrave Corres., vol. 27, Letitia to Mrs. Mactavish, 14 Dec. 1851.
75   P.A.B.C., D. Ross Corres., A. E. Pelly to Ross, 1 August 1850; "Foss vs. Pelly", 185, 196.
76   "Foss vs. Pelly", 183, 193, 213-14.
77   P.A.C., Hargrave Corres., vol. 15: 4533, 4581; "Foss vs. Pelly", 187; MacLeod, *Letitia's Letters*, 255.
78   "Foss vs. Pelly", 207.
79   *Ibid.*, 199. Black's motives for forcing the case into the open were also highly suspect. One observer declared that Black hoped to disgrace Ballenden so that he would be obliged to resign and Black would regain charge of the fort as he was to have had in Ballenden's temporary absence (P.A.B.C., D. Ross Corres., Wm Todd to Ross, 20 July 1850).

80 MacLeod, *Letitia's Letters*, 247; "Foss vs. Pelly", 202-203.
81 "Foss vs. Pelly", 181.
82 P.A.B.C., D. Ross Corres., J. Ballenden to Ross, 1 August 1850; H.B.C.A., D.5/28, fo. 437d.
83 The suit against the Blacks was dropped. The Pellys were required to pay damages of £300 and the Davidsons £100, but Foss declined to collect from the Davidsons.
84 H.B.C.A., D.4/71, fos. 265-266d.
85 P.A.B.C., D. Ross Corres., R. Clouston to Ross, 17 Dec. 1850.
86 MacLeod, *Letitia's Letters*, 256.
87 P.A.B.C., D. Ross Corres., R. Clouston to Ross, 23 Sept. 1850.
88 E. E. Rich, ed., *Eden Colvile's Letters, 1850-1854* (Toronto: Champlain Society, XIX), 193.
89 Pannekoek, "Churches in Red River", 174.
90 Rich, *Colvile's Letters*, 195, 197. The published version mistakenly reads Jane instead of Lane.
91 Rich, *Colvile's Letters*, 201-02. This Donald McKenzie had been a lesser officer in the Company's service and was married to a mixed-blood woman, Matilda Bruce.
92 If such was actually the case, however, it is curious that Pelly never instituted a counter-suit against Foss for redress of damages.
93 Rich, *Colvile's Letters*, 204, 210; H.B.C.A., D.5/30, fos. 47-53, 203.
94 H.B.C.A., D.5/31, fo. 206.
95 H.B.C.A., D.5/32, fo. 323.
96 H.B.C.A., D.5/31, fo. 206.
97 P.A.B.C., D. Ross Corres., George Barnston to Ross, 22 July 1852.
98 Healy, *Women of Red River*, 195.
99 "Foss vs. Pelly", 181.
100 J. J. Hargrave, *Red River* (Altona, Man., 1977), 90.

Epilogue: A World We Have Lost

1 H.B.C.A., D.5/37, fo. 458d.
2 For further details, see Clifford Wilson, *Campbell of the Yukon* (Toronto, 1970), 146-53.
3 In Red River, Hector McKenzie, a well-connected clerk, had formed a liaison with Letitia Bird, perhaps a younger mixed-blood daughter of Chief Factor James Bird. A child was born of this relationship in 1842, but the couple did not marry. In 1851, McKenzie contracted an advantageous match by marrying Annie Bannatyne, a sister of the novelist Robert Bannatyne who had spent some years in the service of the Company. Another clerk Bernard Rogan Ross, after a liaison with a native girl, married Christina Ross, daughter of Chief Factor Donald Ross, in 1856.
4 It should be noted that a number of well-educated English mixed-bloods were able to attain prominence in Red River society prior to 1870; some occupied significant positions in government and teaching, see W. L. Morton, *Manitoba, A History* (Toronto, 1967), 90.
5 W. J. Healy, *Women of Red River* (Winnipeg, 1923), 132.
6 W. L. Morton, "Donald A Smith and Governor George Simpson", *The Beaver*, Autumn 1978, 9; W. J. Healy, *Women of Red River*, 25-37.
7 H.B.C.A., D.5/38, fos. 342, 372d-373.
8 P.A.M., Alexander Ross Papers, vol. 1: 121.
9 Healy, *Women of Red River*, 194-98.
10 Arrangements for the education of young ladies at the Red River

Academy fell into disarray in the 1850's, see T. F. Bredin, "The Red River Academy", *The Beaver* (Winter 1974), 17.

11   P.A.M., Miss Davis' School Collection, 129; Healy, *Women of Red River*, 135, 159.

12   Healy, *Women of Red River*, 116-117.

13   P.A.M., Alexander Ross Papers, Vol. 1: 200.

14   Marion B. Smith, "The Lady Nobody Knows", *British Columbia: a centennial anthology* (Vancouver, 1958), 477-78.

15   *Ibid.*, 472.

16   P.A.B.C., Canada Official Census Records, Victoria, 1881.

17   Irene Spry, ed., *The Palliser Papers* (Toronto: Champlain Society, XLIV), 169. James Ross also observed, "Perhaps Halfbreed children are not respectful enough towards their Indian mothers".

18   W. L. Morton, ed., *Alexander Begg's Red River Journal and other papers relative to the Red River Resistance of 1869-70* (Toronto: Champlain Society, XXXIV), 396.

19   P.A.M., Alexander Ross Papers, Vol. 2: 364.

20   Morton, *Begg's Red River Journal*, 10-11.

21   Irene Spry has emphasized that the transition from the old fur trade economy to a modern agrarian one took longer than has been appreciated and that the mixed-bloods had an important role to play in this transition, see her article "The Transition from a Nomadic to a Settled Economy in Western Canada, 1856-96", *T.R.S.C.*, Fourth Series, VI, 11 (1968): 187-201.

22   See Douglas Sanders, "Indian Women: A Brief History of Their Roles and Rights", *McGill Law Journal*, 21, 4(1975): 659-660 and Maria Campbell, *Halfbreed* (Toronto, 1973).

23   Hugh Dempsey, ed. *William Parker, Mounted Policeman* (Edmonton, 1973), xiv.

24   Nellie McClung, *Clearing in the West* (Toronto, 1976), 52.

25   "Connolly vs. Woolrich, Superior Court, Montreal, 9 July 1867", *Lower Canada Jurist*, XI: 230, 248.

26   *Ibid.*, 257.

27   Louis Knafla, "Marriage Customs, Law and Litigation in the Northwest, 1800-1914," Paper presented to the Canadian Historical Association Annual Meeting, London, 1978, 11.

28   *Ibid.*

29   P.A.C., Hargrave Corres., vol. 21, Hargrave to his uncle and cousin, 20 Aug. 1827.

Index

INDEX